The Textual Tradition of the Canterbury Tales

The Textual Tradition of the Canterbury Tales

N.F. Blake

Professor of English Language
University of Sheffield

Edward Arnold

© N.F. Blake 1985

First published in Great Britain 1985 by
Edward Arnold (Publishers) Ltd,
41 Bedford Square, London WC1B 3DQ

Edward Arnold (Australia) Pty Ltd,
80 Waverley Road, Caulfield East,
Victoria 3145, Australia

Edward Arnold, 300 North Charles Street,
Baltimore, Maryland 21201, USA

**British Library Cataloguing in
Publication Data**

Blake, N.F.
   The textual tradition of the Canterbury
   Tales
   1. Chaucer, Geoffrey. Canterbury
   tales
   I. Title
   821'.1   PR1874

   ISBN 0-7131-6448-4

Text set in 10/11pt English Times
by Colset Private Ltd, Singapore
Printed and bound by Billing & Sons
Limited, Worcester

Contents

	Acknowledgements	vi
	Abbreviations	vii
	Preface	ix
1	Editions of **The Canterbury Tales**	1
2	Scholarly Opinion of the Manuscript Tradition	24
3	Problems and Proposals about the Manuscript Tradition	44
4	The Earliest Manuscripts	58
5	The Formation of the Text: Hengwrt	79
6	The Development of the Text 1: Corpus, Ha7334 and Lansdowne	96
7	The Development of the Text 2: Dd 4.24, Gg 4.27 and El	123
8	Other Developments in the Text	150
9	A Matter of Copytexts	165
10	The Evidence of Other Chaucerian Texts	179
11	Conclusion	187
	Bibliography	203
	Indices	
	a) Index of lines	215
	b) General index	219

Acknowledgements

I should like to thank the British Academy for providing me with a research grant to acquire microfilms of the manuscripts of *The Canterbury Tales* and other Chaucerian works in order that I might work on this book. I am grateful to the many librarians in Great Britain and America who have supplied me with the microfilms. I have spoken at many universities and conferences on topics which receive fuller treatment in this book. I am grateful to my audiences for their criticisms and suggestions. I have discussed the general thrust of this book with many scholars who are too numerous to mention. I am, however, particularly grateful to David Burnley and Derek Pearsall who read the book in draft and made various suggestions for its improvement. I alone remain responsible for the views expressed in it. I should also like to thank Sandra Burton for her help in preparing the typescript.

N.F. Blake
Sheffield, 1984

Abbreviations

Manuscripts and early prints

Cx76   The Canterbury Tales published by William Caxton
       c. 1476
Cx82   The Canterbury Tales published by William Caxton
       c. 1482
El   The Ellesmere manuscript (Huntington Library, San
       Marino)
Ha7334 British Library, MS Harley 7334
Hg   The Hengwrt manuscript (National Library of Wales,
       Aberystwyth)

Other manuscripts are indicated through a short library or
collection reference, e.g. Corpus = Corpus Christi College,
Oxford, MS 198, and Lansdowne = British Library MS
Lansdowne 851. Further details of these manuscripts can be
found in Manly and Rickert 1940 vol. I.

Pilgrims and tales

Ck	Cook	Pd	Pardoner
Cl	Clerk	Ph	Physician
Fk	Franklin	Pr	Prioress
Fr	Friar	Pro	General Prologue
Kt	Knight	Ps	Parson
Mc	Manciple	Re	Reeve
Me	Merchant	Rt	Retraction
Mel	Melibeus	Sh	Shipman
Mi	Miller	Sq	Squire
Mk	Monk	Su	Summoner
ML	Man of Law	Th	Thopas
Nn	Nun	WB	Wife of Bath
NP	Nun's Priest		

When added to the above abbreviations P = Prologue and T = Tale, e.g. MLP = Man of Law's Prologue, TMel = Tale of Melibeus.

Modern titles

References to modern studies are by author's surname and date of publication only. When more than one work was written by an author in the same year, the date is followed by an a, b, etc. to indicate the first, second, etc. title listed for that year in the bibliography at the end of this book.

The following abbreviated titles are used in the bibliography:

ChR   *The Chaucer Review*
ES   *English Studies*
JEGP   *Journal of English and Germanic Philology*
MLN   *Modern Language Notes*
MLR   *Modern Language Review*
MP   *Modern Philology*
NM   *Neuphilologische Mitteilungen*
PMLA   *Publications of the Modern Language Association of America*
SAC   *Studies in the Age of Chaucer*
SB   *Studies in Bibliography*
SP   *Studies in Philology*
STC   A.W. Pollard and G.R. Redgrave, *A Short-title catalogue of books printed in England, Scotland, & Ireland and of English books printed abroad 1475-1640.* London: Bibliographical Society, 1926. 2nd edn edited by W.A. Jackson *et al.*, 1976—.

Preface

The two most widely used editions of Chaucer's *The Canterbury Tales*, at least in the universities in Great Britain, are the second edition of Robinson (1957) and the Everyman edition by Cawley (1958), both of which are reasonably cheap and the first has the advantage of containing all Chaucer's poems. Not only are these editions now somewhat outdated, but they both use as their base manuscript for *The Canterbury Tales* the Ellesmere manuscript (El). Recent scholarship has indicated that El is an edited manuscript and that the Hengwrt manuscript (Hg) has a more reliable text. It was partly for this reason that I edited a text of the poem based on Hg which was published in 1980. This edition brought into the open a problem which had been largely pushed aside until then. The editions which are used for teaching and as the basis for most scholarly discussion are based on El, which has a different order, a different allocation to pilgrims of certain pieces of the poem and some additional links and tales as compared with Hg. The status of these changes and additions is consequently a central problem in establishing the text of the poem, and any decision would affect many critical studies of the poem.

Not unnaturally these parts of the poem are referred to constantly in this book, and so it may be helpful to the reader to indicate what they are. First, however, it is necessary to note that the poem consists of tales which are joined by links. These links are from the pilgrimage frame. In modern editions these links are most often referred to as prologues, though a few are described as endlinks and some simply as links. Inevitably some of these links have been allocated to different pilgrims at various times, and consequently the links may appear under differing titles in modern editions. In this book pieces will also be referred to by their line references in order to prevent confusion. The system of reference employed is that all parts of the poem in Hg included in my edition are referred to by the lineation system used in that book, so that 5:61 means section 5 line 61. Parts of the poem not in my edition are referred to by the group lineation introduced by Furnivall and popularized through Skeat's 1894 edition. These references are included in square brackets and consist of a capital letter and a number. Thus [E2012] means Group E line 2012.

In the order found in El and most modern editions, the following parts of the poem are those which appear frequently in the pages which follow. The first is the link which occurs after the Man of Law's Tale, in modern editions usually called the Man of Law's Epilogue [B^{1}1163-90]. This link was used to introduce the following tale and the name of the speaker of that tale is introduced at [B^{1}1179]. In most manuscripts this speaker is the Squire and so the link is referred to in them as the Squire's Prologue. In some manuscripts the speaker is the Summoner, though his tale does not follow immediately after the link; and in one manuscript the speaker is the Shipman. This link is missing in many manuscripts besides Hg. In the Wife of Bath's Prologue there are five passages which are found in some manuscripts, but not in Hg. These passages are [D44a-f, 575-84, 609-12, 619-26, and 717-20].

In Hg the Clerk's Tale ends with an envoy entitled 'Lenuoy de Chaucer' (8:1177-1212) followed by a stanza from the pilgrimage frame known as the Host-stanza or the Clerk's Endlink (8:1213-19). This stanza is omitted in some manuscripts, and the envoy is also re-arranged by some scribes. In El and other manuscripts the Clerk's Tale is followed by the Merchant's Tale, and they have a link to join the tales together which is referred to here as the Clerk−Merchant link [E1213-44], though in many modern editions it is referred to as the Merchant's Prologue. Two couplets within the Merchant's Tale differ considerably from one manuscript to the next; they are 5:61-2 and 5:985-6. In El the Merchant's Tale is followed by the Squire's Tale, whereas in Hg the order of these two tales is the reverse. In El there is a link between them, which in many modern editions is divided into two parts known respectively as the Merchant's Epilogue and the Squire's Prologue [E2419-40 and F1-8]. In Hg this link (for it really is one and not two pieces) was introduced late into the manuscript in a gap left by the scribe between the Merchant's Tale and the Franklin's Tale. The names in the link differ as to which speaker is coming next. The link is referred to here as the Merchant−Franklin link. In El the Franklin's Tale follows the Squire's Tale and a link is found in that manuscript and hence in most modern editions to join the tales together [F673-708]. Since the first part of the Franklin's Tale is often separated from the tale to act as a prologue, this link has no specific title in modern editions. It was, however, introduced late into Hg in a gap left by the scribe between the Squire's Tale and the Merchant's Tale and is there given the title of the Merchant's Prologue. The pilgrims are changed according to the function of the link. It will be referred to here as the Squire−Merchant link. In the Franklin's Tale itself El contains two passages which do not occur in Hg and most other manuscripts; they are [F1455-6 and 1493-8]. As the Pardoner's Tale has a separate prologue, the link between the Physician's Tale and the Pardoner's Tale is referred to as the Physician—Pardoner link. This link has undergone some revision in a number of manuscripts, though El agrees with Hg here.

A number of possibly interlinked changes occur in the Monk's Tale and Nun's Priest's Tale. In the former, which contains a series of 'tragedies', there is in Hg no account of the tragedy of Adam. In El and most later manuscripts a stanza about Adam is included in the tale [B²3197-3204]. It is referred to as the Adam stanza. As part of the Monk's Tale there is a series of four tragedies dealing with fourteenth-century figures, and this series is usually known as the Modern Instances. In Hg and many other manuscripts including El the Modern Instances occur at the end of the tale. However, in some manuscripts they are placed in its middle between the tragedies of Zenobia and Nero, and this positioning is followed in some modern editions. When the Modern Instances are in the middle of the tale, its last tragedy is that of Croesus. This tale is followed by the Nun's Priest's Prologue, which exists in a long and a short form. The long form consists of an additional twenty lines [B²3961-80] which introduce the Host who has some fairly hard things to say to the Monk. Hg has the short form. After the Nun's Priest's Tale most manuscripts have the Manciple's Tale, and so its prologue forms the link between the two tales. However, in El and some other manuscripts the Nun's Tale (which in many editions is known as the Second Nun's Tale) follows the Nun's Priest's Tale. One manuscript, Dd 4.24, has introduced the beginning of a link [B²4637-52], though this link does not mention who the next speaker is going to be. It is sometimes included in modern editions, and when it is it is known as the Nun's Priest's Epilogue.

In El, as we have seen, the Nun's Priest's Tale is followed by the Nun's Tale, which in other manuscripts came before the Physician's Tale. The Nun's Tale has no prologue from the pilgrimage frame, but in some manuscripts a prologue for the tale was created out of the tale itself. This tale is followed in El and most other manuscripts by the Canon Yeoman's Prologue and Tale, which are not found in Hg. Their authenticity is therefore a matter of controversy. Finally, after the Parson's Tale most manuscripts have a concluding piece for the poem, now known as the Retraction. This piece is not found in many manuscripts because their final leaves are often missing. Because this is true of Hg and some other early manuscripts, the status of the Retraction is difficult to establish.

As this book uses a system of reference dependent upon the sections and lineation in my edition of 1980, it may be helpful to

include a table of correspondence between the section arrangement
and the traditional group/fragment, lineation.

Group (Fragment)	Section
A1-252	1:1-252
A252ab	1:253-4
A253-2680	1:255-2682
A2681-2	*om.*
A2683-2778	1:2683-2778
A2779-82	*om.*
A2783-3154	1:2779-3150
A3155-6	*om.*
A3157-3720	1:3151-3714
A3721-2	*om.*
A3723-4422	1:3715-4414
B^{1}1-1162	3:1-1162
B^{1}1163-90	*om.*
D1-44	2:1-44
(D44a-f)	*om.*
D45-574	2:45-574
D575-84	*om.*
D585-608	2:575-98
D609-12	*om.*
D613-18	2:599-604
D619-26	*om.*
D627-716	2:605-94
D717-20	*om.*
D721-2294	2:695-2268
E1-1212	8:1-1212
E1212a-g	8:1213-19
E1213-44	*om.*
E1245-2418	5:1-1174
E2419-40	*om.*
F1-8	*om.*
F9-672	4:1-664
F673-708	*om.*
F709-1454	6:1-746
F1455-6	*om.*
F1457-92	6:747-82
F1493-8	*om.*
F1499-1624	6:783-908
C1-296	9:1-296
C297-8	*om.*
C299-968	9:297-966
B^{2}1191-3196 (VII.1-2006)	10:1-2006

Group (Fragment)	Section
B²3197-3204 (VII.2007-14)	*om.*
B²3205-3564 (VII.2015-2374)	10:2007-2366
B²3565-3652 (VII.2375-2462)	10:2671-2758
B²3653-3956 (VII. 2463-2766)	10:2367-2670
B²3957-60 (VII. 2767-70)	10:2759-62
B²3961-80 (VII. 2771-90)	*om.*
B²3981-4636 (VII. 2791-3446)	10:2763-3418
B²4637—52 (VII. 3447-62)	*om.*
Gl-553	7:1-553
G554-1481	*om.*
Hl-362	11:1-362
Il-1092	12:1-1092

Finally, it should be noted that, in those texts which employ a yogh and/or thorn, these symbols have been modernized to *y*(or *g*) and *th* respectively.

1

Editions of The Canterbury Tales

Although the editorial tradition of *The Canterbury Tales* may be said to start with the first manuscript written after Chaucer's death, I shall in this chapter be concerned solely with the printed editions for they introduce a new phase in the readership of Chaucer's work. A continuity between the various editions can be traced, for each editor had available the preceding edition or editions to work from. Because of the large number of copies produced, printed editions have a much wider distribution than manuscripts and can thus have a more marked influence on modern attitudes to the text. Consequently they are often granted an authority which is not bestowed on the manuscripts. In the history of the printed editions those by Tyrwhitt, Skeat and Manly–Rickert represent important stages so that the development of the edited text may be described as falling into four periods.

William Caxton returned to England with a printing press in 1476 (or possibly even late 1475), and after issuing a few quarto volumes he produced the *editio princeps* of the poem. Although this edition has no date or place of printing, it almost certainly appeared in 1476 at Westminster.[1] That Caxton issued this text so soon after his return to England is an indication of its popularity, for he needed to sell many copies of any printed work if he was to make a financial success of his publishing venture. Cx76 begins with Pro and the tales which make up section 1. CkT is incomplete, though this is not indicated in the rubric. MLPT follow; the tale itself is not divided into stanzas. Then comes SqT which is introduced by the headlink [B¹1163-90] known usually today as the Man of Law's Epilogue; it naturally has the reading 'Squire' at [B¹1179]. There is no indication that SqT is unfinished. MeT comes next and it is introduced by the headlink [E1213-44]. This tale has no endlink and is followed directly by section 2, in which WBP contains [D44a-f, 575-84, 609-12, 619-26, and 717-20], and then by the Clerk's prologue, tale and endlink, the latter of which is

---

[1]On the dating of this edition see Hellinga 1982 p. 83.

introduced by the rubric *Verba hospitis* (8:1213-19). The tale is not divided into stanzas and contains both the Wife of Bath stanza and the envoy, which has no rubric. Then we get the Franklin's prologue (6:1-20) and tale. After this comes NnT; the rubrics refer to the teller as the Second Nun. Her tale is divided into prologue (7:1-119) and tale (7:120-553), but it is not divided into stanzas. This tale is followed by CYPT and by the two tales which make up section 9. The words of the Host to the Physician and the Pardoner (9:287-326) are described as The Pardoner's Prologue, and his tale includes what today would be considered his prologue and the tale. There is no prologue to PhT. Section 10 with its tales in the usual order follows. ShT has no prologue and there is no rubric at the end of TTh. In MkT the Adam stanza is missing and the Modern Instances (10:2671-758) are placed in the middle except that the first two of those Instances (i.e. three stanzas, 10:2671-94) are omitted. The tale is not arranged in stanzas. NPP has the shorter form, but the final rubric to MkT has no reference to the tale's possible incompleteness. There is no endlink to NPT. Sections 11 and 12 follow the usual pattern, and the poem concludes with the Retraction.

The rubrics introducing and concluding the various prologues and tales are generally in English, but they have not been spaced out to set them off from the narrative. There are no running heads. Few of the tales are divided into separate books, though many have divisions indicated by painted capitals; ClT has five rather than six books. As a result of the arrangement of tales certain links that have appeared in most twentieth-century editions are not present. Because the Man of Law's endlink serves to introduce SqT, there is no room for the alternative headlink for his tale [F1-8]; and similarly since MeT is introduced by the Cl−Me Link [E1213-44], there is no room for the alternative one [F673-708], although that in many modern editions introduces FkT. The tales of the Merchant and the Nun's Priest have no endlinks, because the prologues to the tales which followed were thought to provide the necessary linking sequences and because the concept of an epilogue had not yet developed. The tales of the Physician and the Shipman have no prologues. The edition contains certain lines which are no longer considered genuine, and often these provide extra emphasis for the more blatant sexual descriptions. Thus when Damian copulates with May in MeT, Hg simply has:

> Gan pullen vp the smok and in he throng.
> And whan that Pluto saugh this grete wrong, . . .
> (5:1109-10)

Here Cx76 inserts eight lines between these two:

A greet tente a thrifty and a long
She sayde it was the meriest fytte
That euer in her lif she was at yet
My lordis tente seruith me nothing thus
He foldith twifolde be swete Ihesus
He may not swyue worth a leek
And yet he is ful gentil and ful meek
This is leuyr to me than an euynsong.

There are countless other changes and omissions of either whole lines or words. It has been shown that Cx76 is related to Trinity R.3.15, though this was not Caxton's exemplar.[2] He almost certainly followed his exemplar closely and did little or no editorial work for this edition.

Caxton's second edition was produced six years afterwards in 1482, though it too has no indication of date or place of publication. He did, however, include a prologue in which he repeats many of the traditional phrases in praise of Chaucer.[3] He also claimed that this edition 'I have dylygently oversen and duly examyned to th'ende that it be made acordyng unto his [Chaucer's] owen makyng, for I fynde many of the sayd bookes whyche wryters have abrydgyd it and many thynges left out, and in somme place have sette certayn versys that he never made ne sette in hys booke.'[4] This statement is a prelude to the announcement that he has used a different manuscript as exemplar for Cx82, which consequently has a better text and is closer to what Chaucer wrote. He gave no examples of what changes he had made. In fact, although he did have a different manuscript, what he apparently did was to correct a copy of Cx76 against this manuscript and then to use the corrected copy of Cx76 as his exemplar.[5]

Cx82 begins like the first edition with section 1 complete followed by the Man of Law's headlink and tale; there is no indication that CkT is incomplete. MeT follows the Man of Law and it is introduced by its headlink [E1213-44], which had served as headlink to that tale in Cx76. The Squire's headlink (or the Man of Law's endlink [B¹1163-90]) follows MeT and introduces SqT which is now divided into three books; it therefore retains the reading 'Squire' at [B¹1179]. At the end of SqT there is the rubric. 'Ther is nomore of the Squyers tale'. FkPT are then joined to SqT by the link [F673-708]. Next come section 2 with its usual components including [D44a-f] in WBP and the Clerk's headlink, tale (now consisting of six books) and endlink (or Host-stanza); the Wife of

[2]Manly and Rickert 1940 I.80, 530.
[3]Blake 1967.
[4]Blake 1973 p. 62.
[5]Dunn 1940.

Bath stanza and envoy (introduced by a rubric in French) are part of this tale. Then follow the Nun's prologue and tale, in which the rubrics refer to the Second Nun but the running heads simply to the Nun. Next come CYPT and sections 9 and 10 in their normal sequence. PdPT are now divided as in modern editions and introduced by 'the wordes of the Hoost' as a separate unit. In MkT the Adam stanza is included and the three stanzas of the first two Modern Instances missing in Cx76 are inserted immediately before the story of Croesus which concludes the tale. Presumably the editor noticed the omission of the three stanzas, but did not accept that they had any necessary connection with the other Modern Instances. Although these three stanzas themselves could not have completed the tale in the alternative manuscript available to Caxton because the other stanzas which make up Modern Instances would follow them, presumably the Modern Instances as a whole came at the end of the tale in that manuscript since he decided to insert these missing stanzas as near the end of MkT in Cx82 as possible. There is no indication in the rubric that MkT is incomplete, though the long form of NPP is included. After NPT Cx82 includes the endlink which is run together with McP to form a single link. The edition concludes with sections 11 and 12 complete.

The two major changes of order introduced into Cx82 are the placing of firstly the Merchant's headlink and tale between MLT and the Squire's headlink (or Man of Law's endlink), and secondly the Franklin's prologue and tale between SqT and WBP. Because of this new order the link [F673-708] between the Squire and the Franklin is introduced. The Nun's Priest's endlink is also included. What is today known as the Man of Law's endlink was clearly regarded then as the Squire's headlink and goes with SqT when that is put later in the order. Many of the additions within the tales in Cx76 have been eliminated, though the two editions are alike in which tales have divisions into books. The rubrics are usually in English, though a few are in Latin. The printing of the lines as stanzas in those tales which have them, the spacing out of the rubrics and the introduction of woodcuts set a standard of excellence in the presentation of this edition which was not to be matched for some time.

From these two editions it is apparent that there was relative agreement about the order at the beginning and end of the poem. Both commence with sections 1 and 3, and both end with the sequence section 7, CYPT, and sections 9 to 12. It was the central sections which caused the editorial uncertainties. The contents of section 2 were constant, but its position was not definitively decided. The other four sections each contain a single tale and these occur in different positions. The order that is followed influenced what links are provided, for particular links were regarded as belonging to individual tales. Tales, prologues and links are generally provided with introductory and concluding rubrics in English, though a few are still in Latin. These are generally purely descriptive, though at the end of TTh Cx82 has the rubric. 'The hoost interrupteth his tale'. There are fewer book divisions within the tales than we today are used to. The text contains some lines in the tales no longer considered genuine and omits others that are; and in this respect Cx76 is far worse than Cx82.

Cx82 formed the basis of two editions by Pynson, one printed about 1492 and the other in 1526, though it remains possible that he also had access to a manuscript. The edition of 1526 was one of three volumes of Chaucer's works published by Pynson in the same year, and although the three volumes were apparently sold separately, together they amounted to a composite edition of Chaucer's collected works. Pynson included a modified version of Caxton's prologue in his editions of the poem, although his general presentation is not as clear as that in Cx82. The stanzas are indicated only through indentation of the first line, and the rubrics are often cramped. The Nun is so called in the rubrics and running heads to her tale; there is no rubric after TTh; and the Retraction is not included. An edition by Wynkyn de Worde, Caxton's assistant and eventually successor, appeared in 1498. This was apparently set up from a defective copy of Cx82, which had to be supplemented by a manuscript for part of section 10, including the end of PrT and all of TTh, TMel and MkT.[6] The manuscript was a good one, closely related to Hg, and it is interesting to speculate whether this manuscript was the same one used by Caxton to revise Cx82. However, de Worde's edition differs from Cx82 in that he moved sections 2 and 8 to follow section 3. In this way the Merchant headlink [E1213-44] serves with the Host-stanza (8:1213-19) at the end of ClT to unite the tales of the Clerk and Merchant. This order is not one which de Worde could have acquired from Hg or a manuscript close to it, though it is found in El and Ha7334. For the rest de Worde kept the order and contents of Cx82. The 1498 edition is the first to be printed in double columns which remained standard till the eighteenth century.

In 1532 appeared the volume *The Workes of Geffray Chaucer newly printed* by Thomas Godfray at London and edited by 'Wylliam Thynne chefe clerk of your [Henry VIII's] kechyn'. This edition, frequently reprinted and augmented, remained the main text of Chaucer till Tyrwhitt's edition of 1775-8. Chaucer is the first English poet to have his works issued in a collected edition – a fact which underlines his considerable reputation. In the volume *The Canterbury Tales* has pride of place as the first text. Thynne

[6]Garbaty 1978.

based his edition on de Worde's 1498 edition, though he evidently had access to one or more manuscripts as well. The poem opens with section 1 with its normal sequence and although CkT is incomplete there is no reference to this in the rubric. This is followed by the prologue, tale and endlink of the Man of Law, the latter having the reading 'Squire' at [B^{1}1179] and introducing SqT. The concluding rubric of this tale which is based on that in de Worde's edition is 'There can be founde no more of this foresaid tale/ whiche hath ben sought i dyuers places'. This tale is followed by the links [F673-708] (with the reading 'Merchant' at [F675]) and [E1213-44] which are printed as separate units, although both serve to introduce MeT. Then comes section 2 with its normal contents, and that leads into the prologue, tale and endlink (Host-stanza) of the Clerk. These are followed by the prologues and tales of the Franklin, the Nun (called the Second Nun) and the Canon's Yeoman. PhT which comes next is introduced by a fourteen-line headlink, which is also found in several manuscripts but had not appeared in a printed edition previously. This headlink introduces section 9 which otherwise has its normal contents. ShT which follows is introduced by a twelve-line headlink, which is also found in some manuscripts but here makes its appearance in print. It introduces section 10. In MkT the Adam stanza is included and the Modern Instances are at the end. The tale has two rubrics, one saying simply 'Here endeth the Monkes tale' and the other stating 'Here stynteth the knyght the monke of his tale'. This is the first time this has been suggested in a printed edition, and is somewhat surprising in that the rubric at the end of TTh does not suggest that it was broken off by the Host. The Nun's Priest's endlink is run together with McP. Then sections 11 and 12 follow as usual except that Thynne following Pynson does not include the Retraction, which did not reappear until Urry's 1721 edition.

The rubrics that begin and end the prologues and tales are now all in English, but the divisions into books in the tales are in Latin except that the envoy in ClT has a rubric in French. Although KtT is still without book divisions, all other tales which now have them have been provided with divisions. ClT has six books. In this edition every tale is separated from the next one by at least one link passage, and in some cases by two. The edition therefore presents the poem in what is ostensibly a complete form apart from the incomplete tale by the Squire, though as the Merchant praises him for his tale in the link which follows there is little sense of incompleteness. Anyone coming upon the poem in this edition would readily come away with the impression that the poem was complete apart from one minor blemish. However, Thynne restored some of the extra lines found in Cx76 which has been eliminated in Cx82 such as the obscene lines found in MeT quoted earlier in this chapter.

Following Thynne's edition the poem was printed as part of the collected works of Chaucer for the next two hundred years. Often indeed new editions were no more than reprints of Thynne. The first of these came out in 1542, and in it *The Canterbury Tales* differs from the 1532 edition only in having the Ploughman's prologue and tale added after PsT. The prologue indicates how the Ploughman had decided to go on pilgrimage to Canterbury and was asked by the Host to tell his tale. His tale is a satire on the abuses of the religious orders. It occurs in no extant manuscript of the poem. As Thynne's edition did not have the Retraction and as the Parson and Ploughman are said in Pro to be brothers, the addition of the latter's tale immediately after the former's does not create much sense of being an addition. This edition was reprinted in 1550, but on this occasion The Ploughman's Tale was inserted before PsT, as though it was accepted that that tale was the concluding one of the poem. The edition of 1561 prepared by John Stow shows no change in *The Canterbury Tales* even though Stow was familiar with many manuscripts and had a large collection of his own. Stow also knew of Gg 4.27 which he brought to the attention of Thomas Speght who was mainly responsible for the edition of 1598. This edition is essentially a reprint of 1561 except that Speght added a glossary, a biography and some notes; he also included a series of 'arguments' to the poems which doubles as a table of contents. The argument of The Ploughman's Tale is 'A complaint against the pride and couetousnesse of the cleargie: made no doubt by Chaucer with the rest of the Tales. For I haue seene it in written hand in Iohn Stowes Library in a booke of such antiquity, as seemeth to haue beene written neare to Chaucer's time.' Further editions were published in 1602 and 1687 without essential difference to the text of the poem.

John Urry's edition of Chaucer appeared in 1721, though Urry was dead by then and the edition was seen through the press by others. Urry was aware of previous editions of Chaucer's works and he knew of at least fourteen manuscripts of *The Canterbury Tales*. He followed the general order of Thynne's edition, but he included Gamelyn and The Ploughman's Tale. Because of its appearance in so many manuscripts Urry expressed surprise that previous Chaucerian editors had not included Gamelyn in their editions. 'If they had any of those MSS in which it is, I cannot give a Reason why they did not give it a Place amongst the rest, unless they doubted of its being genuine. But because I find it in so many MSS, I have no doubt of it, and therefore make it publick, and call it the Fifth Tale. In all the MSS it is called the Cooke's Tale, and therefore I call it so in like manner: But had I found it without an Inscription, and had been left to my Fancy to have bestow'd it on which of the Pilgrims I had pleas'd, I should certainly have adjudg'd it to the Squire's Yeoman' (p.36). Of the Ploughman's prologue and tale he wrote that they were 'in none of the MSS that I have seen, nor in any of the first Printed Books; Caxton and Pynsent, I presume, durst not publish it: The former printed this Poet's Works in Westminster-Abbey, and both before the Abolition of Popery; and the MSS being before that, I fancy the Scriveners were prohibited transcribing it, and inioyn'd to subscribe an Instrument at the end of the Canterbury Tales, call'd his Retraction' (p.178). The Mery Adventure and the Tale of Beryn were also included in the volume, but at its end after all the other poems. Doubts as to their genuineness are expressed, and they are said to have been found in a manuscript on loan from Mrs Thynne. It has not since been located. Textually the poem is bad because Urry made numerous corrections to the language and metre for he felt that Chaucer's text had been corrupted by generations of scribes. Urry numbered the lines in the tales, though the numbering is erratic. The General Prologue and The Knight's Tale share a lineation, as do the other tales in section 1. Gamelyn has a separate lineation, but the tales of the Man of Law, the Squire and the Merchant share one. Finally many of the original rubrics are discarded so that most of the poem is divided simply into the prologue and the tale of the particular speaker. The edition does contain a full glossary compiled by Timothy Thomas and it was the first to abandon black letter.

The editions in this first phase of printed copies of the poem are characterized by the use of a preceding edition as exemplar with the occasional use of a manuscript for modifications to the order and content. The producers of these texts had little idea of editorial scholarship, for their concept of a good text was not one as close as possible to what the author had written, but one which was as full as possible. These editions are inclusive rather than exclusive so that pieces are continually being added rather than dropped. The only exception to this is the Retraction which dropped out of editions from Pynson onwards. Naturally there is an element of chance as to what is included, for that depends on what manuscripts were available. As far as the tales are concerned Gamelyn and Beryn are included by Urry, but the Ploughman's Tale, which is found in no extant manuscript, was added in the sixteenth century. The tales of the Cook and Squire are incomplete, but it is only the latter which arouses comment. The order of the tales of the Squire, Merchant, Clerk and Franklin keeps on undergoing revision together with the position of section 2; the beginning and end of the poem remain stable. Each tale has a headlink or prologue to introduce it. Since SqT is always introduced by the link [B^{1}1163-90] there is no room for the alternative headlink to the tale [F1-8] which makes no appearance in these editions. However, other links are introduced into the poem over the course of time. Sometimes two links are combined to form a single link, for it would appear that the preferred arrangement was the sequence prologue – tale – prologue – tale, though the symmetry was interrupted by the presence of more than one link on some occasions. The Modern Instances come finally to be placed at the end of MkT, though that tale is usually followed by the long form of NPP and is accepted from Thynne onwards as being incomplete. Many variant readings occur within the tales, though some of the grosser additions were purged from the printed editions as early as Cx82, only to be reinstated by Thynne.

Thomas Thywhitt broke with the immediate past in many ways. His edition in five volumes, published 1775-8, was the first for many years which did not form part of a collected works of Chaucer. More importantly he did not rely upon the editions of his predecessors, though he was familiar with them; indeed he used a heavily annotated copy of Speght's 1602 edition as copy for his printer. He criticized Thynne's text and he himself went back to the manuscripts, for his object was to present the text of the poem 'as correct as the Mss. within the reach of the Editor would enable him to make it' (vol. 1, p. i). In this he followed the lead of Thomas Morell who in 1737 had anonymously published an edition with manuscript variants of the Prologue and The Knight's Tale based on an examination of about fifteen manuscripts. Tyrwhitt knew of twenty-six manuscripts, mainly in libraries in London, Oxford and Cambridge, and these he compared as the basis of his text. El and Hg were not available to him, but Ha7334 was. However, he put particular faith in five manuscripts: Additional 5140, Dd 4.24, Egerton 2726 and 2864, and Ha7335. The last of these was his major source, though the choice was not entirely happy since it is a later fifteenth-century manuscript with an unfinished text. Even so, Tyrwhitt focused attention again on the manuscripts, and the text he established differs in only small particulars from many available today, partly because he has continued to influence editorial decisions. Tyrwhitt was the first editor to discuss the proper order of the tales, and he provided reasons for his various decisions. The poem opens with section 1 in its usual order. The lines are now numbered, though the numbering (which does not extend to the prose) runs continuously through the poem. In Section 1 he included 1:253-4, but omitted [A3155-6 and 3721-2] without comment. CkT is followed by a line of asterisks to indicate its incompleteness. Gamelyn is not included, though found in many manuscripts, because its manner, style and versification are inferior to Chaucer's. MLPT follow, but there is no endlink to the tale. Then comes section 2 with its normal order. WBP omits [D44a-f], but it includes the four passages [D575-84, 609-12, 619-26 and 717-20] which are found in only a few manuscripts. Tyrwhitt accepted that [D44a-f] were in Chaucer's manner, but fitted in awkwardly in the prologue; he suggested that Chaucer 'wrote them, and afterwards blotted them out' (vol. 4, p. 262). After section 2 come the Clerk's prologue and tale (in six books); and although the Wife of Bath stanza and envoy (without rubric) are included, the Clerk's endlink or Host-stanza is omitted. This is the first time the stanza has been omitted from a printed edition and Tyrwhitt's decision influenced later editors. No specific reason for its omission is offered, though Tyrwhitt felt that 'Wepyng and waylyng, care and oother sorwe' [E1213] was a direct echo of 'And lat hym care and wepe and wrynge and wayle' (8:1212) so that these two lines had to be placed in direct proximity. This meant that MeT, introduced by the headlink [E1213-44], followed immediately after ClT. The tales of the Clerk and Merchant had to come after the section with the Wife of Bath because they refer to the Wife in their tales, and so Tyrwhitt felt that the order in his better manuscripts was vindicated by the logic of the poem. In MeT 5:61-2 are omitted. The tale is followed by the endlink [E2419-40] and the Squire's headlink [F1-8] which are run together to form the Squire's prologue; it is the first time these two are associated in a printed edition. SqT which follows lacks the last two lines (the first two of the otherwise incomplete third book) and a line of asterisks advertises its unfinished state. This tale is followed by the Franklin's prologue, which in Tyrwhitt consists of the link [F673-708] and 6:1-20 which are run together as a single unit; naturally there is the reading 'Franklin' at [F675]. Tyrwhitt claimed that this prologue was rightly the Franklin's rather than the Merchant's because this was the position in the best manuscripts and because the speaker refers to his grown-up son [F682] whereas the Merchant refers to his recent marriage [E1233-4]. Furthermore, the tone of this link suits a gentleman like the Franklin better than the Merchant. In FkT two short passages [F1455-6 and 1493-8] which are found only in some manuscripts are omitted. Tyrwhitt expressed confidence that the tales of the Clerk, Merchant, Squire and Franklin were arranged in his edition in accordance with Chaucer's intentions. He was less confident in the decision to put the tales of the Nun and the Canon's Yeoman after that of the Nun's Priest; he did so because the reference to Boughton under Blee in CYP must follow the reference to Rochester in MkT; and this was the order found in many good manuscripts. Hence FkT is followed by PhT which is introduced by a six-line prologue from Ha7335, which is itself an adaptation of the longer fourteen-line prologue to PhT found in some manuscripts. Tyrwhitt expressed scepticism about the genuineness of the prologue, particularly its last five lines, but he felt it would serve a turn until the right prologue was discovered. The rest of section 9 follows PhT as normal, though the link between the Physician and the Pardoner is run together with the Pardoner's prologue. Then comes section 10, in which ShT is introduced by what had been the Squire's headlink in previous editions (or the Man of Law's endlink in many modern editions), namely [B¹1163-90]. The reading 'Shipman' has replaced 'Squire' at [B¹1179], and it was probably found by Tyrwhitt in Selden, the only extant manuscript in which it occurs. The numbering of the lines in TTh differs from modern editions because Tyrwhitt printed some of the stanzas in a way not used today. The tale ends with dashes to indicate its incompleteness, but there is no rubric to underline this state of affairs. MkT contains the Adam stanza, and the Modern Instances are placed at the end. Tyrwhitt knew that in some manuscripts they came in the middle and realized that this had the virtue that the last line of Croesus's story 'And couere hir brighte face with a clowde' (10:2670) was then placed in close proximity to the Host's words 'He spak how fortune couered with a clowde' [B²3972]. Since this forms part of the Host's interruption of the tale it provides an effective echo. But as the Host said he had been half asleep, Tyrwhitt thought there was no reason why he should not refer back to a passage some eighty lines earlier. Furthermore the Modern Instances fit awkwardly in the middle of the tale, and Tyrwhitt decided to follow the lead of the best manuscripts which have them at the end. NPP has the longer form, and his tale is followed by the endlink which has no rubric. Tyrwhitt felt these lines were the prologue to some tale, but did not know which one since only one manuscript refers to the following Nun's tale and so he did not accept that reading. The endlink is followed by a line of asterisks to indicate some incompleteness at this point. Since NnT follows here, Tyrwhitt could not run the Nun's Priest's endlink together with McP as earlier editors had done. The Nun is called the Second Nun in the rubrics to her tale, but simply the Nun elsewhere in the edition. Her prologue and tale are followed by those of the Canon's Yeoman. His irruption on the scene at this point is considered 'a little extraordinary' (vol. 4, p. 181) by Tyrwhitt, though he does not question the genuineness of the prologue and tale. Instead, he suggests that some sudden resentment on Chaucer's part against alchemists led him to interrupt the regular course of his poem. Then follow McPT, but Tyrwhitt rejects The Ploughman's Tale as spurious because it occurs in no manuscript. PsPT with the Retraction complete the poem.

Tyrwhitt believed Chaucer had written only half his poem, for there was nothing for the return journey. Even so, he accepted that apart from one or two unfinished tales, the poem as it stood was a complete entity which is why the lineation ran continuously throughout. He did away with all manuscript rubrics and arranged the poem as a continuous sequence of prologue–tale–prologue–tale introduced by his own regularized rubrics. To achieve this he was forced to amalgamate various links such as [F673-708] and 6:1-20; to omit links like the Clerk's endlink or Host-stanza; to adapt links so that [B^{1}1163-90] was made into the Shipman's prologue because the Squire already had a prologue; and to include links like the Physician's prologue even though he was not convinced that they had been written by Chaucer. The result is a poem which is presented as a complete whole and in a logical sequence of prologue–tale–prologue–tale. Tyrwhitt brought the matter of the order of the tales into scholarly discussion, and he tried to provide answers partly from the manuscripts and partly from what he considered the logic of the poem. Although he returned to the manuscripts for his text, the principles he followed are not clear because the art of textual recension had not been properly established by his time. His text is eclectic in that he examined a number of manuscripts and took from each the reading he considered most satisfactory. Similarly he accepted certain lines or passages as genuine because he felt they were Chaucerian or because they fitted in with the scheme he imposed on the poem. His knowledge of Chaucer's language and metre was insufficient for any well-based decision. Even so his decisions were extremely influential on succeeding scholars. As is true of so much eighteenth-century work, his edition is particularly strong on annotation and the discovery of sources; he was also the first editor to provide an extensive and reliable glossary. In these three matters modern editions still rely heavily on his work. Chaucer had become a classical English writer whose work needed elucidation if it was to be understood.

Once Tyrwhitt focused attention on the manuscripts, other editors followed his example though they did not necessarily rely on the same ones. In the early nineteenth century Ha7334 became popular. It formed the basis of the edition by Thomas Wright which appeared in the Percy Society in three volumes in 1847-51. Wright criticized Tyrwhitt for using late fifteenth-century manuscripts when he knew of earlier ones, and he claimed that Tyrwhitt was 'entirely unacquainted with the palaeographical and philological knowledge necessary for an appreciation' of the manuscripts (I.xxxiii). Wright claimed that Ha7334 was 'by far the best manuscript of Chaucer's *Canterbury Tales* that I have yet examined, in regard both to antiquity and correctness' (I.xxxv), and suggested it was written shortly after 1400. In his edition he followed Ha7334 as closely as possible in order to 'give Chaucer, as far as can be done, in his own language, which certainly has not yet been done in print' (I.xxxix). He nevertheless valued Tyrwhitt's edition and kept its lineation by putting spurious lines in square brackets and not numbering additional lines. The tales have modern titles as in Tyrwhitt. He starts with section 1 as usual. At the end of that he includes Gamelyn in a smaller type and with its own lineation. He comments 'Tyrwhitt omits this tale as being certainly not Chaucer's, in which judgment he is perhaps right. It is however found in the MS. Harl, and all the MSS. I have collated' (I.176). MLT followed without its endlink and then comes section 3. He omits [D44a-f] though he puts them in a footnote; the other lines in WBP are included though they are not in Ha7334. Then comes ClT (in six parts) with its envoy but without the Host-stanza. The Merchant's prologue [E1213-44] and tale (but without 5:61-2) are followed by the Squire's prologue, consisting of [E2419-40] and [F1-8], and tale. His tale lacks its last two lines which are replaced by a line of asterisks. Then come the Franklin's prologue (consisting of [F673-708] and 6:1-20 as one unit) and tale, which lacks [F1455-6, 1493-8]. Then there follow section 7, the prologue and tale of the Canon's Yeoman, and section 9. The spurious Physician's prologue is put in square brackets. The Pardoner's prologue consists of the words of the Host and the actual prologue as a single unit. Section 10 comes next. The Shipman's prologue is marked as spurious and TTh ends with a dash but no rubric. MkT includes the Adam stanza and has the Modern Instances in the middle. In this matter Wright preferred to ignore Tyrwhitt's example and to retain the order in Ha7334 'not only because I think it the best authority, but because I think this to be the order in which Chaucer intended to place them . . . When Chaucer wrote his grand work, the eventful history of Pedro the Cruel of Aragon was fresh in people's memories, and possessed a special interest in this country, from the part taken in the events connected with him by the Black Prince; we can easily suppose the monk, who professes to disregard chronological order, wandering from the story of Zenobia, to some events of his own time, and then recalling other examples from antiquity' (III.21). NPP has the long form, but the tale has no endlink. Sections 11 and 12 complete the main poem, though Wright added the Mery Adventure and the Tale of Beryn at the end, with the former acting as the prologue to the latter. He accepted that these ludicrous accounts were added after Chaucer's death. Wright followed Tyrwhitt in having modern rubrics, but he also believed that the poem was unfinished at Chaucer's death and had been arranged in the order found in Ha7334 only after that event. He understood that considerable tampering with the text had taken place after Chaucer's death. It was probably a fifteenth-century editor who had arranged the fragments and added such extra material as Gamelyn. Although Wright was dominated by Tyrwhitt, there are features of his edition which point to the future. His text represents a single, early manuscript and it allowed the language and metre of the poem to be appreciated in a quite different way from what had gone before.

At the end of the eighteenth century collected editions of the works of major British poets began to appear, and generally Chaucer was the first poet in such editions. The poems included were not specially re-edited for them but were taken over from existing editions. For the most part *The Canterbury Tales* was taken from Tyrwhitt and the rest of Chaucer's poems from Urry. Although these editions used Tyrwhitt, they often included the other tales printed by Urry though they are regarded as spurious. In John Bell's collection from 1782 Tyrwhitt's text is used for *The Canterbury Tales,* though Gamelyn is included from Urry though its genuineness is questioned. Robert Anderson, whose collection appeared in the next decade, followed the same procedure. In his introduction he wrote:

> The present edition of the *Canterbury Tales* is from Tyrwhitt's incomparable edition, and his valuable and learned Glossary is copied with little variation, except in the omission of the numerical references. *The Plowman's Tale, Tale of Gamelyn, Adventure of Pardoner and Tapster,* and the *Merchant's Second Tale,* omitted by Tyrwhitt, have been retained, though all evidence, internal and external, is against the supposition of their being the production of Chaucer.[7]

Although the case is not argued in detail, it is clear that Tyrwhitt's claims for the genuineness or otherwise of certain tales have been accepted even though these editors print the extra tales from Urry. These tales were never again to compete seriously for a place in the poem. However, collected editions of English poetry in the nineteenth century followed Wright's use of Ha7334. This applies to Robert Bell's edition (1854-6) and the New Aldine edition prepared by Richard Morris (1867).

In 1894 W.W. Skeat produced his collected edition of Chaucer in six volumes; a seventh with the apocrypha appearing in 1897. During the nineteenth century certain scholarly developments had taken place which profoundly influenced this edition, though in most respects his text differs little from that of Tyrwhitt. That century made enormous strides in philological knowledge so that the historical development of the English language became better documented and mapped. Work on the New English Dictionary (later the Oxford English Dictionary) began. Numerous studies on

[7]Anderson 1793 p. vi.

Chaucer's language and metre appeared, and the dating of the various manuscripts of the poem was put on a proper footing. Developments also took place in editorial technique, for the method of textual recension was now more convincingly practised. Equally important was the foundation of the Chaucer Society under the aegis of F.J. Furnivall, for it sponsored many studies on Chaucer and published several manuscripts of *The Canterbury Tales* in diplomatic editions. Particularly important was its publication of the eight manuscripts which it considered to be the earliest testimonies to the poem: Corpus, Dd 4.24, El, Gg 4.27, Ha7334, Hg, Lansdowne and Petworth (although the second of these had not been published when Skeat issued his edition). These manuscripts have dominated editorial discussion ever since. Skeat was aware of the existence of over fifty manuscripts, but he relied on these eight with an occasional reference to another manuscript for the solution to a particular problem. To this extent editorial work with Skeat was less advanced than with Tyrwhitt, who had collated far more manuscripts for his edition.

The manuscript chosen by Skeat as the basis of his edition was El, a manuscript discovered and printed by the Chaucer Society. The reasons he advanced for this choice were that it gave good lines and good sense; it was grammatically accurate; it was splendidly produced; and it contained one of the most complete texts. This last point is the most important, for it meant that by using El the editor would need to make fewer emendations and editorial interventions in the text. Having made a decision about what parts of the text were to be included, the editor then selected as his base the manuscript which reflected that choice most completely. This process of manuscript selection does not of course explain how the editor decided which pieces were genuine and hence to be included; that question was left extremely vague. It is important to emphasize that El was not chosen because it was the earliest manuscript or even necessarily because it was closest to what Chaucer had written; it was chosen for editorial convenience. Another problem in editorial method was presented by the existence of what amounted to different versions of the poem in various manuscripts. These varied not only in the order of the tales, but also in what links were included and in lines within the tales. Skeat recognized that there were four different types, which he labelled A, B, C and D. His edition does not try to reflect one of these types, but is a composite of several. Although some passages which were considered genuine had to be relegated to footnotes, as far as possible he incorporated in his text all pieces that he considered genuine. His text is an amalgam which is not reflected in any manuscript or even for that matter in a type of manuscript. El was chosen as the base manuscript because it was the most conflated of the early manuscripts, though even it did not contain all the lines which Skeat wanted to include in his edition.

Skeat also decided to follow the Chaucer Society in its division of the poem into nine groups, labelled from A to I. Each group was numbered separately in his edition. This editorial decision was not only very influential, but it was also unfortunate and restrictive. While it affirmed the principle that the poem is fragmentary rather than a complete whole, it also fossilized future editorial and critical discussion into certain fixed channels. For example, the tales of the Clerk and the Merchant occur in different orders in many manuscripts and early editions of the poem; but because they were united in Furnivall's Group E, many scholars came to accept that this was Chaucer's own grouping. If this group division did not pre-empt future discussion of tale order, it directed the way in which it was conducted. Equally the lineation adopted by Skeat, following the Chaucer society, led many to accept that certain lines were genuine and others not. Thus in WBP there are five additional passages which are missing from most of the early manuscripts other than El, Dd 4.24 and Gg 4.27, namely [D44a-f, 575-84, 609-12, 619-26 and 717-20]. Since the last four passages are in El they were included in Skeat's lineation, whereas the first one was not, though in his notes he described it as genuine. In most subsequent discussions, therefore, the first passage is only too readily regarded as spurious and the other four as genuine (even though only three of them are found, for example, in Gg 4.27). It appeared to many subsequent scholars as if the problem of what was genuinely part of the poem had been decided and the only matter remaining for discussion was the order of the tales. What might seem a subordinate matter thus became the primary object of scholarly investigation after Skeat's time.

Skeat's edition commences with section 1 as usual. CkT is shown to be incomplete with a row of dots and the rubric, taken from Hg, 'Of this Cokes tale maked Chaucer na more'. Because the poem is edited as fragmentary, there is no hesitation in pointing to its incomplete nature. Then follow MLPT. After that comes section 10, because the Chaucer Society grouping had joined sections 3 and 10 as Fragment B. The Man of Law's endlink (which is not in El) is converted into the Shipman's prologue, following Selden, the only manuscript in which this join occurs. The reading 'Shipman' is given at [B¹1179]. In MkT the Modern Instances occur in the middle, although that arrangement is not found in El. NPP has the longer form. After NPT Skeat printed the endlink (which is not in El) under an editorial title 'Epilogue to the Nonne Preestes Tale'. This is the first time the concept of an epilogue appears in the poem, for previously editors had thought each tale had only a prologue, other links being described as 'The words of the Host' or something similar, though they were always seen as linking devices. The acceptance of the idea of an epilogue allowed for links which did not lead on to another tale to be incorporated in the text as genuine, for the epilogue to NPT concludes Fragment B and can therefore only look backwards. PhT which follows has been stripped of the prologue it had in previous editions; section 9 then proceeds as usual. Next comes section 2 with its usual order; as noted, WBP has [D 575-84, 609-12, 619-26 and 717-20] but not [D44a-f]. This is followed by the Clerk's prologue and tale, the latter including the Wife of Bath stanza and the envoy. The Clerk's endlink or Host-stanza is relegated to a footnote as 'genuine, but rejected' by Chaucer. Skeat suggested that Chaucer's first intention was to end the tale without the Wife of Bath stanza and envoy, but with the Host-stanza, even though El contained both forms of what Skeat understood to be alternative endings. The link with MeT which follows is provided by the Merchant's prologue [1213-44]. This tale is followed by its epilogue [E2419-40], which is separated from the prologue to SqT [F1-8], even though El starts the Squire's prologue at [E2419]. Here Skeat has been influenced by the Chaucer Society's arrangement of groups to break up what is clearly a single link in Ellesmere into two editorial links. Once again he has had recourse to the new arrangement that tales can have an epilogue. The incompleteness of SqT is indicated by a row of dots, and as the tale was unfinished it could not be followed by an epilogue. Consequently the link [F673-708] is introduced by El's rubric 'Here folwen the wordes of the Frankelin to the Squier, and the words of the Host to the Frankelin'. FkPT are then followed by the prologues and tales of the Nun (called the Second Nun) and the Canon's Yeoman. Sections 11 and 12 complete the edition with their normal order including the Retraction.

Skeat printed in his edition many lines which were not in Tyrwhitt but which are found in El such as [A3155-6 and 3721-2], and this is hardly unexpected since El was his base. More surprisingly he included a number of lines which are not in El in addition to the two major passages [B^{1}1163-90 and B^{2}4637-52]. Some of these lines are found in Tyrwhitt, and that may have influenced Skeat regarding their inclusion. They include 1:253-4, [A2681-2, C103-4 and C297-8] among others. No reason is offered as to why these lines are included, though naturally they are claimed as 'genuine'. As we saw, Skeat made no attempt to work out a textual recension for the poem so that he could base his text on solid evidence. One can only agree with Hammond who wrote: 'It is evident to any close student of the Canterbury Tales that Skeat has not devoted to the MSS such examination as Morell or Tyrwhitt made, and that his editorial procedure, a century and more after Tyrwhitt, is guided by the erroneous supposition that the true

Chaucerian readings may be picked out intuitively, instead of by the laborious and impartial comparison of all the authorities. We find in him still the view of Bentley, "Nobis et ratio et res ipsa centum codd. potiores sunt" '.[8] Yet Skeat instituted the modern preference for El as the base manuscript of modern editions – a preference which still lingers on among scholars, even though Skeat had made his choice not on grounds of a manuscript recension, but simply because it contained the highest number of the lines which he intuitively felt should be included in a modern edition. Before his time other manuscripts like Ha7334 were more influential. Skeat also influenced ideas about the poem because he institutionalized the group numbering of the Chaucer Society which has been used in discussions of the poem until very recently. Yet that numbering makes certain assumptions about the links between some tales and so is better discarded. Skeat had a mixed system of rubrics to the tales. He takes over some rubrics from El and Hg, but he also invents modern rubrics when he feels it necessary. Finally he also confirmed the policy of making editorial changes on metrical grounds, in particular in relation to final – e. For example, at 1:8 all the early manuscripts except Ha7334 agree with Hg in reading *his half cours*. Skeat argued that the metre needed the reading *halfe*, which is what he put in his edition. Some metrical changes were even more far-reaching than this one. These alterations were made on the assumption that one had a complete understanding of Chaucer's language and metre; and it is only recently that this assumption has been called seriously into question.

That Skeat was influenced by Tyrwhitt is clear not only from his own words, but also from his treatment of some editorial problems. Thus Tyrwhitt had omitted the Clerk's endlink (or Host-stanza) partly because it did not fit in with his scheme of prologue – tale. Although Skeat allowed for the possibility of a tale having an epilogue, he did not include this stanza even though it occurred in El, his base, and in Hg, which he later recognized as the earliest manuscript. Instead he suggested that the stanza had been part of the earlier ending of the poem, even though his manuscripts did not support this idea. El, for example, has the Wife of Bath stanza, the envoy and the Host-stanza. The omission of the stanza in Tyrwhitt led Skeat to omit it and to devise an explanation of alternative endings – an explanation that has remained a potent force ever since.

The influence of Skeat can be seen in the Globe Chaucer which was first published in 1898 and frequently reprinted. It remained one of the most popular one-volume editions of Chaucer's works.

---

[8] Hammond 1908 p. 146.

The Canterbury Tales was edited by Alfred Pollard, and although it claims to be a critical text it follows Skeat's edition in almost all particulars. Pollard kept Skeat's order with all the links accepted in that edition; he edited from El; and he used the Chaucer Society group numbering and lineation. Even the passages not in El accepted by Skeat reappear in the Globe edition with the sole exception of the couplet 1:253-4 which is relegated to a footnote. Pollard repeats the Hg rubric at the end of CkT, but otherwise is more restrained than Skeat in the use of modern rubrics. He accepts that Gamelyn is not by Chaucer. He places the Modern Instances in the middle of MkT for in El they come at the end 'wrongly as the Host's talk shows'. The Nun's Priest's endlink is included, though its 'authenticity is not above suspicion'. In accepting the authority of El Pollard claims it is a 'a most carefully written MS, well spelt and observant of grammatical forms, with readings always straightforward and intelligible'.[9] Scholarly acceptance of the excellence of El was now firmly established, although relatively recent.

In 1940 the eight-volume *The Text of the Canterbury Tales* edited by John Manly and Edith Rickert appeared. This edition was based on an exhaustive investigation of all known manuscripts which were arranged into groups to illustrate the development of the text. However, the editors believed that Chaucer had issued parts of the poem separately, sometimes in more than one version, and therefore they believed that each tale had a separate textual history. In principle, therefore, the technique of textual recension could not be applied to the poem since that approach presupposes that all copies of a text go back only to a single archetype. Nevertheless, Manly and Rickert applied the technique of textual recension to the poem. They proceeded by determining first which parts of the poem they considered genuine, although the principles used to decide this are not at all clear. Then they subjected the poem to the technique of textual recension by ignoring the fact that some parts of the poem went back, according to their theory, to different archetypes or versions. Having arrived at a manuscript history, they restored to the text those parts of the poem which did not appear in the original archetype but which were added to the text later by Chaucer. Hence they had the worst of both worlds. Their textual recension showed that El was an edited text with many alterations made by a scribe or supervisor. This was hardly a surprising decision, for Skeat had chosen it because it was the fullest manuscript which would need least editing; its status as a conflated text was clear. However, because they accepted Skeat's general views on the text of the poem, they incorporated in their

[9]Pollard, Heath, Liddell and McCormick 1898 p. xxix.

text much that occurs only in El or related manuscripts. They were not influenced by their own textual recension as to what formed genuine parts of the poem; they were only influenced as to particular readings within the lines. Hence they were forced to print very complicated textual traditions for the individual tales to accommodate those passages which were not in the best early manuscripts, but which they considered to be genuine. They followed Skeat in adopting the Chaucer Society groups and their lineation; and this naturally influenced the order of the tales they followed. They adopted modern rubrics to each part of the poem, though they also included the rubrics from El. Although they accepted that Hg was probably the earliest manuscript which contained an excellent text, they were not swayed by its rubrics, order or divisions within the tales to include them in their edition.

They begin the poem with section 1 as usual. Lines 1:253-4 are relegated to a footnote and dubbed 'genuine but cancelled'. In KtT [A2681-2] are included, though they are in neither El nor Hg, and [A2779-82] are also included though they are found in most early manuscripts except Hg and Dd 4.24. KtT is divided into four books, as in El. In MiP [A3155-6] are included in square brackets in the text and it is suggested they 'may be editorial', though what that might mean is not explained. In MiT [A3721-2] are included though they are found only in El of the early manuscripts. There is nothing at the end of CkT to suggest its incompleteness, though this is indicated in the notes. Gamelyn is omitted as 'certainly spurious' though the reasons are not given. Then come the Man of Law's prologue and tale, followed by his endlink with the reading 'somnour' at [B^{1}1179], a reading found in Ha7334 and a few other manuscripts. The reading 'Shipman' is dismissed as spurious. This is followed by section 2 in its normal order. In WBP [D44a-f] are included with that lineation as are the other four passages found only in El and a few other manuscripts. This section is followed by the prologue and tale of the Clerk, which includes the Wife of Bath stanza, the envoy, and the endlink or Host-stanza (but lineated as [E1212a-g]) although in the critical notes the editors say that Chaucer 'discarded this stanza' in a later version. The link [E1213-44] serves as the Merchant's prologue which introduces his tale. At 5:61-2 they include only the first half of the first line; and at 5:986 they include a line found in some manuscripts, but not in Hg or El, both of which originally had blanks for it. The tales of the Merchant and Squire are linked by the Merchant's endlink [E2419-40] and the Squire's prologue [F1-8] which are treated as independent units. SqT includes the last two lines, though there is nothing in the text to indicate its incompleteness, which is referred to in the notes. Then follow [F673-708] as a link with the reading 'frankeleyn' at [F675]; and 6:1-20 act as the Franklin's prologue.

In this tale [F1455-6 and 1493-8] are included although they are found only in El and Additional 35286. The editors took the two passages together, although they would clearly have preferred to regard the first two lines as spurious because 'so unpoetical'. They felt constrained to include them since they wished to include the second passage which is 'thoroughly Chaucerian in thought and style'. FkT is followed by section 9, in which PhT has no prologue. In the link between the Physician and the Pardoner they omit [C297-8] as a couplet belonging to the other version of the link which Chaucer wrote. After section 9, we get section 10 in which ShT has no prologue. In MkT the Adam stanza is included; its omission in Hg and other manuscripts is noted, but no reason for its omission is given. The Modern Instances are put in the middle of the tale even though this is not their position in the better manuscripts. The editors felt that the Host's reference in [B²3972] to the ending of the story of Croesus (10:2670) should not be widely separated from it and that as 10:2665-70 indicate a formal conclusion to the telling of the tragedies nothing should follow it. They suggest that the Modern Instances were written for a different purpose before the poem started, and when Chaucer included this section in the tale he did not make his intentions sufficiently clear, so that the scribes placed it in different positions. In NPP they include [B²3961-80] which they accept as part of the later expanded version. The Nun's Priest's endlink is included, though in the notes it is suggested that it 'though genuine, was rejected'. This is followed by the prologues and tales of the Nun (called the Second Nun) and the Canon's Yeoman. The genuineness of the latter is not questioned, though it is considered a late piece and though it has more textual problems than usual. This may be because it was 'an uncorrected copy upon which Chaucer was still working'. Then come sections 11 and 12 which complete the poem, the latter section including the Retraction.

The editors are not consistent in the way they handle the text. Thus 1:253-4 are relegated to a footnote, although they are genuine but rejected, whereas the endlink to NPT [B²4637-52] is included though it too is genuine though rejected. During the course of the edition they refer to different Chaucerian versions, though it is never made clear which of these versions they are trying to reproduce. Often it seems as though they are trying to edit a later version, but the inclusion of some 'rejected' passages makes that unlikely. To some extent they wish to include as much as possible of what Chaucer wrote, though this does not extend to passages like 1:253-4. It is clear that in their choice of what they considered genuine they were influenced by Skeat, and although they showed he was wrong to prefer El as a base text this new dicovery does not seem to have influenced their ideas about what was Chaucerian. As with so many previous editors, they exercised their own discretion in deciding what was genuine; and like many previous editors, they were therefore strongly influenced by previous editions and decisions. They did not let themselves be guided by their own manuscript recension in this matter. However, as far as order was concerned they rejected the Chaucer Society and Skeat order. Sections 9 and 10 were returned to the second half of the poem and the use of the Man of Law's endlink as the Shipman's prologue was rejected, for it had support only from one late manuscript. But the tales of the Nun and Canon's Yeoman remained immediately before McT because of the reference to Boughton under Blee in CYP.

Since the Manly—Rickert text was produced, there has been little change in editions of the poem until very recently. As far as order is concerned some editors have reverted to Skeat's scheme of having section 10 after section 3, but section 9 has not been moved from its place in the latter half. Where section 2 follows section 3, some editors have emended [B^{1}1179] to give it the reading 'Wife of Bath' to link up with the following prologue, even though that reading is found in no manuscript. The order after section 2 has invariably been the tales of the Clerk, Merchant, Squire and Franklin. Usually section 9 follows at that point with the tales of the Nun and the Canon's Yeoman placed immediately before the Manciple's prologue. Editions have tended to vary slightly over what lines to include in the text, often on no systematic basis. What are described as genuine, but cancelled, passages may be in the text, in square brackets in the text, or in the footnotes, though why is not always evident. It is now customary to include 1:253-4, even if in square brackets. The passages [A2681-2, 2779-82, A3155-6 and A3721-2] are generally included without comment, though Fisher believes the first was marked for excision by Chaucer. In WBP the lines [D44a-f] are more often in the text than not, sometimes in square brackets; the other four passages in this prologue found only in Ellesmere and related manuscripts are included without comment. The endlink or Host-stanza to ClT is often put in the footnotes or placed in square brackets, for it is seen as an earlier ending of the tale or as a cancelled link. In MeT 5:61-2 is either left incomplete or filled from El, but there has been a trend to follow Ha7334 in 5:986. In FkT [F1455-6 and 1493-8] are regularly included. In section 9 [C297-8] are often omitted because they represent the earlier of Chaucer's versions for this link. In MkT the Adam stanza is included and the Modern Instances are placed in the middle; the long form of NPP is a standard feature. The Nun's Priest's endlink is included, though it is noted that it was marked for excision by many editors. CYPT are included without comment.

Hence a fairly standardized text has continued to be presented to readers of the poem, with the differences largely being a matter of deciding whether passages which are accepted as cancelled by Chaucer should be included in the text or not. Increasingly editors have preferred to use Hg as their base text for the readings of individual words and spelling conventions, but this new preference for Hg has not led them to reconsider what parts of the text are genuine and in what order the tales should be arranged. So although Manly and Rickert showed that El was an edited text, it has not lost its appeal for modern editors. The Variorum Edition now in progress uses Hg as its base manuscript, but tends to follow the contents and order of El. It was only in 1980 that a text based exclusively on Hg was published; and the claim of that edition to reflect the state of Chaucer's text at his death as against the standardized text of other modern editions remains a primary concern of this book.

2

Scholarly Opinion of the Manuscript Tradition

In the first chapter I reviewed the way in which editors have presented the text of *The Canterbury Tales* to the reading public. Yet many scholars have expressed views about the manuscript tradition, even if they have never themselves produced editions; and many editors have produced editions without apparently paying much attention to the work on manuscripts and the textual tradition which has been carried out. It is, therefore, also necessary to consider how and why scholarly views about the textual tradition have changed. For the most part this is a story which is confined to the nineteenth and twentieth centuries; before that time there was no discussion of textual problems outside the covers of particular editions. The survey can be arranged for convenience into three periods, which may be associated rather arbitrarily with the Chaucer Society, the edition in 1940 by Manly and Rickert, and the contemporary Variorum Edition. Only the broad outlines of the scholarly debate can be presented here.

The starting point of any survey must be the establishment of the Chaucer Society by F.J. Furnivall in 1868. The Society issued two series of publications, one containing diplomatic editions of various manuscripts of Chaucer's poems and the other devoted to contributions to the study of the poet and his work. As part of the latter Furnivall published *A Temporary Preface to the Six-Text Edition of Chaucer's Canterbury Tales* in 1868.[1] This work was prompted by the need to provide some basis for the diplomatic editions of the early manuscripts of the poem. It must be remembered that Furnivall brought several manuscripts unknown to earlier editors into the discussion of the editorial tradition, of which Hg and El are the two most famous. He accepted that the poem was incomplete and could not be edited as though it were finished. He therefore divided it into various groups or fragments, each of which was provided with its own lineation. What constituted a group and what its position in the poem should be were more difficult problems. Furnivall believed that all the extant

[1]Furnivall 1868.

tales were intended for the outward journey, even though in Pro both an outward and a return journey are planned. He accepted that some of the tales could have been designed for the return journey, but he could see no overriding reason to accept this possibility. As he wrote of PsT 'if any one likes to put the Parson's Tale at the end of the back journey, no one can find fault with him. I prefer to take the Tale as written for the last of the down journey' (p. 38). His acceptance of only an outward journey, which has been generally followed since with a few notable exceptions, to some extent counter-acted the effect of his other opinion that the poem was fragmentary. Since the start and conclusion of the journey were present as well as many intermediate stages, it has been easy for many to assume that the extant fragments added up to what was virtually a complete poem, which had simply been modified by the author as he grappled with his project. This view was further accentuated by Furnivall's insistence on geographical consistency in the representation of the journey. Such consistency could be achieved by his acceptance that no manuscript contained the fragments in their correct order so that any editor was at liberty to rearrange the groups in the order which he felt was the one intended by Chaucer. There is naturally a certain illogicality in assuming that those parts of a poem which had been composed by the time of the author's death and before he could revise them must be coherent in matters of geography, time and fictional reality, particularly as there are many other features in the fragments which were in Furnivall's opinion clearly wrong and needed authorial revision, such as the Nun, or the Second Nun as she is traditionally known, referring to herself as *vnworthy sone of Eue* (7:62).

Furnivall's documentation of his position was neither full nor cogent. He believed that the journey had taken $3\frac{1}{2}$ days and he used contemporary documents to support this contention. The pilgrimage was a leisurely one. He accepted the following order. Section 1 came first because of Pro. Other tales may have been intended to complete the first day's telling, for the pilgrims spent the first night at Dartford. The second day commenced with section 3, which thus came after section 1, partly because that section occupied this position in many manuscripts. The only internal reference to its position is the indication in MLP that the time is about 10 a.m. Furnivall concluded that 'The Pilgrims had evidently 'made a night of it' at Dartford, or been very tired with their journey, so that they started late next morning' (p. 20). This proposal shows that Furnivall did not really accept the poem as fragmentary since in his scheme each section follows on directly from the previous one. If the time was 10 a.m., that could be because Chaucer intended to put some additional tales before this one. Furthermore, the time of day does not tell us which day it is. Because many manuscripts put section 3 after section 1, Furnivall accepted this position. His scheme amounts in practice to accepting the evidence of his favoured manuscript El unless that can be shown to fly in the face of geographical and temporal reality. His problems became more serious with the sequence after section 3, because the manuscripts were themselves at odds over what came next. Furnivall accepted Bradshaw's conjecture that section 10 followed on from MLT, and indeed he thought it was part of the same group since one manuscript has an endlink to MLT to link it with ShT. This enabled the reference to Rochester in MkP (10:1925) to be used to show that the pilgrims spent their second night at Rochester. The third day begins with section 9, for although there is no geographical reference in it Furnivall thought that the Pardoner's request for drink and a cake before speaking implied early morning when people might want a small snack before breakfast. This section provided enough material to fill the gap needed before section 2 which contains a reference to Sitting-bourne, which was the next regular stopping place after Rochester. Once again we can see that Furnivall is motivated by a desire to fill out all the days in a realistic way as though the poem was complete. But sections 9 and 2 were not sufficient for a day's journey and so sections 8 and 5 were incorporated in this day. These two sections which contain the tales of the Clerk and the Merchant were linked together by Furnivall as one group. These tales are linked because both refer to the Wife of Bath and because the first line of the prologue to MeT (which is not in all manuscripts) echoes the last line of the Clerk's envoy. These reasons hardly seem compelling enough to put the two tales into a single group, particularly as the tales are not linked in many manuscripts and as the link which occurs in some manuscripts to join the tales of the Merchant and the Squire has to be divided between two of Furnivall's groups. Links which were regarded as genuine by Furnivall proved the unity of some groups, but did not establish the group unity of the Merchant's and Squire's tales. The reason that Furnivall established a group boundary between these two tales is that he believed the pilgrims made their third overnight stop at Ospringe after MeT, because that fitted in with his geographical and time sequence. Since other overnight stops coincided with group boundaries, he clearly had to establish a group boundary here no matter what the evidence of the link between the tales which he accepted as genuine. The final day began with the Squire, and his tale was placed in the same group as that of the Franklin because some manuscripts have a link which unites them. After that we get section 7 or NnT, which in many manuscripts is linked with CYPT. Since CYP refers to Boughton and the Forest of Blean, in the geographical sequence the group which Furnivall designated to contain NnT and CYPT must occur at this stage. Because McP refers to 'Bobbe-vp-and-down, Vnder the Blee' (11:2-3), it was natural for Furnivall to put it after CYPT, for *Blee* must be Blean whatever precisely *Bobbe-vp-and-down* refers to. This left only PsT to fit into the sequence of the final day, which meant that this tale occupied the concluding part of the day allowing the pilgrims to enter Canterbury before evening. But McT and PsT are not inseparably linked with each other or with other tales and so were allocated to separate groups.

Furnivall also included notes on the six manuscripts printed in the Society's six-text edition, which he compared with Ha7334 which had until then been the manuscript most often used as the base text for editions. He considered El the best manuscript, although he accepted that it was probably not as early as Ha7334. His reasons for preferring El are largely orthographical and grammatical, for its language was more to his taste. It was also more regular in the matter of final $-e$. He compared the two manuscripts in certain readings, and decided that in some cases El was better and in others Ha7334. Hg he took to be the second best manuscript, though his comments on it are brief and hardly illuminating. He also provided a comparison of the six manuscripts with Ha7334 in many readings, but he drew no conclusions from this exercise.

There can be little doubt that Furnivall was impressed with El as an object, because it is a finely produced manuscript, and as containing a text that was written in a language which he thought approximated most closely to Chaucer's, though he failed to offer any proof of this. He consequently adopted it as the most authoritative manuscript and he followed its lead in most textual matters. Hence the links and the order of the fragments in El provided Furnivall with his point of departure, though he was prepared to break away from it where other considerations intervened. One of those considerations was the arrangement of the tales into a $3\frac{1}{2}$ days' journey from Southwark to Canterbury. The division of the poem into groups reflects the position in El, except where the overnight stay in Ospringe forced him to make a break in the link joining the tales of the Merchant and Squire and the link between McT and PsT. There is no very clear argument why these two tales do not occupy the same group, but Furnivall probably felt the time in the tales was not co-terminous. Furnivall offered no textual evidence for preferring El or for arranging the groups in the way he did; even his decision that the poem portrayed only the outward journey was based on personal opinion. Nevertheless, his decisions have been followed by most scholars ever since. For example, those who wish to suggest that some tales are for the homeward journey find it difficult to make much impact on the stranglehold of the single journey. And the group division and lineation have been followed in most editions, even though the reasons for it have been largely discredited and most editors have arranged the tales in a different order. It was nevertheless a great improvement on the continuous lineation of earlier editors.

Furnivall's position did not command universal approval in his own day and he himself comments on Henry Bradshaw's disagreement. But because Furnivall's arrangement was incorporated into the Chaucer Society prints, it became universally known and copied. Bradshaw issued what he considered a working division of the poem into fragments in 1871, but this was not formally published until his collected papers appeared in 1889.[2] It appears to have been circulated in his lifetime only to interested individuals. Bradshaw divided the poem into twelve fragments as follows:

1 Section 1 (to which Gamelyn was sometimes added in manuscripts).
2 Section 3 (with the endlink).
3 Section 2.
4 Section 8.
5 Section 5.
6 Section 4.
7 Section 6.
8 Section 7 and CYPT.
9 Section 9.
10 Section 10.
11 Section 11.
12 Section 12.

It will be seen that this division corresponds for the most part with the arrangement of sections in my own edition, and this arrangement was arrived at by Bradshaw through his study of many manuscripts. As Bradshaw wrote 'Having found between fifty and sixty copies of the Canterbury Tales, and having further noticed that very few of them have the contents in the same order, I have been able, after a minute examination of a good number, so far to break the work up into what I have been led to believe were the fragments as left by the author' (p. 102). He did not provide his reasons for this arrangement, though he clearly had worked through a lot of manuscripts. His knowledge of the manuscripts seems to have been more profound than Furnivall's. He was able to divide the manuscripts into three groups, of which he thought the one followed essentially in Ha7334 and adopted by Wright and Morris to be the most authentic. The order adopted by Tyrwhitt,

[2]Bradshaw 1889 pp. 102–48.

which comprised a second group, he claimed was the result of editorial intervention after Chaucer's death. The order of the third group, followed by Thynne, was the least satisfactory. In placing manuscripts into one of his three groups he recognized that the order of the tales of the Clerk, Merchant and Squire provided the best test. Bradshaw's scheme would have provided a much better foundation for future scholarship than Furnivall's, and it is a pity that it did not become better known.

Skeat, who was familiar with the work of Furnivall and Bradshaw, published his account of the evolution of *The Canterbury Tales* in 1907, which was some time after the completion of his edition of Chaucer's works.[3] In order to discuss the development of the poem he divided it into fourteen fragments. These consisted of the twelve proposed by Bradshaw and two others, largely to accommodate the arrangement in Hg. Bradshaw's fragment 10 was divided into two because MkT and NPT were separated in Hg from the other tales in that fragment and were placed earlier in the manuscript. It has since been realised that this is a case of faulty binding, though Skeat was not aware of this. In addition Bradshaw's fragment 8 was divided into two because CYPT was not in Hg, and therefore it had to occupy a different fragment from NnT in Skeat's arrangement. Starting with these fourteen fragments Skeat based his evolution on the way in which the fourteen were gradually amalgamated so that in the final order there were only eight. He made certain assumptions. The manuscripts are related to one another in their order and show a progression in the development of the text. There is no indication of variant lines of development. Chaucer wrote almost all the poem before he started to arrange the fragments: 'we see that after Chaucer had once begun to put his Tales together, he wrote very little that was new. The only important addition was the Canon's Yeoman's Tale; and the next most important contribution was the new Clerk—Merchant link in the Harleian scheme'. (p. 27). In his orders Chaucer was merely adjusting the bits which he already had. This certainly gives the impression that Skeat felt Chaucer had by this time more or less completed as much of the poem as he was going to, although the poem was still fragmentary. Skeat seems to have thought in terms of a single outward trip only, though he accepted that the geography of the fragments was faulty and would have been revised. For him the presumed geographical arrangements of the journey were less significant than the tale-orders found in the manuscripts. The most coherent order in which the pieces are united to form the fewest fragments is by his definition the last. He understood Hg to be the earliest order because it

[3]Skeat 1907.

contained 13 separate fragments and no CYPT. After Hg, there are a further three Chaucerian orders represented respectively by Petworth, Lansdowne and Ha7334, with Corpus occupying an intermediate position between Petworth and Lansdowne though it did not form a separate arrangement. The orders represented by Hg, Petworth, Lansdowne and Ha7334 were all Chaucerian ones, and as Ha7334 was the last it represents 'the only *authorised* order' (p. 23). El has simply rearranged the units found in Ha7334 and therefore represents 'an "edited" text, *i.e.* one due to some scribe or editor, and not to the author himself' (p. 20). Although Ha7334 had the best order, it also had a text which was far inferior in its readings to those in many other manuscripts.

There are certain problems with Skeat's views which he does not face up to. If Ha7334 has Chaucer's final order, why does it have such a bad text? If Chaucer made these various orders at the end of his life when the poem as we have it was substantially complete, they must have been executed very quickly one after the other. If this is the case, it is not clear why Chaucer had these varying orders written out in manuscripts, since that would be costly, or why these orders should have been 'published' so that further copies of them could be made. Skeat rejects Gamelyn from the Chaucer canon, although it occurs in Ha7334 which contains his most authoritative order. How did an authoritative manuscript come to contain a tale which was not genuine? Although Skeat worked from the group lineation accepted by Furnivall, his work called Furnivall's arrangement into question. Skeat never considered this fundamental problem. It is also not clear why Chaucer should have made all these different orders at a particular time in the composition of an unfinished poem, but the implication could well be that Chaucer knew he had not long to live and wanted to tidy the text up before he died. Finally Skeat referred to the interesting case of *sterres* (1:2039), which in many early manuscripts is corrupted to read something like *sertres* as in Hg. Skeat suggested that the misreadings could result from a misplaced abbreviation mark for *er* in the copytext, though this might imply that the early manuscripts all used the same copytext. Skeat did not draw any conclusions from the misreadings, but they may form one reason for his thinking that the orders of the poem were all closely related to one another.

Skeat's work shows us how strong a hold Furnivall's groups had on scholarship, even though they corresponded to none of the orders which Skeat himself postulated in the poem's evolution. His preference for the order of the text in Ha7334 was not followed, partly because other scholars continued to prefer the text and language found in El and partly because Ha7334 was seen by many as an edited text. Equally his recognition that Hg contained the earliest version seems to have had little impact on subsequent scholarship.

In 1909 Tatlock published his study of Ha7334, because he recognized its crucial position in discussions of the development of the poem.[4] He accepted it was unlikely that Chaucer had produced more than one version of a fragmentary poem like *The Canterbury Tales* so that different manuscript versions were more likely to be scribal than authorial. In Ha7334 itself there is no sign of extensive revision; there are some extra couplets in SuT, but otherwise the changes are of a minor textual nature. CkT and SqT are still fragments, and in any revision it is likely they would have been completed. In addition there are many links which are missing and many inconsistencies which have not been ironed out. Furthermore, Ha7334 includes Gamelyn which is a spurious tale, and so it cannot have been included in a Chaucerian revision. Finally, the order in this manuscript is unsatisfactory. All these points speak against Ha7334 being a Chaucerian revision, and they are of course supported by the state of the text in the manuscript which all scholars had accepted as being inferior in its readings to many other early manuscripts. Ha7334, though an early manuscript, must be considered a scribal revision of Chaucer's unfinished poem. 'The conclusion seems inevitable that most of its important peculiarities are due to some devoted student of Chaucer, well-educated, intelligent and rather sensitive, but somewhat pedantic and liable to lapses of attention and even good sense' (p. 32). Tatlock accepted that there were various groupings of manuscripts, each of which was derived from the original. Rather than a steady development as suggested by Skeat from one version to the next, he envisaged a series of independent texts all deriving from a single source but not otherwise linked.

In the meantime more detailed textual studies of the poem had been undertaken and the results published in the Chaucer Society transactions. The most important of these were those by John Koch, who not only studied PdT in depth across numerous manuscripts but also studied the textual affiliations of the eight earliest manuscripts.[5] He reached these conclusions. The manuscripts can be divided into two major groups, and of the early ones El, Hg, Gg 4.27 and Dd 4.24 belong to one group and Corpus, Petworth, Lansdowne and Ha7334 to the other. El and Hg are closely related in one group, as are Corpus and Lansdowne in the other, but no early manuscript was used as copytext by another. Of the early manuscripts El contains the best text, for its language is closest to Chaucer's, though it does have mistakes. None of the

[4]Tatlock 1909.
[5]Koch 1902 and 1913.

31

scribes seems to have understood Chaucer's metre, and this for Koch was a matter of great importance since the way in which the scribes handled the metre guided him in assessing the textual value of the manuscripts. Although no manuscript acted as copytext for another, the early manuscripts do show agreement in misreadings, and so considerable contamination across these manuscripts has taken place. Thus when a manuscript in one group deviates from the other manuscripts in that group, it will often share readings with the manuscripts in the other group. How this contamination took place is not explained in detail, though Koch thought there were intermediate exemplars between Chaucer's original and the extant manuscripts. The difficulties presented by this contamination across groups, but also within them, could be explained 'on the assumption of *the existence of some better and more complete Ms.* now lost, to which one or the other scribe of the said Mss. had access' (p. 420). Of the early manuscripts only Hg in addition of El had a good text, though parts of Dd 4.24 and Corpus were also reliable. Finally, Koch claimed that the state of the manuscripts precluded the theory that the individual fragments had been circulated independently before the 'complete' poem was published. The manuscripts are too similar for this to be at all probable.

Much of the work from this period is admirably summarized by Eleanor Hammond in her *Chaucer: A Bibliographical Manual* (1908).[6] In this work she related what other scholars have proposed rather than made any of her own suggestions. However, her summation helped to establish a core of accepted scholarship, which recognized El as the best manuscript.

Skeat returned to defend his position in 1909.[7] He added little that was new, though he developed Bradshaw's point that the crucial test in the order of the tales was the position of those by the Clerk and Squire. He represented the development in this way:

Hengwrt.	Man of Law; Squire; Merchant; Franklin; Clerk.
A. Petworth.	Man of Law; Squire; Merchant; Clerk; Franklin.
B. Lansdowne.	Man of Law; Squire; Clerk; Merchant; Franklin.
C. Ha7334.	Man of Law; Clerk; Merchant; Squire; Franklin.
	(p. 46)

This table shows how the Clerk was gradually advanced in the order of tale-telling, and for Skeat this was conclusive proof of Chaucer's rearrangement so that Ha7334 represented his final

---

[6]Hammond 1908.
[7]Skeat 1909.

authoritative version. The changes in the links arose from this re-positioning of these tales.

In this early period of discussion, interest focused on Ha7334 and its relation to El. This was because Ha7334 was the manuscript that had been used as a base text in many nineteenth-century editions and because it contained unusual readings. Although Hg was considered to be an early manuscript with a good text, it was not given much attention. El became widely accepted as the best manuscript, partly because of its language. Its orthography and morphology were thought to reflect what had been Chaucer's usage, though it was accepted by many that it was not the earliest manuscript. Although Skeat thought there was a single line of development of the manuscripts, it was more common to imagine two or more parallel groupings all descended, not necessarily directly, from the author's original. Skeat arrived at his position from a consideration of the order of the tales; other scholars based their position on the textual tradition itself.

In the second period of scholarship, which we may open with Brusendorff's book but which largely revolves around the writings of Tatlock, Manly and Dempster, the regard for Ha7334 slipped. It is no longer accepted as a possible base text; it is an early, but erratic, manuscript. At the beginning of this period El is accepted as the best manuscript, though during it its position is threatened by Hg but it is never dethroned. Also scholars become more interested in the problems of the publication of the poem and the nature of Chaucer's original copy. The geographical details of the route lost their appeal.

Much of this new approach can be found in Brusendorff's book of 1925.[8] He accepted that no Chaucer autograph had survived and that the extant manuscripts had been produced by professional scribes, probably working for some commercial publisher. It is therefore important to understand the nature of scribes, who may emend to regularize and improve the text, and the nature of the original. Chaucer's copy was probably an unfinished draft, which contained inconsistencies and incorrect readings. A modern edition might have to reject a good scribal emendation to restore a bad authorial reading. Even the titles were probably not included in the draft so that the attribution of the tale of Cecilia to the Nun is probably scribal and not Chaucer's. His executor may have added marginal notes on Chaucer's draft which were developed in various ways by the scribes. Chaucer used the pilgrimage frame artistically, and we should not expect factual realism in the journey particularly as the poem was unfinished.

Brusendorff accepted Koch's division of the manuscripts into

[8]Brusendorff 1925.

two major groups, which he called the 'All England' and the 'Oxford' groups. These were further divided into sub-groups, but there was also considerable contamination across the two major groups. The All England group was the better of the two, and of its manuscripts El was undoubtedly the best, though Hg was also a good manuscript. The reason for El's excellence does not lie in its language or metre, but in its textual readings, though Brusendorff does not argue the matter in depth. He accepted many of the extra lines found only in El as genuine and was therefore forced to conclude that it represented a separate sub-group by itself of the All England group. Since all manuscripts go back to the same Chaucerian original, for it is unlikely that he revised the poem in its unfinished state, the extra lines in El must come from additions on the original which were not picked up by other scribes. Some of the variation among the manuscripts can therefore be attributed to the nature of the original as a draft. That may also have contained lines cancelled by Chaucer which were nevertheless incorporated by some scribes, though not by others. Even so, the scribes of the extant manuscripts did not have direct access to Chaucer's original, for at least one copy intervenes in all cases. Because he accepted that El had the best text, Brusendorff assumed that Chaucer's draft was made up of eight sections, perhaps consisting of quires of loose leaves, which were made up of the following parts:

1 Section 1.
2 Section 3, with *Gamelyn* inserted later.
3 Section 2.
4 Sections 8, 5, 4, 6.
5 Section 9.
6. Section 10.
7. Section 7 and CYPT.
8. Sections 11 and 12.

This arrangement is quite different from the group order proposed by Furnivall, but Brusendorff did not question the acceptance of that group division and lineation which he like other scholars adopted for his discussion.

Tatlock's contribution in 1935 to the second phase of scholarly discussion took the form of an article in *PMLA*.[9] He developed Brusendorff's point that Chaucer left the poem in draft form, perhaps on loose sheets. The scribes used that exemplar and they were motivated by commercial pressures to make the unfinished poem appear as presentable and as complete as possible. None of the poem had been published before Chaucer's death and it is likely that it had never been revised. There are no obvious signs of

[9] Tatlock 1935.

revision by the author in the textual tradition, and there are many indications of a lack of revision. It is probable that when Chaucer died the poem was left in various fragments among his papers. After his death 'no one can doubt that immediately the MS of the *Tales* would be sought on his desk or in his chest, and pounced on with intense curiosity and interest' (p. 107). Naturally anything may have happened to the original at that time: parts of it may have been mislaid. Ultimately it would be prepared by some kind of editor for publication. Chaucer left eight fragments of the poem, which are bound together internally by linking devices; these eight fragments correspond to those proposed by Brusendorff. The order of these fragments had not been indicated by Chaucer on the manuscript, though it is likely that he knew how he would have arranged them. The order proposed by Furnivall is the most satisfactory one, though it is not found in any manuscript. This itself is confirmation that the scribes did not have a Chaucerian order to work from, but were inventing their own.

Tatlock thought three manuscripts were the earliest and most important for textual study, El, Hg and Ha7334. He noted that Hg and El were by the same scribe and that Hg was the earlier of the two, though he evidently believed that El was the best manuscript. Hg is earlier because it has an order which is inferior to El's and because it has many omissions, of which CYPT is one. Tatlock added a lengthy addendum on Hg, and by doing so he was the first to give Hg proper recognition. He understood the need for a more elaborate study of this manuscript, which was the oldest and most significant. It was copied from the same exemplar as El probably consisting of loose sheets. It has a bad order, because when it was made the editor(s) had arrived at no set order for the fragments, and so Hg's order may be regarded as a provisional editorial order. Tatlock did not take this argument any further in his article. The problem arises why El should have extra lines and tales if it was copied from the same exemplar as Hg, particularly if those extra pieces are regarded as genuine. His work is the first to pay due regard to Hg's pre-eminence as a good early manuscript without sacrificing the order and extra passages which are found in El.

The Manly–Rickert edition of 1940 contained a lot of introductory matter to explain the basis of the work; and although that introduction is not always clear, some difficulties were explained in an article by Germaine Dempster.[10] The main points of the Manly–Rickert position may be said to be these. Although there was an authorial copy in Chaucer's possession, individual parts of the poem were published by Chaucer and were in circulation in his lifetime. This pre-publication was posited to

[10]Dempster 1946, and Manly and Rickert 1940.

explain the authorial variants in the text, the evidence that some scribes had acquired their copy piecemeal, and the possession of many early manuscripts by friends of Chaucer. The many divergences in the text were explained partly by scribal alteration, but principally by authorial variants, which may have been written in the text or on separate slips. The varying text was needed to explain the extra lines which are found in El and which were accepted as genuine. In principle this meant that the text existed in various authorial forms, and the purpose of their text was to establish and represent the author's final intentions in so far as they could be elucidated. Because of the variants in the text, it followed that each tale, and sometimes parts of a tale, had a separate textual tradition; and this in turn meant that there were lots of exemplars which had been used by the early scribes although none of those exemplars survived. The order of the tales was not decided by Chaucer, and the manuscript orders represent scribal attempts to arrange the extant fragments in a satisfactory system. Hg is the manuscript with the most reliable text, for its scribe was both good and conservative. His order was not Chaucerian, but represents a first attempt at trying to arrange the pieces coherently. The scribe of Hg acquired his fragments piecemeal, which partly explains his order, and some pieces he never got hold of. El has a less good text, but it contains material which comes direct from Chaucer's own copy. Hence, although the Manly–Rickert edition is eclectic in its readings, it may be said to prefer readings in Hg but material in El.

There are difficulties in the position adopted in the Manly–Rickert edition, which would probably not have been resolved even if they had published further work; both died in fact at about the time the edition appeared. One relates to the exemplars which are posited, but which have all disappeared. It seems *a priori* unlikely that this would have happened since so many other manuscripts survive. In addition, there is no evidence of pre-publication in the extant manuscripts. Single tales or groups are not found by themselves in early manuscripts. The editors worked on the principle of recension to establish their text, but that method can succeed only if there is one archetype. Their theory of authorial revision implies more than one archetype, and so recension does not seem an appropriate method to apply to this poem. In fact they used recension to establish the textual readings and ignored the extra lines in El for this purpose. They simply accepted El's lines as genuine without producing any evidence to support their claim, and they incorporated these lines into the text without letting them affect their stemma of manuscripts. Basically they were often motivated more by what they thought was appropriate than what the textual evidence actually suggested. Their claim that each tale has one or more different exemplars is inherently unlikely and is accepted on rather shaky textual grounds. The readings which they regarded as significant were often arbitrarily chosen and usually insufficient to build up the hypothesis of exemplars.[11] In many ways the edition helped to confirm the pre-eminence of Hg, but was otherwise somewhat retrograde in its scholarly direction. In one respect Manly and Rickert did promote further scholarship, in that they arranged the manuscripts into certain groups which have been used ever since as the basis of manuscript discussions. They thought some manuscripts were anomalous, such as Hg and Ha7334, and these were left outside the main lines of descent. Otherwise the manuscripts were divided into four major groups, known as *a, b, c* and *d*. The alphabetical sequence does not necessarily imply primacy. El was associated with group *a*, though it was not identical with it. The *b, c* and *d* groups can be represented by Helmingham, Corpus and Petworth respectively.

Mrs Dempster continued Manly's work, but her conclusions basically modified many of the positions he had adopted. One article dealt with the change of ink in Hg after 5:1074 in MeT.[12] The change of ink by the scribe must represent a break in copying, perhaps only overnight, which suggests that in his exemplar there was something which led him to make a break there. The importance of this feature in Hg is that group *c* manuscripts lack the end of MeT; everything from 5:1075 is missing. This indicates that there was something in the exemplars of both Hg and group *c* manuscripts which encouraged a break at this point in MeT. Presumably the exemplar was the same, for it was unlikely that such a distinctive feature would have been reproduced in one exemplar after the other. Possibly the exemplar was Chaucer's own copy; and if it consisted of loose sheets, then one of those sheets must have started at 5:1075. A new sheet would be a natural point for a scribe to pause in his copying overnight or longer, and it is quite understandable that odd sheets at the end of the tale had been lost (if only temporarily) from the exemplar. Mrs Dempster concluded from this that 'the very great majority of the manuscripts postulated as heads of genetic groups . . . were copies made after Chaucer's death from the papers he had left' (p. 329). If so, this would mean there was no pre-publication of manuscripts, and the groups established by Manly and Rickert would be much more integrated than those editors had assumed.

This latter point was developed in two further articles by Mrs Dempster. In the first of these she examined how the group *d* manuscripts are derived from group *c*.[13] Manly and Rickert had

[11]Blake 1983, and Kane in Ruggiers 1984.
[12]Dempster 1948b.
[13]Dempster 1948a.

shown that textually these two groups were very similar, but they were different in the middle section of the poem containing the tales of the Squire, Merchant, Clerk and Franklin. But the *c* group had no links for these tales, which the original scribe of the *d* group borrowed from Hg. It was the availability of these links which encouraged the *d* scribe to modify the *c* order. The scribe of the *d* order was trying to make the poem as complete as possible and this accounts for his order and for additional spurious links which he included. Since it was accepted by Manly and Rickert, and further confirmed by Dempster, that the *b* order was a development of *d*, this article went to show that at least three groups, *b*, *c* and *d* were closely linked in order and that their scribes had some access to Hg. This could only mean that at least the *c* and *d* groups orginated from the same scriptorium, and it helped to show that the production of the manuscripts of the poems was more unified than had been indicated in the Manly–Rickert edition.

In the second article Mrs Dempster concentrated on the whole question of tale order, but with particular reference to the relationship between Hg and El.[14] She accepted that Hg's order was bad and had arisen through the way in which the scribe acquired the pieces. Although El's order was a good one, it seemed to be dependent on Hg. In Chaucer's original papers sections 1, 2, 9 and 10 (at least until TMel) were constant; their contents were fixed. The other tales stood by themselves and were not part of a Chaucerian constant group. But various sections like 3 and 9 have no indication as to geography and yet tend to come in the same place in most orders. Furthermore FkT is frequently followed by NnT, even though there is no link to join them. This can mean only that there was some coordination in the orders of the tales, which were editorial. Dempster proposed that the order developed from Hg to El and the *a* group, which was then developed by the *c* group, to which Ha7334 is closely related. The *c* group leads, as she showed in her previous article, to *d* and *b*. She concluded that all orders were therefore related and that the tale order development was a relatively simple one. Moreover, her theory assigned a large role to Hg in the order, even though it played a small part in the development of the text. Many scholars have denigrated the scribes of the poem for not reproducing a sensible order, but Dempster proved that they were not without interest in the problem or unintelligent in trying to solve it. They did, however, have a different set of assumptions to which they worked. Although Dempster tried to work within the framework of the Manly–Rickert textual proposals, her conclusions called into question many of their assumptions. The development of the

[14]Dempster 1949.

manuscript tradition was much simpler than they had supposed, and Hg was clearly a manuscript of great importance in that tradition.

The end of our second stage of scholarship left the manuscript tradition in some confusion. El was still used as the basis for editions and its order was considered a good order. But Hg was the earliest manuscript and had the best text. Although its order was arbitrary, it formed the basis of El's, though both orders were scribal. Ha7334 was no longer regarded as such an important manuscript. Since then little work has been done on the manuscripts or the manuscript tradition until the last few years. It is not without significance that a modern *Companion to Chaucer Studies*, which has already appeared in a second edition, contains no chapter on the manuscripts or the manuscript tradition of any Chaucerian poem.[15] Most modern studies on the poem have been concerned with criticism and its reference to the relationship of two or more tales. These studies usually take the traditional editorial order based on El as their model, but as they are largely critical in their emphasis they do not concern us here. That two tales may have similarities in theme and approach does not mean that Chaucer meant one to follow the other in the order of tales. Although such studies have accepted the Manly–Rickert position on manuscript tradition, they accept, implicitly or explicitly, that there was only a journey to Canterbury and that the tales were related probably in El's order. Several studies have taken the pilgrimage frame as an important feature of Chaucer's moral and religious purpose, and so a journey ending at Canterbury has supported their critical opinion. In the early 1970s a group of scholars under Professor Ruggiers embarked on a programme to produced a variorum edition of the works of Chaucer as well as facsimiles of the more important manuscripts. The latter have naturally prompted more interest in the manuscript tradition. Other scholars have turned their attention to detailed matters like the palaeography and spelling of the manuscripts. Often these have emphasized the importance and priority of Hg. Even so, the attempt to work out the relationship between Hg and El so that Hg is given proper recognition is a long and painful one; El still commands the support of sentiment, tradition and some conviction. It is partly to help elucidate this relationship that I have written this book. In it some of the views I have already published are repeated, usually in a modified form, so there is no need to review them in detail in this chapter.

Some scholars have tried to break away from the traditional El pattern in ways which do not involve Hg. Thus Charles Owen has

[15]Rowland 1979.

noted, quite correctly, that Pro envisages a journey out and one back and that none of the manuscript orders are authorial.[16] He has proposed that the extant tales should be allocated over an outward and return journey. His suggestion is for a journey of five days with the tales in sections 11, 2, 9, 8, 5, 4 and 7 being told on the return journey in that order. If the order in the manuscripts is not Chaucerian, then this is a perfectly possible solution, though this has nothing to do with the order found in the manuscripts. The same is true of other suggestions which base their order on such premisses as medieval story telling.[17] The rearrangement may be what Chaucer had in mind, but there is no means of proving whether that is so or not.

That El and its order still exercise an immense attraction is indicated by an article by Larry Benson in 1981.[18] His view is that there are two genuine orders established by Chaucer and that all manuscripts' orders derive from these two. It follows from this that Chaucer established these orders in his lifetime and that consequently he had completed the poem: 'we have the work in what Chaucer regarded as its final state; unfinished, unrevised, and imperfect as *The Canterbury Tales* may be, Chaucer was finished with it' (p. 81). The two orders were basically the El-group *a* order of sections 1, 3, 2, 8, 5, 4, 6, 9, 10, 7 (with CYPT), 11 and 12, and the other order in which section 7 (with CYPT) is placed before section 9. Manuscripts of group *a* are not related textually according to Manly and Rickert, and so in them uniformity of order is significant. Benson follows Dempster in accepting that the *b, c, d* groups came from one source and were related; they are scribal developments of a different order. He criticizes the idea proposed by Dempster that the El order is developed from Hg. On the contrary, he sees Hg as being a later order, perhaps later than most of the other manuscripts. This arises in part because he accepts that many passages and links not in Hg are genuine, and because where Hg has adapted links found also in El he accepted that the El versions are better metrically and therefore written by Chaucer. He also finds it improbable that Hg was used by so many later scribes in their orders, even though they made no use of his text. Consequently the relationship between groups *b, c,* and *d* is the reverse of what Dempster proposed. Since Hg is an early manuscript, it follows that the manuscript tradition of the poem was well established by the time it was written, and this implies that it was started in Chaucer's lifetime. Since the *a* order is 'of considerable artistic merit' (p. 111) showing an intimate

---

[16]Charles A. Owen Jr, 'The Design of the *Canterbury Tales*,' in Rowland 1979 pp. 221–42.
[17]Allen and Moritz 1981.
[18]Benson 1981.

knowledge of the contents of the tales, then it would be ridiculous to assume that it was put together by anyone else than Chaucer himself. Much of Benson's argument rests on the assumption that there is a correct order and that only Chaucer could possibly know what that correct order was to have been. This assumption runs counter to that generally accepted today, though it needs careful attention. More importantly, Benson's theory deals very unhappily with Hg which he accepts as an early manuscript but which he places at the end of the manuscript tradition.

Many other scholars have also accepted the El order as the best, because Keiser notes 'it is almost impossible not to find special significance' in the fact that a credible tale order is found only in El and related manuscripts.[19] He noted also that the manuscript is very beautiful so that whoever commissioned it must have had great affection for the poem. He may even have heard it recited at court. Such assumptions suggest that El had special authority. A vigorous rebuttal of this position has been maintained by Owen.[20] He has repeated that Hg and El are closely related textually, by the same scribe, and not far apart in date. More importantly they share the same type of glossing and marginalia, except that El's is more thorough than Hg's. The two manuscripts reflect an attempt to collect all the genuine material and then to arrange it in a satis-factory way — satisfactory by fifteenth-century standards of text display.[21] The same principles motivated the other early editors. The evidence of the manuscripts suggests that only the text came from Chaucer; the ordering was made by the editors after his death. But there is a progression in that ordering as in the marginalia and other accompaniments of the text from Hg through the other early manuscripts. Even though parts of the poem circulated before Chaucer's death, neither he nor anyone else tried to arrange the poem into an order until after he had died, the neat arrangement and order of the poem found in El which some critics attribute to Chaucer are not his.

An important contribution to the early history of the poem has been made by the palaeographers Doyle and Parkes.[22] Apart from providing an account of the make-up of Hg as a manuscript, they have discovered from the extant manuscripts information about how the scribes worked. It was clear that there was a flurry of activity to produce vernacular texts at the beginning of the fifteenth century. Scribes in the London and Westminster area collaborated to produce some of these. With texts like *Confessio Amantis* the text could be broken up and particular stints sent to different

[19]Keiser 1977-8.
[20]Owen 1982.
[21]See especially Parkes 1976.
[22]Doyle and Parkes 1978 and in Ruggiers 1979.

scribes. That text, unlike *The Canterbury Tales,* was sufficiently standardized for this procedure to be followed. The scribes did not work together in a particular scriptorium, but were probably employed *ad hoc* by an entrepreneur on a piecework basis. The book trade was essentially a bespoke trade and relied on the cooperation of independent members of several crafts. The entrepreneur may himself have been a scribe or illuminator who employed his fellow artisans for a certain project. Some of the scribes like Thomas Hoccleve may have done copying for such entrepreneurs as a kind of second job to supplement the income of their main profession. The conclusions of Doyle and Parkes call into question the Manly–Rickert hypothesis of private and commercial production, for there is no evidence of large commercial scriptoria copying vernacular texts speculatively. The production and apparent standardization of texts does not come from a commercial scriptorium, but from independent scribes working to the requirements of an entrepreneur. The number of manuscripts copied does not suggest that many copies of a text were produced on a speculative basis; the trade responded to the demands of its clients.

A topic which has receiving increasing attention recently is the spelling systems of the manuscripts. Professor Ramsey published a study of the spellings of Hg and El which led him to suppose that they were written by different scribes.[23] He imitated the technique used in studying early printed books of trying to identify the compositors by their spelling habits. By a study of certain forms throughout the text such as *thow* or *thou* and *&* or *and,* he concluded that the spelling systems of the two manuscripts were so different that this could only be explained by the assumption that they were written by two people. Although palaeographers have claimed that the same man wrote both, Ramsey believes the spelling evidence to be stronger and that at best the two men were trained in the same scriptorium. Ramsey also went on to study the variants in El and concluded with Manly and Rickert that these are largely editorial and probably introduced by El's scribe. Its text is far less reliable than Hg's, even when they were using the same exemplar. There is no evidence of supervision in El and so its readings must originate with the scribe. Ramsey was satisfied that the editorial reliance on El is quite unjustified. Recently Samuels has criticized Ramsey's conclusions and shown that Hg and El were written by the same man.[24] The differences in spelling can be explained by the lapse in time between them for El was written perhaps ten years later than Hg. The languages of the manuscripts

[23]Ramsey 1982.
[24]Samuels 1983b.

have also been investigated. For example, David Burnley has studied the inflexions of the adjectives.[25] He showed that there is a grammatical system in these inflexions in Chaucer's language which is preserved in the manuscripts with considerable fidelity. But Hg is the manuscript which preserves the system most completely and may in that respect at least be said to be closest to Chaucer's language. Studies such as these, and others are promised, have helped to prove the standing of Hg as both an early and a very reliable copy of what Chaucer wrote.

Although I will discuss the implications of these scholarly proposals and counter-proposals in the next chapter, the present position reveals how urgently we need a thorough study of the textual tradition of *The Canterbury Tales*. Some modern scholars have reacted against the Manly–Rickert edition to uphold the claims of El's primacy, whereas others have developed their work to suggest that Hg represents most satisfactorily the poem in its form at Chaucer's death.

[25]Burnley 1982.

3

Problems and Proposals about the Manuscript Tradition

In the last chapter I reviewed some of the suggestions that have been made about the manuscript tradition; in this one I will try to isolate the various problems that scholars have highlighted which have to be faced in any discussion of that tradition. I will thus be able to indicate what solutions I will adopt in this book. The basic problem is how one refers to the parts which make up the poem. This way of posing the problem presupposes that there are parts and that the poem is not a complete whole as was implied in those early editions with a continuous system of lineation for the whole work. Some modern scholars, admittedly only a minority, have claimed that the poem is complete in its incompleteness and have suggested that Chaucer had finished with the poem. Yet these scholars also think that the poem underwent several rearrangements, many of which were not authorial. So even for those who adopt this position it is necessary to have a system which allows us to discuss these later arrangements sensibly; hence a continuous system of lineation is not satisfactory. Since it was introduced in 1868 most scholars have used Furnivall's system of nine groups, each with their separate lineation, although many have expressed their dissatisfaction with it and some have proposed alternative solutions. The objections to Furnivall's scheme are that it does not reflect the situation and order of tales in any manuscript and that it does not readily allow for discussion of alternative arrangements because it tends to suggest that a particular arrangement is correct. It has encouraged the acceptance that certain parts of the poem are genuine, and in the recent variorum edition of MiT based on Hg some lines from El were included by the editor simply because of the traditional lineation, which he did not wish to disturb.[1] Furnivall's system reflects an order in a manuscript which most scholars agree is not the earliest, and so it faces the methodological problem of deciding why the group lineation should reflect that stage in the poem's development rather than another.

Already in the nineteenth century Bradshaw realized that to

[1]Ross 1983 p. 226.

discuss the tale order and development of the text it was necessary to have more groups than Furnivall had allowed. In particular he noted that the tales of the Squire, Merchant, Franklin and Clerk were frequently moved and needed to be kept in separate categories. In view of this and because Hg is considered by scholars to be the earliest extant manuscript, I have decided to base the numeration system used in this book on Hg. This is not meant to imply that Hg contains the only genuine pieces by Chaucer. But it does indicate which pieces are in Hg and which are not; the question of what is genuine must be decided later. However, two pieces which were added later in a different ink to fill blanks in Hg have been omitted from the numeration, namely the links that occur in it between the Squire's and Merchant's tales [F673-708] and between the Merchant's and Franklin's tales [E2419-40, F1-8]. Since the three tales which these links join belong to the four which constantly changed their position in the order and their association with other tales, it is not possible to include the links without also implying the tales are part of constant groupings. The links are therefore excluded without at present implying anything regarding their genuineness or otherwise. These links like all pieces found in other manuscripts but not in Hg are referred to by Furnivall's group and lineation system, where that system includes them. Thus a passage which is referred to by numbers only (e.g. 1:115) is in Hg, whereas one referred to by letter and number (e.g. A115) is not (except of course for the two links mentioned above). Those tales have been allocated to the same section which are part of a single continuous grouping in Hg and other early manuscripts, because the tales are joined by the same links without change from one manuscript to the next. These groupings are referred to as sections to distinguish them from the groups, which was the name employed by Furnivall. They are numbered in accordance with their position in Hg, but again this numbering is not intended to imply that the sequence of tales it represents is either correct or Chaucer's. The resulting sections are given below, and in the list it may be assumed that where there is more than one tale in one section those tales are joined by a link which is an integral part of the section. All other links which form part of the system are indicated so that those not mentioned at the beginning or end of a section are not part of the system or numbered.

Section 1	Pro, KtT, MiT, ReT, CkT (incomplete)
Section 2	WBP, WBT, FrT, SuT
Section 3	MLP, MLT
Section 4	SqT (incomplete)
Section 5	MeT
Section 6	FkT

Section 7	NnT
Section 8	ClP, ClT followed by *envoy* and Host-stanza
Section 9	PhT, PdT
Section 10	ShT, PrT, TTh, TMel, MkT, NPT
Section 11	McP, McT
Section 12	PsP, PsT, Rt

It will be observed that some tales such as Gamelyn and CYPT which occur in some early manuscripts are not included in this numeration system. It would be possible to extend the system by referring to these as sections 13 and 14, but this would destroy the purpose of the numeration of isolating what was in Hg as its basis. Consequently these tales are referred to by their names or abbreviations as are those links found neither in this system nor in Furnivall's. It should be emphasized that this numeration is simply one of convenience as a means of discussing the development of the text; it is not intended to pre-empt that discussion or to imply what is or what is not original. It may also be mentioned at this stage that Hg does not contain the end of PsT or Rt, because the last folios of the manuscript are missing. The problem of whether Rt was in Hg will be discussed later, but it seemed convenient to include it in a section since it is found in early manuscripts which are complete. A text based on this numeration and the Hg manuscript can be found in my edition of the poem from 1980.

There are a series of interlocking problems which revolve around the genuineness of its parts and how Chaucer actually wrote the poem. It is universally agreed that not everything that is included in the majority of manuscripts as part of the poem was written by Chaucer, and usually it is assumed that Chaucer left the poem in an incomplete state and that various scribes and editors did their best to fill in the gaps. Inevitably, therefore, there will be a mixture of genuine and spurious material. Although this is a state of affairs which can arise in any medieval text, it is peculiarly characteristic of *The Canterbury Tales* because of the many places where addition and interpolation could occur and because of the interest the text generated. In the past attempts were made to analyse what was Chaucer's own contribution on the basis of metre, style or language. Although the proponents of such attempts have made claims about genuineness on this basis, it is now realized that such studies are unreliable. In the first place, we know little about Chaucer's language, style and metre. Secondly, his own usage could have changed over the period of the poem's composition and many of the tales have different styles because of their subject matter. Thirdly, it may have been possible for others to imitate his language and style sufficiently to deceive a modern scholar. Finally, the poem survives in no autograph copy and so there is no firm basis for comparison. Other attempts to prove what is Chaucer's have been based on what passages fit in well from a critical point of view, for it is often assumed that only Chaucer could produce texts of literary sophistication and subtlety or those which fitted in expertly with what particular critics have felt was his intended development of the poem. Often these views represent little more than a critical justification of those parts of the text which have traditionally been included in editions of the poem. No test has so far been devised which can with confidence distinguish a Chaucerian line from a spurious one − and it is useless to pretend that any solution to the problem of genuineness exists. Nevertheless, the literature is scattered with claims that this or that passage is Chaucer's. Even such a distinguished scholar as Donaldson can write of the manuscripts of *The Canterbury Tales*: 'Fifteen of them are "perfect" in the sense that they contain all the tales, though it should be emphasized that no manuscript is perfect in the sense that it contains every line that Chaucer wrote'.[2] This statement implies that Donaldson can distinguish what Chaucer wrote from what he did not, though how he can do so is not made clear. The idea that we can tell what is genuine from what is not may be alluring, but it is quite unachievable. It has bedevilled study of the poem for too long. It has hampered studies of the development of the manuscript tradition, because particular answers have been required from the data. It is more satisfactory to leave the whole question of genuineness on one side until the manuscript tradition has been elucidated. The latter may help us to come to some decision about the former.

The question of genuineness is related to the way in which Chaucer wrote the poem. There are basically two opposite ways of approaching this problem. One is to propose that Chaucer had a plan of the poem and that he had mapped out the tales and tellers before he commenced writing. If it is put in such a bald way this method is unlikely to command much support. This is because many scholars think that what is left of the poem represents only the outward journey to Canterbury and that consequently Chaucer changed his plan which envisages an outward and a return journey in Pro during the course of the poem's composition. However, it is not certain that there is only an outward journey, and so an overall plan is possible if not widely regarded as likely. Nevertheless, those who see an attempt on Chaucer's part to match tale to teller do envisage a certain amount of planning. The other way is to propose that Chaucer had no plan and constructed his poem on a piecemeal basis. In its most extreme form this method would entail that Chaucer wrote his tales first and then fitted them to a suitable teller

[2]Donaldson 1974 p. 94.

and in this way gradually built up his sections. If the poem actually survived as fragments at Chaucer's death, the latter seems the more attractive possibility. If he had a plan one might have supposed that he would have started the poem at the beginning and then proceeded with its other parts in their correct sequence. He seems rather to have composed the parts in no such regular way. This would suggest that he composed tales as he came across sources that he thought he could use. Some allowance for arbitrariness and lack of planning in the enterprise is probably an unavoidable conclusion. Such a conclusion need not mean that he took up everything that crossed his path, but it does mean that he had to fit the tales he composed to his tellers rather than the other way round. It is unlikely that his sources for tales were so large that he could readily pick and choose only those which were ideally suited for those pilgrims he had included on the way to Canterbury. In fact scholars have not speculated much on Chaucer's method of working, though what has been written by other scholars often presupposes a higher degree of planning than is intimated above.

Whether Chaucer had a master plan or not, did he nevertheless revise those bits of the poem he had written? Many of the tales and links exist in differing states and so it is clear that someone revised them. Whether that reviser was Chaucer, at least in some parts of the poem, is a problem that has provoked considerable discussion. Those who think that he was responsible have based their position on two general contentions. The first is that Chaucer in his short poem to Adam shows an interest in a correct text, for he portrays himself there as emending what the scribe had miscopied. If he took trouble to make this type of correction, he probably revised the text at the same time as he went over it. The texts mentioned in the poem to Adam are the *Boethius* and *Troilus and Criseyde*, and it need not follow that *The Canterbury Tales* had got to the stage when it was copied by a scribe. The second is that many manuscripts do not contain all the lines that editors believe genuine. As we saw above no manuscript contains everything that Donaldson believes Chaucer wrote for the poem. There are various ways of trying to resolve this difficulty, but the most common approach is to claim that the extra lines form part of Chaucerian revisions written either after the first draft was issued or in the margins of the original and hence not included by all scribes. In essence this view of recension comes back to the question of whether we can tell which parts of the poem are Chaucer's and which scribal. Since that matter has been put on one side because it is virtually insoluble, it is sensible also to leave the matter of revision to one side until the textual tradition itself is clearer. Before doing that, we ought to remember that some scholars have argued vigorously against the possibility of Chaucerian revision on general grounds. Since there is so much that is unfinished and unrevised (such as the geographical references), some believe that none of the poem was revised. It does not follow that, because some parts are unrevised in the opinion of modern scholars, no revision on the poem had been carried out by the author. After all revision does not necessarily lead to improvement.

The revision in the poem I have been considering so far is that which is represented by a varying text in different manuscripts; its evidence comes from the failure of the manuscripts to agree on what was the text of a particular passage. There is, however, a different kind of revision which has been proposed for the poem and that is a change of plan which was carried through in all the extant manuscripts. Thus it has been claimed that ShT was originally written for the Wife of Bath. This is because in that tale the narrator apparently uses female personal pronouns as though he were a woman. Thus after saying that a husband has to pay for his wife's expenses, he continues:

> He moot vs clothe and he moot vs arraye
> Al for his owene worship richely:
> In which array we dauncen iolily.   (10:12-14)

Because the narrator appears to speak of himself as a woman, the tale must have been intended, so that argument runs, for a female narrator. Since there is only one secular, married female on the pilgrimage, namely the Wife of Bath, it follows that the tale was designed for her. But the passage, which continues for another five lines, does not have to be interpreted as the narrator's own words or opinion. It is a rhetorical dramatization of a set situation which happens to be put into the Shipman's mouth, but has no bearing on the gender of the narrator.[3] The hypothesis that this tale was intended for the Wife of Bath lacks firm support and may be discounted. Evidence of this kind has been used to decide the textual tradition of the poem, but most of it is very dubious and should not be used as it cannot be substantiated. This type of revision, like the other type, must be put on one side until the manuscript tradition itself has been unravelled.

There is a problem in leaving the question of revision aside until the textual tradition is clearer, namely that the presence or absence of revision could affect the way in which one tackles the problem of the development of the text. The technique of recension, by which through such features as textual error one tries to build up a stemma of the manuscripts' relationships, can only be undertaken if all manuscripts go back to the same archetype. If there had been

[3]Chapman 1956 discusses this point in some detail.

revision, it would not be possible to employ recension, for revision would imply that there were two or more versions of the poem or parts of it so that one would have to take into account a *Canterbury Tales A* and a *Canterbury Tales B* at the very least. If this were true each version of the poem would have its own archetype and stemma. As we saw in the last chapter Manly and Rickert thought that each tale had its own stemma, though they accepted that ultimately all tales went back to a common Chaucerian original despite the fact that they accepted there had been authorial revision in the poem. It is not possible to work in that way. As we shall see in a moment it is possible to work with the assumption that the manuscripts go back to Chaucer's working copy. It is therefore a sensible solution to start with tale orders in the manuscripts, which usually involve additional links to provide the necessary connections to the rearranged tales, and with the passages which are found in some manuscripts rather than others. Conclusions derived from this analysis should provide some indication of the development of the text and a working basis for the provision of a stemma.

Since the time of the Chaucer Society scholars have accepted that there are eight early manuscripts of the poem: Hg, El, Ha7334, Corpus, Gg 4.27, Dd 4.24, Lansdowne and Petworth. Of these only three have been given special prominence either because of an early date or because of a posited excellent text. These are Hg, El and Ha7334. It will therefore be appropriate to consider these three manuscripts and their order and texts in some detail before considering the other early manuscripts. Of these three, Hg and Ha7334 are considered to have a somewhat anomalous order or text. They did not fall into any of the groupings established by Manly and Rickert, who divided most manuscripts into four main groups, labelled *a, b, c* and *d;* the others were anomalous and formed a group which had no special affiliations. Even though the Manly–Rickert methodology has flaws, I will retain their grouping of the manuscripts for the time being, since it conveniently tabulates information mostly about the later manuscripts. There is no point in repeating work which has been generally accepted as far as the composition of the four main groups is concerned. Of the early manuscripts El, Gg 4.27 and Dd 4.24 belong to their group *a*, Corpus and Lansdowne to group *c*, and Petworth to group *d*; Hg and Ha7334 belong to the anomalous group.

The date when the poem was begun or how long it was in progress cannot be determined. It is generally agreed that Chaucer was working on the poem when he died, and this is usually offered as one reason for the incompleteness of tales like SqT. If we accept the poem as incomplete we shall probably not be far wrong; and it may be assumed that incompleteness arose through his death. It is possible as Benson has argued that Chaucer tried to give it a finish before he died, though there do not seem to be any compelling arguments to adopt this position. The fact that many people after Chaucer's death took a hand in rearranging the text would seem to indicate an incomplete poem. If Chaucer had issued an authoritative version and order, there would be less reason for the scribes to tamper with the poem. The more interesting question is when Chaucer commenced the poem. The usual chronology suggests a date about 1385 — a date when he had finished his other writings. This date is an arbitrary one based on the assumption that Chaucer was working on only one text at a time. There are, however, references in other poems to what have been interpreted as earlier versions of what were to become tales in *The Canterbury Tales*. In the *Legend of Good Women* F420 a reference to Palamon and Arcite is taken to imply the existence of an early version of KtT which was written before the poem as a whole was conceived. This interpretation is quite possible, but it is just as likely that *The Canterbury Tales* was begun much earlier than the accepted chronology allows and that the reference in the *Legend of Good Women* is to the tale as we know it. There is no reason to believe that the composition of individual works was kept in watertight compartments by Chaucer, and we may accept *The Canterbury Tales* could have been embarked upon long before the accepted date of 1385. This is an important point which may influence attitudes regarding the pre-publication of parts of the poem, a theory which has extensive implications for its manuscript tradition.

The concept of pre-publication is linked particularly with Manly and Rickert, though it has been supported by some recent scholars like Benson. It has been dismissed as improbable by a wide range of scholars from the time of John Koch onwards. Ultimately the acceptability of this hypothesis depends upon the posited manuscript tradition, for it was invented to explain certain features Manly and Rickert found in it. It helped for example to explain why some genuine pieces were not found in all manuscripts, for revision could have been effected in the text after some tales had been released. Other arguments in favour of pre-publication were the assumed piecemeal way that the scribe of Hg had acquired the fragments of the poem and the fact that many of the early manuscripts were owned by Chaucer's friends. Neither of these arguments is convincing. Other explanations have been offered to explain the arrangement in Hg. If Chaucer's friends owned early manuscripts, it could be because they knew of the poem's existence and ordered copies from the scribes after his death. A further point concerns the references to individual tales which are found in other Chaucerian poems. These references, it has been argued, presuppose that people knew the tale in question and that therefore they must have had access to at least part of the poem – a state of affairs that implies some kind of pre-publication. We have just noted one of these references, that to KtT in *Legend of Good Women.* A second example occurs in the *Envoy to Bukton,* in which the recipient is reminded of the misfortunes of marriage and to emphasize the point a recommendation is given:

The Wyf of Bathe I pray yow that ye rede (29).

If Bukton could read the views peddled by the Wife of Bath, it follows that he would have had access to a manuscript of her tale at least. As this *Envoy* is traditionally dated *c.*1396, It would indicate that this tale was available at least by then. Several points need to be made in this connection. The Bukton *Envoy* cannot be dated accurately and may be later than is assumed, though naturally if it is genuine it would date from Chaucer's lifetime and so the argument as such would not be unduly affected by its date. There were several ways of publishing in the medieval period, of which one was verbal delivery. Bukton may have known of the Wife of Bath in this way, but not necessarily read her tale. We do not need to take this kind of reference too literally in that we have to accept that the recipient could indeed read the work to which he was referred. There are references to many of Chaucer's works in several of his poems and yet there is no evidence that any of them were published in his own lifetime. With *The Canterbury Tales* there is the added problem that the poem in unfinished and therefore it is unclear how the tales would circulate. If they were published individually, it would presumably be without any link or any indication that the tale was part of a longer section. For if Chaucer was gradually building up his sections, there is no way of deciding when he thought a section would be sufficiently complete to be released. There are no extant manuscripts with individual tales that can be dated before 1400. If the tales had circulated individually before 1400, one might have expected the tales even in the constant sections to have become muddled up and many of their links to have been lost. If there was an early version of KtT which was published, why does that text not appear in other sections of the poem? Every scribe knew the position of KtT which came after Pro and before MiT; but this situation could hardly have arisen if copies of KtT had been circulated in Chaucer's lifetime. The same goes for WBPT. Similarly the links associated with these two tales are always found in the manuscripts. If a group of tales is constant, its order is not disturbed in the manuscripts as would surely have happened if the tales were circulated before his death. In the fifteenth century when tales were copied individually, they were copied without their links; and this is what one would expect to have occurred in the earlier period if pre-publication had taken place. As things stand, the external evidence does not seem strong enough to make the theory of pre-publication acceptable. It is only the textual tradition which is able to prove or disprove it; and so this theory cannot be fed into the textual analysis beforehand. It may well be that when a textual tradition has been sorted out, it will suggest that pre-publication was likely; but that is something that can come only after the analysis is complete. It may be said now, though, that the absence of any manuscripts from before 1400 means that the evidence from the textual tradition would have to be very conclusive to make the theory of pre-publication tenable.

Pre-publication also has a bearing on the question of Chaucer's copy. If Chaucer was working on the poem until his death, he would have had a copy of it in his possession when he died. It would only be if one assumed that the poem, though unfinished, had been issued as though complete that one could possibly imagine that Chaucer did not retain a copy. In fact no one has accepted this hypothesis which seems *a priori* unlikely. The only possible view is surely that Chaucer had not finished his poem and that he had at least one copy of all the pieces which he had so far written as part of it in his possession when he died. It would not follow that all these pieces were included in the earliest manuscript or even manuscripts, since that would depend upon the state of the sections in Chaucer's residence and how careful the executors were in collecting the various pieces. It does, however, have an important implication for pre-publication. If a complete set of pieces was available in Chaucer's residence, is the theory of pre-publication necessary? Why would a scribe go to the trouble of trying to collect bits and pieces of the poem from different readers, particularly as he could not be certain he had all the bits, when there was a complete set available elsewhere in London? It would seem very strange if the manuscript tradition depended on such pieces which had been published in Chaucer's lifetime rather than on the more authoritative text that was in his possession. And many scholars do refer to the alterations made by Chaucer in his copy as though the scribe did have access to his own working copy. Pre-publication may be an attractive theory if it can be shown that there are two separate strands in the development of the text, one of which could come from Chaucer's copy and the other from the fragments issued in his lifetime. There have indeed been theories which propose two such strands in the manuscripts. Koch divided the manuscripts into two groups and the same thing was done by Manly and Rickert. However, it is also clear that there was considerable contamination across these two groups suggested by these scholars, and Manly and Rickert accepted that all the manuscripts went back to the same archetype. Their acceptance of two different manuscript strands reflects their opinion of the private and commercial production of the manuscripts in the fifteenth century and has no bearing on pre-publication. More recently, scholars have generally accepted that all manuscripts are related in their order, which would tend to militate against the theory that there were two groups of manuscripts with separate lines of descent. We saw in the previous paragraph that there was little to support the concept of pre-publication, and the views expressed in this one strengthen that conclusion.

Recent studies by palaeographers have highlighted the means in which the manuscripts were made. The majority of the early manuscripts of the poem were written in the London/Westminster area, and the scribes that executed them also worked on other texts. From time to time they worked together on some texts in an *ad hoc* way. There are thus traces of cooperation among the scribes, which is what one might expect in view of the small size of the population at the time. If Chaucer had employed such scribes in his lifetime, as his stanza to Adam implies, then it is possible that some scribes knew of Chaucer and the sort of poetry he was composing, even if *The Canterbury Tales* was not issued in his lifetime. The circle of writers and scribes in London and Westminster was restricted, perhaps consisting of not more than 250 people, and each side must have dealt with the other quite often. If so, some scribes would probably know of the existence of Chaucer's poem. It is hardly likely that they or anyone else would assemble bits piecemeal rather than get access to his copy. In an investigation of the manuscript tradition it is most sensible to start with the assumption that the manuscripts are derived from the copy preserved in Chaucer's residence and made more generally available because of his death. This assumption fits in with the absence of manuscripts before 1400 and the explosion in the production of manuscripts after that date. It would also imply that the earliest manuscript or manuscripts were copied from Chaucer's own copy, though it is naturally possible that a working copy was made to be used by the scribes. It may never be possible to decide that question definitively, but if the existence of an intermediate copy cannot be proved it is naturally more sensible not to posit it. Until the existence of such an intermediate copy is proved, I will work on the basis that the manuscripts were based on Chaucer's personal copy.

It will be part of the investigation to examine the nature of that copy, whether the extant manuscripts derive from it radially or vertically using another copy as model, what the relationship among the scribes was, and whether the copy was itself unchanging. Palaeographers have shown that some manuscripts were copied by the same scribe. Hg and El were both copied by one scribe, and Corpus and Ha7334 were also copied by a single scribe. Yet these manuscripts belong to different textual groupings: El belongs to the *a* group, Corpus to the *c* group, and the other two are both anomalous. They differ equally in their *ordinatio*, the way in which the text was presented on the page. The headings and tale divisions differ, and a manuscript like El has illuminations of the pilgrims. There are therefore points of contact between manuscripts, but also important differences among the same ones. This is a problem that has to be tackled in a discussion of the manuscript tradition. The use of the same scribe to copy the same text twice suggests a close-knit organization and perhaps the same exemplar. On the other hand, the differences in text and layout suggest separate exemplars. Any theory must explain the close interrelationship among the manuscripts as well as their wide divergences. The usual explanation has been either that the scribes used different exemplars or that they imposed their own, somewhat arbitrary, ideas on the poem. The difficulty with the theory that they used different exemplars is that, if the text is derived from the copy in Chaucer's possession at his death, we have to assume the existence of a large number of exemplars that have subsequently disappeared. Since the earliest manuscripts date from five to ten years from Chaucer's death, there would need to have been a large production of manuscripts which did not survive. It would be surprising if all the manuscripts of what might be termed the first generation disappeared, leaving only those from the second. Such a thing could have happened, but its improbability will mean that we need reliable evidence to accept it. Another possiblity is that the scribes themselves altered their exemplar as they copied the text. This is normal practice in the copying of medieval manuscripts and is something that must have happened at least to some extent. The *ordinatio,* the titles and the spelling system at least were no doubt imposed by the scribes. It is likely that they also changed the text on occasion, adding and deleting bits as they went along. Nevertheless there are extensive alterations in the poem, such as extra links between tales and the extra lines in WBP, which appear only in some manuscripts. It is usually accepted that these passages are so long that they can have come only from a different exemplar. Thus it might be argued that as El has the extra passages in WBP and extra links not found in Hg, the same scribe must have used different exemplars for his copies. On the other hand, the texts share certain textual features, of which the common copying error at 1:2039 is the best known; and these similarities suggest a common exemplar, for otherwise we have to assume that at 1:2039 the faulty positioning of an abbreviation was carried through several exemplars — a supposition which seems on the face of it extremely improbable. Some scholars have come forward with a compromise by suggesting that the original copy contained corrections by Chaucer in the margin, and that these corrections were picked up by some scribes and not by others. This seems a possible explanation, though in this particular form it cannot explain why some scribes neglected to include lines which were in their copy even though they were in the margin. The theory has been put forward in this way because its proponents wish to claim that the extra lines are Chaucerian. The question of what is genuine is, as we noted above, best left aside in any consideration of the manuscript tradition. It may nevertheless, be possible to develop the theory by suggesting that the changes were made gradually in the copytext. This is a view that has not been canvassed and will perhaps be difficult to prove. If we accept that the early copies of the poem are linked, as the similarity in order and the various textual interrelationships indicate, we would need a theory which allowed the scribes to use what was basically a similar copytext, though it was not static. If the copytext was undergoing revision by some kind of editor, this could explain the similarities and the differences among the resulting copies. It is a possiblity that will need serious consideration, even though in this form it has not been proposed by other scholars. If the copytext was Chaucer's own draft, it may well have been in some confusion. The editor may well have tried various possibilities before arriving at a relatively stable text and these possibilities could have been indicated on the exemplar itself, which would be the obvious place for them to appear. In some instances the additions might have to be on separate sheets with an indication in the exemplar where they should come; in other cases they could be entered directly on the exemplar. A theory along these lines might help to explain why a good text like that found in Hg was not used by subsequent scribes, a fact which has puzzled many commentators. We also need to bear in mind that the scribes and editor, if there was one, were intelligent people trying to make sense out of what was a collection of disparate fragments. Their aim was probably to give the poem a sense of completeness as far as this was possible, and the changes introduced were designed to make the parts of the poem relate to one another more sensibly. We do not have to assume that because we approve of an order or arrangement it is therefore Chaucr's own; and we may also accept that scribes were quite willing and able to turn out lines in the Chaucerian manner to fill in what they considered gaps in the poem.

In view of what has been discussed above I shall proceed as follows in the rest of the book. I shall first examine the text and make-up of Hg, El and Ha7334 in some detail and then go on to look at the other early manuscripts more briefly. Then I shall consider the extra lines found in the various early manuscripts and their different orders to decide whether they are all related, as has been suggested. Then it will be necessary to review the question of the exemplar or exemplars used by the early scribes, a discussion which will naturally also lead to a consideration of the textual traditon and the nature of the copytext. After that, it will be helpful to set any decision reached about *The Canterbury Tales* in the context of Chaucer's career and the problems posed by the textual tradition of his other poems.

4

The Earliest Manuscripts

In this chapter I shall give brief descriptions of the eight earliest manuscripts. Other early manuscripts probably existed. The Merthyr fragment which contains three leaves with parts of NPT come from a manuscript which has been dated shortly after 1400, but the fragment is not extensive enough to be used in textual studies. It is a reminder that not all manuscripts have survived. In this chapter I shall concentrate on quiring and peculiarities of how the manuscripts were put together. Ink, handwriting, decoration, date and the type of manuscript will be commented on. Some idea of the textual character of the manuscript with its rubrics and annotations will be given and its affiliation in the Manly–Rickert grouping of manuscripts will be noted. The textual problems of each manuscript will be treated more fully in the following chapters; and some readers may prefer to proceed straight to the next chapter. As Hg has always been regarded as the earliest manuscript since its discovery in the nineteenth century, I shall start with it. Because El was written by the same scribe, I shall tackle it second. Ha7334 and Corpus are both early manuscripts written by the same scribe, and they will be treated next. I shall deal then with Lansdowne and Petworth, since they are clearly related to Corpus; Lansdowne is a group *c* manuscript. Finally Dd 4.24 and Gg 4.27 will be treated together since both belong to the Manly–Rickert group *a*.

Hg needs rather greater consideration than some manuscripts because it is regarded as the earliest extant one and because important textual assumptions have been made from it. Two major and several minor descriptions of the manuscript have appeared earlier, though these have been flawed in part because of assumptions about prior publication which have been fed into them.[1] The manuscript now consists of 249 leaves, though it is defective at the end where some leaves of PsT are missing. It is not possible to decide whether Rt was originally part of this

[1]The two major descriptions are Manly and Rickert 1940 I.266-83 and Doyle and Parkes in Ruggiers 1979; an important minor description is in Tatlock 1935 pp. 133–9.

manuscript. There is no evidence that Hg was designed to contain anything else than *The Canterbury Tales*. In comparison with other early manuscripts, Hg has a rough and ready character; it has none of the sophistication of El. There is some decoration, which is found most extensively on the first leaf and less flamboyantly at the beginning of individual tales. The leaves are of vellum. The scribe of Hg has been identified as the man who wrote El and part of Trinity College Cambridge MS R.3.2., a copy of Gower's *Confessio Amantis*.[2] El and Trinity R.3.2 are dated to the early fifteenth century, the latter after Gower's death in 1408. However, palaeographers suggest that the scribe's handwriting is old-fashioned by early fifteenth-century standards and that the scribe probably learned his trade in the fourteenth. The style of the illumination in Hg is also more characteristic of the late fourteenth century, for it shows no signs of early fifteenth-century developments. There are additions in Hg in different hands, one of which has parallels from 1412-13. It has consequently been suggested that the bulk of the work in Hg 'was mostly done after 1400, perhaps in the first few years of the fifteenth century'.[3] That is, the manuscript was written shortly after Chaucer's death. Recently on the basis of the spelling systems Samuels has dated Hg to 1402-4 and El to about a decade later (1410-12).[4] Since the scribe also wrote part of Trinity College Cambridge R.3.2., he was active in the London area for that manuscript may definitely be allocated to London or Westminster. He was a professional scribe who copied other English and Latin texts, probably to order. He may have been employed, like Hoccleve, in some semi-official capacity as a scrivener.

Although fairly utilitarian in character, Hg is written in a clear script and is easily legible. The manuscript has deteriorated partly through the loss of its final leaves and partly through lack of care. The bottoms of some leaves are missing, caused perhaps by the gnawing of rats. There are stains and traces of damp here and there, but otherwise the manuscript is in good shape. Pricks for the ruling which is mainly blind survive on some leaves, but the line ruling is irregular so that varying amounts of text are accommodated on different pages. It is evident that the manuscript was not prepared with as much care as went into El. There is no ruling in Hg for marginalia, running titles or catchwords. In the Manly—Rickert classification it is put into the anomalous group of manuscripts.

The manuscript contains five separate parts, which are made up as follows:

[2]Doyle and Parkes 1978.
[3]Doyle and Parkes in Ruggiers 1979, p. xx.
[4]Samuels 1983b.

I   The whole of section 1; it consists of eight quires of eight leaves each except for quires six and seven which consist of two and six leaves respectively. Since these two would make up a quire of eight leaves, it may be that they represent some technical mistake in the production of the quires. The incomplete CkT finishes on fol.57^v, and the rest of that page, the last in the quire, is left blank. According to Manly and Rickert the quire signatures allowed for another quire to be included after part I, which they assumed indicated that the scribe anticipated including the rest of CkT. Later the scribe added in the bottom margin of fol.57^v the words 'Of this Cokes tale maked Chaucer na moore' in the yellowish ink characteristic of part III.

II   The whole of section 2; it consists of four quires, of which the first three are of eight leaves and the final one of six. The last leaf of the final quire is blank. The quiring suggests that this part was written as a unit independently of the rest of the manuscript; the ink in this section is of a slightly browner colour than that used elsewhere.

III   Contains the end of section 10, commencing 'Here bigynneth the prologe of the Monkes [tale]' and including MkT and NPT, and the whole of section 11. It consists of three quires of eight leaves each. McT commences in the middle of the final quire, and is thus clearly linked to section 10. McT finishes at the bottom of fol.111^v. This part is written in a yellowish ink which differs from that found in the rest of the manuscript except for isolated pages in part IV.

IV   This, the largest part, contains sections 3, 4, 5, 6, 7, 8, 9 and the beginning of 10, which concludes 'Here is endid Chaucers tale of Melibe'. This part consists of fourteen quires, of which the majority are of eight leaves. But the sixth quire has an added singleton; the seventh consists of sixteen leaves; and the last contains ten leaves. TMel, which is in prose, runs to the end of the final leaf of this quire which may have been expanded to ten leaves to accommodate the end of the prose tale which demanded a different ruling from the other tales. As there is no coincidence of quire and section endings in this part, the tales were intended to proceed in this order. Some leaves were originally left blank, a few of which were filled with material written in the yellowish ink characteristic of part III. MLT ends at the bottom of fol.128^r, and fol.128^v was left blank; it was filled in the seventeenth century with genealogical notes. SqT begins at the top of fol.129^r. SqT finishes with the two lines of its *Tercia pars* at the top of fol.137^v; the rest of the page was left empty, but was subsequently filled with a Sq–Me link [F673-708] serving here as MeP written in the yellowish ink. This prologue occupies the rest of the page. MeT begins on the top of fol.138^r. MeT finishes halfway down fol.152^v and the rest of that page was left empty, as were all of fol.153^r and the top half of fol.153^v. FkT begins halfway down fol.153^v. The bottom of fol.152^v was filled with seventeenth-century genealogical notes. A link to join MeT and FkT [E2419-40, F1-8] was copied in yellowish ink later on fol.153^{rv}, though it was not long enough to fill the space available. The scribe spaced out the prologue with gaps to make the insufficiency of the text less obvious. It is evident that the passages in yellowish ink were added after the rest of part IV was written. After 5:1074 the ink which had been dark becomes much lighter; and it is likely that this represents a short break (possibly only overnight) in copying. The seventh quire is anomalous in consisting of sixteen leaves. It contains the end of FkT, the whole of NnT, and the beginning of ClT. The leaves containing NnT are in a slightly different coloured ink from that used for FkT and ClT, and presumably it was copied later. The quire was enlarged to take NnT which was inserted after FkT and ClT had been copied. Since NnT adequately occupies the space provided, the scribe must have known its length beforehand.

V   Contains PsPT which is incomplete only because the end of the manuscript has been lost. At present there are two quires of eight leaves in this part. Manly and Rickert estimated that there would have been two further quires of eight leaves, but Doyle and Parkes think that a single quire of ten leaves would have sufficed for the rest of PsT. The first line of PsP contains a reference to the Manciple which is written on an erasure as though PsT was not originally designed to follow on from McT.

The present order of the manuscript does not represent its intended order. Part III is clearly misplaced. In the first line of MkP there is reference to TMel; and in PsP as we have seen there is a reference to the Manciple. So part III is misbound and should be placed between parts IV and V. The order intended by the scribe when he finished copying was I−II−IV−III−V. There are, however, quire signatures in the manuscript, though these are not always very legible and have not survived in all cases. From those that can be interpreted, it has been deduced that part IV was originally intended to follow part I, perhaps with the addition of a single quire after the incomplete CkT. Since part II is written in a different ink, the evidence of ink and quire signatures complements each other. Part II was inserted in the sequence of quires at a later date. If it was intended for another position, it can have occupied only one other position in Hg. Part I is the beginning of the poem, and part V was almost certainly the end of the poem, though in the absence of its end we cannot be certain of that. Nevertheless the Host in PsP does indicate that there needs only one more tale to complete the project and he invites the Parson to 'knette vp wel a greet matere' (12:28). Part III follows directly on from part IV. The only gap available for part II is thus one between parts III and V. There is no endlink to McT and so no indication as to which tale should follow. Although the first line of PsP refers to the Manciple, this as we saw is written on an erasure and so something else must originally have come immediately before PsPT in part V. It is possible, therefore, that the scribe originally intended to include part II between parts III and V. Since part II ends with SuT which concludes 'We been almoost at towne' (2:2268), this may have been taken to refer to Canterbury. Attempts have been made to read under ultra-violet light what was erased in the first line of PsP. The attempts have not yielded much that is concrete, though what is visible has not usually led scholars to suggest that the reading was originally 'Somnour' or one of its other spelling variants.[5] Despite this, no other teller from the material available in Hg could so readily have occupied this position originally.

The manuscript thus consists of five separate parts which are identifiable entities; but it need not follow that they were written in the order in which they now appear. The different inks suggest that this was not so. Parts I, IV and V are written in one ink, apart from minor variations and the additional passages in the yellowish ink. Part III is in this yellowish ink, and part II in a browner ink. It is probable that part III was copied directly after part IV, because MkT refers back to TMel as the scribe would see and because both tales belong to a constant section. If so, part IV was written after part V, for otherwise one would expect part V to be in the same yellowish ink used for part III. It is therefore likely that the parts were written in the order I−V−IV−III−II with the yellowish and brown inks being employed after the original black was exhausted. This sequence of copying is understandable only if Hg represents the first attempt to arrange the extant fragments of the poem in a sequence and if that attempt was made by someone after Chaucer's death. For the order of copying indicates a lack of familiarity with the contents. If this were not so, one might have expected the poem to be copied in the order in which it was to be read, as is true of other manuscripts. If parts I and V were copied first, this is explicable on the basis that they were the beginning and end of the poem and so occupied fixed points. These could be copied while some order was being introduced into the remaining fragments, for their sequence was more problematical. Section 1 which formed the contents of part I is incomplete for it finishes with CkT, for which the scribe could find no end. Hence he left the rest of the final quire of part I blank and made allowance for the addition of a further quire. It has been suggested that the scribe expected to find the rest of CkT before completing his copying, though this is only one possible solution. At this point in some early manuscripts Gamelyn is inserted in the sequence of tales; and it is possible that this solution was considered for Hg. Another possibility is that the scribe made space for something to follow without knowing what it

[5]See Doyle and Parkes in Ruggiers 1979, p. xxviii and Tatlock 1935 p. 138.

would be, though this seems less likely in view of the way he treated the incomplete SqT. He evidently never expected to find the conclusion of that tale. Hence one may accept that he left a space for either the end of CkT or the whole of Gamelyn. As he later inserted a note to the effect that Chaucer did not complete CkT, the former solution is preferable.

From part I he went to part V, which contains only section 12 which in Hg may not have included Rt. This part contains no signature numbers, or if it did they have not survived. The absence of signatures is understandable if part V was copied before part IV, since the scribe could not have known what their signatures would be when he copied the quires. The only problem with writing this part at this point in the copying sequence was that the first line of PsP contained a reference to the preceding teller. As we do not know what the copytext was like we cannot tell whether it contained a name in this line or not. It may have had a blank or the name of a pilgrim to whom no tale had been allocated or the name of a pilgrim who did tell a tale. If the last of these possibilities was correct, one might have expected the scribe to copy that tale also as part of part V since it should form a constant group with PsT. If the first possiblity applied, then one might expect the scribe to have left a gap as well. So there is something to be said for the possibility that the name was that of a pilgrim who had no tale among the extant fragments. It is also conceivable that PsT constituted a separate fragment in the copytext and so the scribe decided to copy only that tale as the conclusion and ignored whatever name was in the first line of the prologue. Because we do not know what name was erased, it is difficult to be certain what happened at this point in the copying.

The placing of parts I and V at beginning and end respectively was straightforward since there were indications in the poem itself where these tales should come. The intermediate parts presented more difficulty since there was little to guide the scribe as to where to place the individual tales. We may work from the assumption that the tales of constant sections were arranged by Chaucer in order. Thus the tales of section 10, starting with ShT and ending with NPT, would have been positioned by Chaucer. The scribe's problem was where to put this section in the sequence of sections. It was suggested by Manly and Rickert, and the view was repeated by Doyle and Parkes, that the arrangement in Hg is haphazard and reflects the fact that the scribe acquired the pieces in a piecemeal way. This view is based on the assumption that there was prior circulation of the tales before Chaucer's death. As we saw in the last chapter, the evidence for prior circulation is not very strong, and we have no indication if there was such prior circulation whether it would be by constant section or by individual tale. If the latter, then it would be extraordinary for the scribe to acquire the tales haphazardly in the correct sequence of the constant sections. It is not likely that the tales of section 10 would arrive with the scribe in the correct order if they had been circulating independently. If the former, we should want to know why a section was considered sufficiently complete and self-sufficient to be circulated in that form. Furthermore, this theory ignores the fact, which has been accepted by all scholars, that there was a set of fragments in Chaucer's possession when he died. It would be strange if this set, which might be supposed to represent Chaucer's final intentions, was disregarded in favour of circulating fragments, whose number the scribes would not be certain of. In any event the way in which Hg was written seems to argue against this theory. Part IV contains the bulk of the tales from the middle part of the poem. This part was written as a unit, and there is no junction of tale and quire boundaries within it. It seems improbable, to say the least, that a scribe would copy the tales in an indivisible unit if he was acquiring them piecemeal, for he would then not be able to rearrange them when he had acquired all the tales. It is unlikely that he would be so unconcerned with the poem that he would behave in this way, particularly as the composition of the manuscript in five parts shows that he took some trouble over the arrangement of the poem. As we shall see, his acceptance of an order for the tales in part IV did cause him problems. Consequently, we may dismiss the theory that the scribe of Hg acquired the tales or sections of the poem in a piecemeal way. He is likely to have had access to all the pieces he included in Hg (except for those passages inserted later in a different coloured ink) before he started copying. This is what one would expect, and one would need strong evidence to abandon that expectation. The evidence is simply not there.

A feature of Hg is that it contains small gaps left by the scribe, many of which were filled in subsequently in a different hand. These gaps are of individual words or they can be as long as a line or two. In some instances the gaps may represent scribal error, but in most they probably reflect something missing in the exemplar the scribe was using. The later additions do not occur on erasures and they are not alterations to the text. The gaps are indicated in the table below by the italicized words, which represent that part of the text added in a later hand. If the scribe omitted a line or lines and left no gap, this is naturally not recorded.

MiT (1:3316)	Ful faire and thikke been the pointes *set*.
FrT (2:1285-94)	They sholde syngen if *that they were hent*.
	And smale tyth*eres were foule yschent:*
	If any persoun *wold vpon hem pleyne*

Ther myghte *asterte hym no pecunial peyne.*
For smale *tithes and for smal offryng*
He made the *peple ful pitusly to syng.*
For er the *bysschop caght hem with hys hooc*
They were *in the erchdeknys book*
And thanne *had he thurgh hys iurisdiccion*
Power to *do on hem correccion.*

SuT (2:1762)   I haue today been at youre chirche *at messe.*
(2:2022)   A lord is *lost if he be vicius.*
MeT (5:61-2)   And if thow take a wyf *she wole destroye*
Thy good substance and thy body annoye.
(5:985-6)   Folwynge his wyf, the queene Proserpyne
Whos answer hath doon many a man pyne.
TMel (10:1777)   And he seith in another place: [*gap in Hg not filled*] that hath shame of his synne and knowelicheth it.

The larger gaps must reflect an omission or imperfection in the copytext. It is not credible to suppose that in FrT for example Chaucer composed his lines by thinking only of the first three words or so of each line before he completed them. Presumably the copytext was damaged so that the second half of each line was illegible. The scribe's unwillingness to complete the lines shows he was a conscientious copyist who was copying what was in front of him. No doubt the gaps could have been filled, because this happened to the gaps he left between certain tales for links to be provided. But as these gaps were smaller, they may have been overlooked; or rather the scribe may have forgotten to tell the supervisor that they needed filling. This behaviour suggests that the scribe of Hg did not add anything to the text on his own initiative.

Textually Hg has, since the Manly–Rickert edition, been regarded as reliable and authoritative. Its spelling system and grammar are reasonably consistent and appear to be close to Chaucer's own.[6] It has not been followed by most editors simply because it does not contain parts of the poem they prefer to include. It does not contain, for example, Gamelyn or CYPT, the Cl–Me link [E1213-44], or the Adam stanza in MkT. It has a few omissions through eyeskip such as 1:639-40 in Pro. Otherwise it has a good text with few of the additional passages found in other manuscripts. It has subdivisions in some tales, though not as many as are found today. Its subdivision in KtT is unique among the early manuscripts. It has rubrics for the tales and links and marginal annotations in some tales. Running heads are also provided. But most of these were added later after the manuscript was finished.

El was written by the same scribe as Hg. It is the manuscript

[6]Samuels 1983a and 1983b.

which is followed by most modern editors in tale-order, if not in its readings, even though it was written later than Hg. As we have seen, it may be a decade later than Hg. It consists of 232 leaves on which *The Canterbury Tales* is written, together with a further four leaves at the beginning and four at the end which are contemporary with the manuscript but may not have been intended to be found in this way originally. Manly and Rickert suggest they were intended as a final quire of the manuscript, but some of its leaves were moved forward to protect the manuscript. These leaves then acted as flyleaves and were filled with various material in different fifteenth-century hands. One of these additions is a copy of Chaucer's lyric *Truth*. The 232 leaves are divided into 29 gatherings of eight leaves each; there are no irregularities in the make-up of this manuscript. There are no examples of coincidence of tale and quire boundary. There are, however, two breaks in the continuous copying of the tales. After CkT, which finishes on the verso of a leaf, the scribe left the rest of that page and the whole of the next leaf blank. MLP which follows commences on the top recto of the next leaf, which is the first leaf of the second half of the quire. It would, therefore, have been possible to insert extra leaves in the middle of the quire. The second break occurs after SqT. This incomplete tale finishes on the verso of one leaf, and the rest of the page (about three-quarters) is left blank so that FkP which follows commences on the next recto at the top. As FkP refers to the Squire and as there is no coincidence of tale and quire boundary, the gap does not indicate any uncertainty in the order. It may be that the scribe envisaged some brief conclusion to the tale. The other small gaps in the manuscript are technical, for the scribe did not start a new tale at the bottom of a page if there was not much room there.

In El allowance was made for marginal notes and running heads, and there is a series of rubrics. The *ordinatio* is more completely realized than in Hg, and this suggests a later manuscript with a text that has reached a more settled condition. The most striking feature of El is its illumination; it is the most elaborate found in any manuscript of the poem. Not only are there ornate initials at the beginning of prologues and tales, but there are also pictures of individual pilgrims at the start of each tale. The pictures may have been added as an afterthought. The illumination resembles that found on the initial leaf in Hg and shares some of its old-fashioned qualities. It provides another link between these two manuscripts and supports the contention that they were written by the same man. In view of this close connection it might be expected that the scribe used the same copytext for both manuscripts, though it does not prove that was so.

El is a group *a* manuscript and contains the order and contents characteristic of that group. It has CYPT, but not Gamelyn; and it has four of the additional passages in WBP. The order and contents of El are those usually found in modern editions.

Though the text of El has been considered excellent by some, since the time of the Manly–Rickert edition it has been accepted as an edited text which does not reflect its copytext adequately.[7] As compared with Hg, the text has been modified in several ways. There are in *The Canterbury Tales* several examples of *rime riche,* but El has considerably expanded their number. In KtT we find these extra cases in El:

1:1833-4	Ech of you bothe is worthy doutelees To wedden whan tyme is *doutelees* (cf. *but nathelees* Hg)
1:2277-8	Hir maydens that she thider with hire ladde Ful redily with hem the fyr they *ladde* (cf. *hadde* Hg)
1:3085-6	For gentil mercy oghte to passen right Thanne seyde he thus to Palamon *ful right* (cf. *the knyght* Hg)

Although it is conceivable that some instances may be attributed to dittography, examples are so common and so often involve other minor adjustments to the line that they must have been introduced deliberately by the scribe. In El additional words are often introduced which help to create parallelism in the line, though in some instances the demands of the metre may have precipitated the addition. At 1:49 where Hg reads 'As wel in cristendom as hethenesse' El has 'As wel in cristendom as in Hethenesse', and this example is typical of many more. In this case the wish to create parallelism seems the more likely cause of the alteration, for the metre in Hg is preferable to that in El. There are indications that in El alliteration is avoided if possible, and lines are lengthened if they are too short. There are frequent changes to the personal pronouns, to the tenses of verbs, and to individual words, though it may well be that the majority of such changes are without significance since they fall within the acceptable range of changes in medieval manuscripts. Nevertheless, El has a smoother and more polished text than Hg. With the other changes to be considered in a subsequent chapter, El exhibits considerable editorial improvement as compared with Hg. These changes indicate that El is later than Hg.

Ha7334 was regarded as the most authoritative manuscript by many nineteenth-century editors, though the state of its text caused many scholars problems of interpretation. It is one of the anomalous manuscripts in the Manly–Rickert classification. It is

---

[7]This is why modern editions do not use it as a base text, see also Blake 1980.

written in one hand, which has been identified as that of the scribe who wrote Corpus. The scribe, who also wrote many *Confessio Amantis* manuscripts, worked in the London/Westminster area where he was active from the 1390s to 1426.[8] He was a professional scribe, though his spelling system suggests an origin in the West Midlands. Ha7334 was probably written in the first decade of the fifteenth century. The manuscript consists of 286 folios of text with a single flyleaf at the beginning and two at the end. It has 38-9 lines per page and probably contained nothing else than *The Canterbury Tales*. Trimming of the leaves has led to many of the catchwords and signatures being cut away. Its illumination is similar to that found in Corpus and Lansdowne and consists of initials and demi-vinets at the beginning of tales. This illumination is slightly later in style than that found in Hg and El.

Although the manuscript has lost a quire which contained the end of SqT and the beginning of FkT, it is otherwise complete. The quires are of eight leaves each except for three. The first of these, quire 9, consists of only six leaves and contains Gamelyn which comes after CkT. CkT is missing a few lines at the end and the scribe crowded in two lines as one at the bottom of the last page of quire 8. He tried to make a break here so that something could be included; clearly Gamelyn was known of when the manuscript was copied. Gamelyn itself finishes on the last page of quire 9, but the last twelve lines of that page are blank. There is no catchword on this page. MLP begins on the top recto of the first leaf of quire 10. Quire 9 was inserted into the manuscript after quires 8 and 10 had been written, although it is in the same ink and hand as the rest of the manuscript. There is a note in French in a different hand at the end of CkT which reads 'Icy commencera le fable de Gamelyn', which is presumably an instruction from the supervisor. Quire 19 also consists of six leaves. It contains the end of MeT and the link adapted to fill the MeT—SqT link [E2419-40, F1-8]; SqT commences on the top recto of the first leaf of quire 20. Since the manuscript has a different *ordinatio* here, there is a break between quires 19 and 20. The final page of quire 19 contains the Me—Sq link, which consists of thirty lines and with its associated rubrics was insufficient to fill the page. The scribe wrote the text in a larger script and left space before and after the rubrics to create the illusion that the text filled the page. This behaviour proves that quire 19, or at least its final page, was written after SqT was written in quire 20.

The third short quire in Ha7334 is the final one which consists of only two leaves. The major part of the last page is blank and clearly nothing was designed to follow *The Canterbury Tales* in this

[8]Doyle and Parkes 1978.

manuscript. Apart from these special quires, there was an attempt to arrange that TMel occupied separate pages. Presumably as with the enlarged quire in Hg this was designed to ease the problem of ruling, since the prose tale demanded a different ruling from the verse. At the end of Th–Mel link there is a gap of five lines so that TMel starts at the top of a separate page, though this is not the first page of a quire. The tale finishes at the bottom of a page and so no gap was necessary before MkP commenced, for that came naturally at the top of the next page. NPP starts on the first page of a quire, though its rubric occurs on the last page of the preceding one; the junction of tale and quire boundary here appears to be mere chance.

Ha7334 shows two types of *ordinatio* – a feature it shares with Corpus. Manly and Rickert thought this difference was caused by two separate rubricators; it is possible though that the copytext or the progress of copying was in some way responsible. They thought that the first eleven quires (which contain sections 1 with Gamelyn, 3 and the first lines of WBP) and quire 20 (which contains the beginning of SqT; its end was on the missing quire 21) and some folios of quire 26 (which contain parts of ShT) were finished by one rubricator, and the rest of the quires by a second. The first set of quires contains no running heads, and the rubrics are not provided with spaces in the text, for where they are included they are inserted against a line of the text. From quire 12 Ha7334 has rubricated running heads, spaces for rubrics, and *Narrat* or its equivalent at the beginning of each tale. This new arrangement involved ruling and the provision of spaces for the rubrics; it must therefore have been allowed for by the scribe before the manuscript was passed to the rubricator(s). This difference in *ordinatio* confirms that quire 20 was written immediately after quire 11.

Ha7334 is not so developed as Hg or El in its subdivisions in the tales. Textually it has many omissions and additions, though these are not the same as those found in El. It contains both Gamelyn and CYPT; it does not have the extra lines in WBP, but it contains extra lines in SuT. It also has many of the links found in El which were not in Hg or which occurred there in a different form. The omissions are mostly attributable to carelessness. Some may be deliberate such as the omission of 2:575-8, though it is difficult to prove. The carelessness is beyond question. The manuscript contains a great many copying errors; Skeat has enumerated a number in KtT and others may be found in the apparatus criticus of the Manly–Rickert edition.[9] Despite these omissions, the alterations in the text led Tatlock to describe the scribe as an intelligent editor of the poem, and in this opinion he had been

[9]Skeat 1909 and Manly and Rickert 1940.

followed by other commentators.[10] The text of Ha7334 is certainly contaminated as compared with that in Hg, but it has been edited and prepared for publication in a different way from that used in El. In some respects, such as sub-divisions of the tales and rubrics, it is less advanced than Hg. It also contains fewer marginal annotations than are found in Hg.

Corpus, a group *c* manuscript, was written by the same scribe and it too has been corrected extensively by at least one supervisor who may be the same person who made corrections in Ha7334. Corpus has been dated to the first decade of the fifteenth century and must date from the same time as Ha7334 or even a little earlier. It has not been so well treated as Ha7334, for it has lost a folio at the beginning and several folios internally as well as up to two quires at the end. It now contains 267 leaves. Its illumination has much in common with that found in Ha7334, and as many of the missing folios contained the beginning of tales it is probable they were torn out of the manuscript because of their illumination. As the manuscript has 36-7 lines per page, it is usually possible to deduce whether Corpus contained various links or not. The manuscript was originally composed of quires of eight leaves except for quire eleven which had only six. As the quire finishes in the middle of MLT, there is no apparent reason for its occurrence, and it may be attributed to an oversight.

An unusual feature of Corpus is that some of the tales have chapter numbers. Those that survive with their numbers are ReT (3), CkT (4), MLT (5), WBT (7), PdT (16), ShT (17), TTh (19), TMel (20), MkT (21), NPT (22) and McT (23). Other manuscripts, though only Petworth of the early ones, have a numeration system except that the chapter numbers which survive differ from one manuscript to the next. In Cambridge Mm 2.5, the other manuscript with the most complete numbering, the following occur: ReT (3), PrT (18), MLT (5), WBT (7), SuT (9), FkT (12), TTh (19), PsT (24). The other manuscripts have fewer extant numbers. It is clear that there was originally a numbering system which went:

1 Knight, 2 Miller, 3 Reeve, 4 Cook, 5 Man of Law, 6 Squire,
7 Wife of Bath, 8 Friar, 9 Summoner, 10 Clerk, 11 Merchant,
12 Franklin, 13 Nun, 14 Canon's Yeoman, 15 Physician,
16 Pardoner, 17 Shipman, 18 Prioress, 19 Thopas, 20 Melibee,
21 Monk, 22 Nun's Priest, 23 Manciple, and 24 Parson.

This numbering sequence reflects the order in Corpus and what may originally have been intended as the order in Ha7334; it is the order which Manly and Rickert attached to group *c* manuscripts.

[10] Tatlock 1909.

The numbering includes CYT, but makes no provision for Gamelyn. This is not significant since Gamelyn is part of CkT in group *c* manuscripts: chapter 4 included both the fragment of CkT and Gamelyn. Later, when both are included in manuscripts with running heads, both are to be found under the heading 'Cook' or 'Cook's Tale'. This numbering cannot be used as evidence for the genuineness or not of either CYPT or Gamelyn.

Corpus shares certain features of *ordinatio* with Ha7334. The running heads in Corpus start with WBPT and it is at this point that the rubrics for the tales become more regular. Before then they appear occasionally, and when they do they usually occur in the margin as though they were an afterthought. With WBPT there is a more regular series of rubrics, though this does not attain absolute regularity immediately. Generally prologue and tale are distinguished and rubrics are given a line to themselves. The rubrics in the earlier part are frequently in Latin, usually in the margin, often no more than 'Incipit fabula'. After WBPT the rubrics are normally in English. Although the change is not so regular or so neatly executed in Corpus as in Ha7334, the two manuscripts do show some agreement. Corpus contains a number of glosses in some tales such as WBPT, though some have been inserted later. In this respect Corpus differs from Ha7334. However, it resembles Ha7334 in the restricted division of the tales into parts. SqT has only two parts, for the third which contained only two lines in other manuscripts is omitted as a part and the two lines are allocated to part 2. Part 2 also has an unusual rubric, 'The Stag of an Hert'. The running heads of NnT refer to 'Cecile' and the concluding rubric has merely 'Here endeth Seint Ceciles Tale'. As the introductory rubric is missing, if one ever existed, there is no evidence that NnT was allocated to a pilgrim in Corpus. There are signs, therefore, in Corpus that it may be earlier than Ha7334. It also contained fewer links than are found in Ha7334.

As noted earlier, Corpus consists of quires of eights except for one. There is no coincidence of quire and tale boundaries, and the scribe evidently knew the order he was going to follow before he started copying. This is what one might expect in view of the chapter numbers. The scribe started a new tale immediately after the previous one without any apparent hesitation except in one instance. Gamelyn is included immediately after CkT without a gap and there is no suggestion of indecision in the order here. When he copied SqT, he included it after MLT and ML endlink. As it happens ML endlink, which serves as SqP since 'Esquier' occurs at [B^{1}1179], finishes at the end of a page and SqT commences on the top verso of the same leaf. When he finished SqT, he left the rest of that page (about three-quarters) blank and commenced WBP on the recto of the following leaf. As WBP starts on the first leaf of the second half of the quire, it would have been possible for the scribe to include extra leaves in the middle of the quire, though there is otherwise no suggestion of any hesitation on his part about the order. The gap, may, therefore, reflect the possibility that some brief conclusion to SqT was to be included.

A feature of Corpus is that it lacks the end of MeT, for it finishes at 5:1074 and FkT commences immediately without a break. Possibly some leaves were missing in the exemplar used by the scribe. This break coincides with the change of ink in Hg in this tale. This coincidence of change of ink in Hg and missing leaves in Corpus suggests that both scribes used the same exemplar, for it is unlikely that other manuscripts echoed this exemplar by starting a new page at that point. Corpus does not contain the extra lines found in WBP associated with the a group of manuscripts. It does, however, have many mistakes and omissions caused through carelessness. The scribe also undertook a number of editorial changes. It is probably the earliest manuscript to contain the Modern Instances in the middle of MkT. Corpus shows many of the same failings as Ha7334 and the text itself is far from satisfactory. It is, however, a manuscript which has organized the poem in accordance with a different principle, namely by dividing it into chapters rather than into prologues and tales – and this feature may be significant for the position of Corpus in the hierarchy of manuscripts. Aspects of its text may depend upon the division into chapters.

The other early group c manuscript is Lansdowne, though it is dated later than Corpus. The state of its text suggests a more finished product. It has illumination which is similar to that found in Ha7334 and Corpus, though a little later in date. It is written throughout in a single hand, and the manuscript is well preserved. It consists of quires of eights, though one leaf has been lost in quire thirty, and the final leaf, which may have been a blank, is missing. Lansdowne follows the contents and order of tales found in Corpus, but it is unique in group c in having a series of links to join together all the tales it includes. These were presumably available to the scribe before he started his work, for there is no evidence of any uncertainty in the order of tales and there is no coincidence of tale and quire boundaries to allow for movement of parts of the manuscript. The extra links include four lines between CkT and Gamelyn, twelve lines between SqT and WBP, sixteen lines between CYT and PhT, and six lines between PdT and ShT. The other links found in Corpus are also found in Lansdowne, though neither contains the Host-stanza, Cl–Me link or NP endlink. Like Corpus, Lansdowne has omitted the last lines of MeT because its exemplar was lacking the last leaves of the tale, but it has divided FkT into a prologue and tale, as is also true of NnT. This tale has the rubric *Incipit prologus 2ᵉ Monyalys* to introduce the prologue, but the tale proper has merely *Incipit fabula*. The tale concludes with the rubric *Explicit vita sancte Cecilie*. The running head reads 'the Nonne'. In this manuscript there is a complete run of tales which are separated by a link from the preceding and succeeding one. This manuscript presents what is a complete poem – the goal to which many early scribes were striving, but had been unable to achieve. If this scheme can be said to break down at all it is between ClT and MeT, for Lansdowne does not contain Cl–Me link [E1213-44] or the Host-stanza (8:1213-19). It does, however, have the envoy at the end of ClT which acts as a link between the two tales.

In omissions and additions Corpus and Lansdowne are virtually identical, though there are some differences. Lansdowne omits the last two lines of SqT, which was perhaps deliberate to make way for the new link which is tacked on to the end of the tale. Lansdowne includes the Adam stanza in MkT, for which Corpus had left a gap; it also includes the extra twenty lines in NPP [B²3961-80]. Occasional lines missing in Corpus are found in Lansdowne. Thus a line in KtT (1:3041) is in Lansdowne but not in Corpus. Equally some lines found in Corpus are missing in Lansdowne, but such omissions are not so significant. Manly and Rickert concluded that Corpus and Lansdowne 'were in all likelihood made in the same shop'.[11] Since the concept of scribal shops has been shown not to be applicable to these manuscripts, this conclusion may be modified by suggesting that Lansdowne was copied from Corpus with extra material available to the scribe rather than from Corpus's own exemplar. Though either solution is possible, it is more probable that Corpus was available to the Lansdowne scribe. The text of Lansdowne is less good even than that of Corpus, for a process of editing has taken place and the language has been altered to fit the scribe's own dialect. Lansdowne has a more thoroughgoing system of rubrics, which are given separate lines. These rubrics are usually in Latin, though occasional ones in English appear. It does not have marked divisions into parts in KtT, MLT or SqT, but the last does have a gap and illuminated initial at part 2. ClT has headings for four parts, though as these come at the end of those parts there are in fact five sections. In addition to containing many gaps, PsT has no headings for the remedies of the seven deadly sins; it is likely that Corpus was the same. Lansdowne contains glosses, some of which have been incorporated into the text itself. Some of the glosses in Lansdowne are not in Corpus.

Petworth is the only early manuscript to belong to group *d*. It is a

[11]Manly and Rickert 1940 I.307.

manuscript in good condition which may have been written slightly later than Lansdowne. It contains three old flyleaves and 307 leaves. The manuscript consists of quires in eights, though the final one has only three leaves. The manuscript is copied out continously by a single scribe as though he knew perfectly well what he had to include before he started. On two occasions he has cramped material in to accommodate it all on the page: at the foot of fol.78^r six lines are crowded into a space which would normally accommodate only four; and at the foot of fol.124^r two lines are written as one. Since the passages in question occur in the middle of ShT and MeT, the reason for this behaviour is uncertain though it can hardly spring from an uncertainty of order or material. There is illumination which is dated rather later than that in the manuscripts already treated, and the text is neatly presented with rubrics and glosses. Petworth contains chapter numbers for three tales, ReT (3), TTh (19) and PsT (24). At the head of PrT there is the abbreviation *Cap*, but no number is included. Although Petworth does not have Corpus's order, it seems to come from an exemplar which had the tales in a Corpus order as is indicated by the numbering system.

Petworth is the first manuscript to break up a constant section. After section 1 to which Gamelyn is added, the scribe has introduced the first two tales of section 10, ShT and PrT. The occurrence of PrT out of sequence may well be why it was given no chapter number. ShT is preceded by a twelve-line link which was designed to join it to PdT rather than to CkT. Petworth has other spurious links not found in the other early manuscripts. In many of its omissions and additions within the tales Petworth resembles Corpus and Lansdowne, though it has further omissions which are probably due to carelessness. But it does not follow Corpus and Lansdowne in all their alterations to the text. It has few glosses, but it does have a comprehensive system of rubrics, generally in English. There are few subdivisions in the tales, but in SqT it echoes Corpus in having the rubric 'The Stag of an hert' at the start of part 2. Petworth has many faulty readings arising from carelessness. Everything points to its being a late manuscript among the early group.

The two remaining manuscripts belong to group *a*. Dd 4.24 differs from all the other early manuscripts in being made partly of paper. This may imply a more utilitarian production, and Manly and Rickert thought that its scribe was an amateur.[12] It could equally represent an attempt to arrange the tales in an order in a utilitarian manuscript so that the resulting order could be taken over direct into more prestigious manuscripts like El. The

[12]Manly and Rickert 1940 I.102.

manuscript consists of quires of twenty-four leaves each, an unusual arrangement in the fifteenth century. Each quire consists of five sheets of paper folded to give twenty leaves. These paper leaves are inserted within a single folded sheet of vellum on the outside of the quire, and another folded sheet of vellum is included in the middle of the quire. The first, twelfth, thirteenth and twenty-fourth leaves in each quire are of vellum; the rest are paper. Unfortunately, Dd 4.24 is mutilated and it has lost leaves at beginning and end as well as some internally. The manuscript is written in one hand and is dated to the early years of the fifteenth century. The watermarks of the paper have been dated to the end of the fourteenth and beginning of the fifteenth century, and so a date fairly early in that century is possible. The text is written in single columns with some variation in the number of lines per page. There is no illumination apart from the odd painted paragraph mark, another feature which increases its rather utilitarian nature.

Dd 4.24 has the same order and contents as found in El except it is the only early manuscript to include NP endlink [B²4637-52]. Textually it differs from El in certain small additions and omissions; in WBP, for example, it includes [D44a-f] which are not in El. It is also the only manuscript to include a line at 10:805 in TTh. It has a comprehensive system of rubrics, which is designed to present the poem as a continuous sequence of prologue and tale. The scribe did not recognize links which were not prologues. Where a tale had no prologue this was noted in the rubric. There are differences in the rubrics in that the early ones are in Latin and the later ones in English. At the end of some early tales one finds a marginal note such as 'Quod Wytton', and this may well be the name of the scribe though he has not otherwise been identified. At the end of SqT the scribe included the rubric 'Here endith the Squyeres tale as meche as Chaucer made' and the rest of that page and the following one were left blank. As the next leaf is missing, it is not possible to know how FkT began or why the scribe left this gap. A similar arrangement was found at the end of CkT, for the scribe left the end of the page after the incomplete tale blank. These gaps may have been left because the tales were incomplete and the scribe did not know how they were supposed to finish. However, blanks left elsewhere in the manuscript were clearly left for the provision of links which were to be provided later. In this the scribe of Dd 4.24 behaved in exactly the same way as the scribe of Hg; and the result was much the same. Some blanks were filled and others were not. The two most important gaps were those between FkT and PhT and between NPT and NnT; the former remained empty, but the latter was filled. Dd 4.24, which may well be earlier than El, is possibly the first manuscript to include the long version of NPP. It has the Modern Instances at the end of MkT, though the colour of the ink suggests that they were inserted in this position later. There may well be some link between these two features. There are no running heads in Dd 4.24, though there is an extensive series of marginal annotations. These differ in some important respects from those found in Hg and El.

Gg 4.27 is the most unusual of the early manuscripts of *The Canterbury Tales*, for the poem is included in a larger collection and the manuscript may have been written outside London. The collection contains mostly Chaucerian material, including *Troilus and Criseyde* and *Legend of Good Women*. Editors are undecided whether the scribes had access to better texts of these Chaucerian poems than were available to others, for although *Troilus and Criseyde* is not a good text, *Legend of Good Women* has a unique prologue which has been generally accepted as genuine. The main scribe also wrote Bodleian MS e Musaeo 116, which contains Chaucer's *Astrolabe* among other texts, so he or his supervisor may have had an interest in Chaucer. However, Gg 4.27 seems to have been written under supervision and is probably to be considered a bespoke text. The manuscript has been vandalized by someone who tore out many of the pages with illuminations; and many of the tales in *The Canterbury Tales* now lack their beginning and end. It is not easy to decide what links and rubrics the manuscript originally contained. As it now stands Gg 4.27 consists of 454 original leaves, though other leaves have been added to make good its deficiencies. *The Canterbury Tales* occupies folios 132^r-443^r; it follows *Troilus and Criseyde* and precedes *Legend of Good Women*. It was probably set off from these texts by at least one blank page in each instance. The manuscript was written by two scribes, though the second wrote only a few pages at the end. The whole of *The Canterbury Tales* was written by the main scribe. Both scribes are of East Anglian origin, and they are remarkably alike in their spelling conventions as though one had trained the other. This raises the question whether the manuscript was written in London or East Anglia. The texts copied may well have been available only in London, but the existence of two scribes might suggest an East Anglian origin for the manuscript. Certainly as far as *The Canterbury Tales* is concerned, the text of Gg 4.27 has much in common with other group *a* manuscripts, and the exemplar used by the scribe must have been similar to, if not identical with, that used by the scribes of El and Dd 4.24. The editors of the recent facsimile date the handwriting to the second half of the first quarter of the fifteenth century.[13] This could make it either contemporary with, or somewhat later than, El. The illumination was dated by Edith Rickert to about 1440, though Beadle and Parkes consider

[13]Parkes and Beadle 1979-80 III.7.

this date far too late for the handwriting.[14]

Like Dd 4.24, Gg 4.27 has an unusual quiring system. Its regular pattern is quires of twelve leaves, though there are variations. Quire 11, which contains the beginning of *The Canterbury Tales,* and quire 37, which contains its end, are anomalous as regards their quiring, and this may be explained by the absence of the next work to be copied when the scribe came to the end of the previous one. He also inserted extra leaves to provide blanks before and after the poem to set it off from its surroundings. Quire 25 originally had sixteen leaves, and in it a page may have been left blank before PhT, though in this as in so many other cases the missing leaves cause problems of interpretation. Quires 30, 31 and 33 all had fourteen leaves originally. It is not easy to offer any explanation for the extra leaves originally included in these four quires, partly because so many of the leaves are now missing. The quiring does not suggest that there was any hesitation about the order of the tales, for there was a probable conjunction of tale and quire boundary only at the beginning of MLP (quire 17), ClT (quire 21) and PrP (quire 27). Of these conjunctions only the first may be significant since other scribes allowed for a break after CkT which was incomplete in case extra material was to be added. Since ClT follows on from ClP and since PrP occurs in a constant group, these two instances of tale and quire junction are probably coincidental. It may well be that blanks existed in the manuscript such as the posited blank before PhT to allow for a link, but in the absence of the leaf itself it would be foolhardy to speculate. The present state of the manuscript prevents us from arriving at any conclusion regarding the anomalous quires.

The manuscript may not have been completed. There are no running heads and there are few marginal notes. Those that are present have been added later. The division of the tales into parts has not been carried out thoroughly. MLT has signs that it was to be divided into parts, but the scheme was not carried out consistently; those divisions which are found do not correspond to those in Dd 4.24 and El. There are directions for the rubricator to insert *Explicit* after 3:322 and 952, but there is no provision for initials to start the new parts. The division into parts in ClT seems also to have been executed after the tale was written. Textually Gg 4.27 is close to, but not identical with, Dd 4.24 and El, though as far as tale order and contents are concerned it reflects these other manuscripts. It does not contain NP endlink. Its text was corrected, but not all the passages rubbed out have been replaced. There are many small omissions through eyeskip and the scribe appears to have made his own editorial improvements. In a recent

---

[14]Parkes and Beadle 1979-80 III.7.

study of his text of *Legend of Good Women,* it has been shown that the main scribe was careless and did make editorial incursions in the text. [15] A similar state of affairs exists in *The Canterbury Tales.* There are rubrics which have naturally not survived because so many leaves have been torn out. The system of rubrics that survives is closer to El than to Dd 4.24, though it is not so well developed as in El.

Gg 4.27 represents a less-developed form of the text and its presentation as compared with that found in El. It is not a good text because of its alterations and improvements. Beadle and Parkes describe the main scribe as conscientious, but liable to disturbing lapses of concentration. [16] The evidence the manuscript has to offer cannot be readily interpreted because of its missing pages, but it may be suggested that it echoes the organization of the text found in El − an organization which was only brought to fruition in that manuscript.

[15]Kane 1983.
[16]Parkes and Beadle 1979-80 III.54.

5

The Formation of the Text: Hengwrt

After the brief description of the manuscripts provided in the previous chapter, the question arises of what criteria to use to arrange them in an order to form the basis of further discussion. At present any order must be provisional, for the evidence to confirm any hierarchy can come only through the further discussion of how the scribes tackled the material they had and what reasons motivated them to behave in the way they did. Certainly if order and presentation of material are significant pointers of date and position in the hierarchy, El may be designated as one of the last of the early manuscripts for it shows no signs of the uncertainty in arrangement which is found in Hg and even Ha7334. However, these criteria need not be regarded as definitive since the presentation of material may have depended as much upon the experience of the scribe as upon the position of the manuscript in the hierarchy. Similarly uncertainty of order which is reflected in a disrupted quiring may have arisen because of a need to adapt what had become a fixed order to a different one rather than because all disrupted orders are earlier than all fixed ones. Nevertheless, those manuscripts with a regular quiring system such as El, Lansdowne, Petworth and Corpus, in which the small break in quiring appears to be fortuitous, may be later than the others. Hg is the only manuscript with significant irregularities in its quiring, and Ha7334 was not written in the order in which it was finally presented. Although Dd 4.24 has regular quires of twenty-four leaves, it shows some uncertainty in its order. The position of Gg 4.27 is more difficult to determine because of its missing leaves. On the criterion of uncertainty in order, the only safe conclusion is that Hg is an early manuscript.

There are also the criteria of the material included in the text and the presentation of the text by means of rubrics, subdivisions of the tales into parts and running heads. The latter of these is imposed by the scribes, and the manuscripts divide up into two groups, with Hg, El, Gg 4.27 and Dd 4.24 in one group and Corpus, Ha7334, Lansdowne and Petworth in the other. But El has a more comprehensive series of rubrics and running heads than other manuscripts, which would seem to confirm its lateness in the hierarchy. Corpus, on the other hand, seems by this yardstick to be earlier than Ha7334. When it comes to extra material, whether that material is Chaucerian or not, which is included in the manuscripts, then Hg is undoubtedly the earliest manuscript for it contains the least material. Corpus must also be early by this criterion since it too has far fewer additions as compared with the other manuscripts. In addition, studies in the spelling systems of some manuscripts have indicated that Hg is much earlier than El and that it is probably the manuscript closest to Chaucer's original.

All these indications confirm that Hg is the earliest extant manuscript and that any discussion of the textual tradition must start with the evidence which it contains. This chapter will therefore be devoted to how its scribe arranged the material he had available. Since Corpus and Ha7334 were written by the same scribe and since Lansdowne is closely linked with Corpus in group *c* of the manuscripts, it is sensible to consider those three manuscripts together in one chapter. The three early manuscripts which belong to group *a* can also be treated in a chapter by themselves, though of these manuscripts El might reasonably be considered late. This will leave Petworth to be discussed on its own, and it can be conveniently included in a chapter dealing with later developments in the textual tradition of the poem.

In my discussion of Hg I will assume that the scribe had access at first to the twelve sections referred to in Chapter 3, and that these twelve sections constituted separate physical entities in the copytext either because they formed individual quires or groups or because they consisted of single sheets pinned or sewn together. The significant fact is their independence as sections, for it was this independence which allowed the scribes to move them as units. Tales within sections were not moved in the early textual tradition, but sections themselves could be. The problem for the scribe was to arrange the tales in a sequence so that the poem was presented in as complete a form as possible even though it consisted of fragments. Since he could see from the constant sections that there was a succession of tale–link–tale in the order, this was the principle he used to guide him in arranging the sections within the poem as a whole. In the previous chapter I outlined the order in which the various parts of the manuscript were copied, and it was deduced from that arrangement that the scribe had all the parts of the poem he included in Hg (except the Sq–Me and Me–Fk links) before he started copying. The next question that has to be decided is how he came to settle on an order before he started copying.

Although some of Chaucer's friends may have known of the poem's existence and even heard or seen particular tales, we could not assume that the scribe knew much, if anything, about the poem before he started copying. As a professional scribe he would be used to copying disparate material, putting it in some order and imposing an *ordinatio* upon it. If, as I have suggested, he started by copying parts I and V of the manuscript, he would have come to certain conclusions about the poem which would help him in organizing the intermediate tales. Section 1 consists of Pro followed by four tales, but each tale is separated by a link from the pilgrimage frame which acts as a connecting device to hold the tales together. The scribe would therefore expect the poem to progress in a sequence of tale–link–tale. This expectation would be confirmed by part V which has a link and the final tale, perhaps with a concluding link to round off the poem, and by the constant sections which proceed in a similar sequence of tale–link–tale. He would naturally assume that the finished poem would have had a continuous sequence of tale–link–tale, and this is presumably how he would seek to arrange the fragments he had available. The pieces he had available were far from uniform: he had tales without links, tales with links, and groups of tales which were joined by links. If we accept that the links in yellowish ink were not available to him when he started copying, he would not have had what in Hg are the Sq–Me link and the Me–Fk link. If we represent the absence of a link by − and its presence by ±, we can deduce that the scribe had the following pieces which he had to arrange in a sequence from the middle of the poem.

- (i) + MLT −
- (ii) − SqT −
- (iii) − MeT −
- (iv) − FkT −
- (v) − NnT−
- (vi) + ClT +
- (vii) − PhT + PdT +
- (viii) − ShT + PrT + TTh + TMel + MkT + NPT −
- (ix) + McT −
- (x) + WBT + FrT + SuT −

A few comments about this table are in order. The plus and minus signs represent what is found in Hg, not necessarily what may be found in other manuscripts and hence in modern editions. A plus signifies that there is some action from the pilgrimage frame, even if that is not always called a prologue or epilogue. Thus the end of PdT contains the exchange of the Host and the Pardoner and has been classified as a link and so is signified by a plus.[1] The plus after

---

[1] It is not difficult to see why this passage was not separated as a link, for it does not introduce another tale; it only concludes a tale. Generally the scribes thought in terms of prologues and tales only, and this piece could clearly not be called a prologue.

ClT represents the Host-stanza which is found in Hg, but not in all other manuscripts. In some later manuscripts tales were divided up into a prologue and tale, whereas in Hg they appear as a tale without subdivision. This applies to FkT and NnT. Since this later arrangement does not apply in Hg and as there is no interaction in these newly formed prologues between the teller of the tale and other pilgrims, it has been disregarded.

From the table of pieces given above it may be noticed that there is a pattern in the arrangement of the tales. The first tale, MLT, has a prologue before but no link after it. It introduces a block of tales which have no links at either beginning or end. It will, however, be remembered from the last chapter that gaps were left between these tales for the provision of links, some of which were subsequently filled. Since the order in the table, apart from the position of (x), represents the final order in Hg, it seems almost certain that the scribe decided to group together those tales which had no connecting links and to place them first in the middle part of the poem. That he left gaps between them indicates that he expected links to be discovered or provided to join the tales together. After ClT the pieces he had are arranged so that each tale is separated from the next by a link. This means that if a piece ends with a plus, it is followed by a piece beginning with a minus; and if it ends with a minus, it is followed by a piece beginning with a plus. It would appear therefore that the principle of organization which the scribe followed was simply that of separating each tale by a link. There is no other way in which the final five sections could be arranged to produce the same result except that the order of (ix) and (x) could be reversed since they have the same pattern.

The organization of the intermediate sections of the poem into two groups, one without links and the other with a constant succession of tale–link–tale, is one that has been superimposed and could under no circumstances be attributed to the arrival of the tales in a haphazard and piecemeal way. It confirms that the scribe had all tales available before he started copying. However, this arrangement is a purely formal one which pays no attention to the contents of the tales or the links. Modern scholars have been reluctant to see an organizing principle in Hg, because they have supposed that any order of the tales and links ought to pay attention to their content. In particular they have expressed reservations about the lack of geographical consistency in Hg's order, and also about the lack of a clear relationship between WBT on the one hand and MeT and ClT on the other. We must remember that we know the poem and its parts much better than the early scribes did, who were faced with the immediate problems of organization on the basis of a rather superficial acquaintance.

It may, however, be appropriate now to consider the position of

WBT. This tale is part of the constant section, section 2, which contains WBT, FrT and SuT. This section constitutes all of part II which is written in the brownish ink in Hg and, it is surmised, was written last by the scribe. If we accept that part III is misbound, then in the final arrangement of Hg part II came before MLT, and if it was to be placed anywhere else in the sequence of parts it could come only before part V. This may well have been its intended position partly because it maintains the sequence of tale—link—tale which we have noted in the final group of the middle pieces of the poem and partly because the references to *towne* in the last line of SuT may have been interpreted to refer to Canterbury. In the purely formal arrangement of pieces we have sketched for the organization of Hg, there would be no problem in placing section 2 immediately before PsT. However, when the scribe copied the various tales, he would have noted that there are references to the Wife of Bath within MeT and at the end of ClT. He would appreciate that it was impossible to keep the order he had arranged, since it is not reasonable for one pilgrim to refer back to a tale which actually comes later in the sequence of tales. WBPT would clearly have to be moved from its position at the end of the middle portion; and if it moved, then it would take with it the other two tales in section 2. As the scribe had embarked on the copying of part IV of his manuscript as a continuous sequence of text which did not allow for the alteration of its various pieces, he could not insert part II anywhere within part IV. This fact itself suggests that he only became aware of the need to reorganize the order of the tales after he had embarked on the copying of part IV. Consequently the only thing he could do was to copy section 2 as a separate unit and to insert it in the only space available earlier than MeT and ClT, and that was between parts I and III. It seems certain that he would not have wanted part II to go there if he could have inserted it within part IV; and so it may be accepted that the final order is a compromise solution to the problem regarding this tale which had arisen in the process of copying. It must be stressed that the Wife is the only person to be referred to within another tale and so this particular difficulty only cropped up once. The scribe's re-positioning of this tale is a purely practical solution to a difficulty which has nothing to do with geographical or temporal consistency. That the names of places occurred in a faulty geographical sequence was evidently something which did not worry him or lead him to make alterations. It is quite feasible that this discovery of the unfortunate first positioning of WBPT caused all subsequent confusion in the order of the manuscripts. If there had been no references to the Wife in MeT and ClT, the order intended for Hg might simply have been carried forward and adopted as standard.

An irregularity in part IV is the double quire which contains the end of FkT, all of NnT and the beginning of ClT. The differences in the colour of the ink indicate that NnT was added after the other two tales were written, and the quire must have been enlarged to accommodate it. However, the enlargement of the quire was carried out before ClT was copied, for FkT finishes halfway down fol.165^r and ClT commences at the top of fol.174^v. A gap which was sufficient to accommodate NnT was provided, which was not difficult to calculate since NnT is in stanzas. When NnT was copied, it was started at the top of fol.165^v so that the bottom half of fol.165^r remained blank. This may have been intended like the other blanks in part IV to be filled by a link. Since a precise space was left in the manuscript for NnT, this tale was available to the scribe when he finished FkT and started ClT. It is not so clear why he should have delayed copying NnT. In other manuscripts NnT is linked with CYPT as part of a constant section. Hg does not contain CYPT. It may be that the delay in copying NnT was connected with CYPT. Since CYPT forms a constant section with NnT elsewhere, one would expect CYPT, if it were Chaucer's, to have been found in his papers after his death and to have been linked with NnT, as is true of the other constant sections. One solution is to accept that CYPT was written after Chaucer's death to be attached to NnT. If the scribe of Hg knew that it was being written, he might have delayed writing NnT to see whether he could also include CYPT. Since this tale has a prologue and no endlink, it would have fitted into the sequence of tale–link–tale at this point, for it comes after NnT which has no endlink and before ClT which has a prologue.

If we may recapitulate the discussion so far, it is probable that the scribe of Hg had access to all the tales he included before he started writing. He copied the parts of his manuscript in the sequence I–V–IV–III–II. He did so partly through lack of familiarity with the material and partly to gain time to organize the middle sections of tales. He thought of the poem as proceeding in a sequence of tale–link–tale and tried to arrange the fragments to produce this sequence. He had more tales than links so that he grouped together the linkless tales and left gaps between them for links to be added.

It is time now to consider in greater detail the order in Hg and some of its implications. Section 1 came first because of Pro, but it ended with the incomplete CkT, whose ending the scribe thought might turn up, though he was to be disappointed in that hope. The problem was how to follow an incomplete tale, to which an ending might be found. He chose MLP, which he commenced on a new quire, because this is a prologue which does not look back to a tale which has just been told. It simply announces what is to follow and so represents a new start in the poem. MLP is followed by MLT. As it happens there are certain features in MLP and MLT which do not harmonize. In particular MLP announces a tale to follow in prose, whereas MLT is in verse. Various attempts have been made to overcome this discrepancy. Some have suggested that MLP was designed for another tale, while others have claimed that 'prose' here refers to the stanzas of rhyme royal in which MLT is written.[2] Furthermore, MLP refers to other stories written by Chaucer all of which are based on classical models and deal with ladies who were betrayed or whose husbands met a violent death. It might well be argued that this prologue should precede a tale about a similar lady rather than about Constance, whose tale not only ends happily but is also placed within a Christian environment. MLP does mention the Man of Law for the Host says:

'Sire man of lawe,' quod he, 'so haue ye blys
Tel vs a tale anon as forward is'. (3:33-4)

However, in Pro there is reference only to a 'sergeaunt of lawe' (1:311), though that phrase is too long to fit into the line in MLP. We may wonder whether Chaucer did actually write MLP for MLT or whether in fact he occasionally wrote free-standing links in which he left a blank for the teller of the tale to follow. We may recall in this connexion that in PsP the word 'Manciple' is written on an erasure. Generally, when tales occur in a constant section, this is reflected in Hg and the other early manuscripts so that if PsP referred to a tale by a particular pilgrim, his tale and PsT should have formed a constant section. Therefore it remains possible that PsP had a space in its first line for the name of a pilgrim to be inserted when the previous teller was decided. If that was the case, the same thing may have happened in MLP, though in this instance it is the following teller who is to be named. Once MLP and MLT were joined, later scribes found no reason to separate them, despite the odd inconsistency between them, and so the hypothesis that the two were separate sections in the Chaucerian fragments cannot be proved from later manuscripts. The hypothesis does, nevertheless, receive some support from the position of MLT in Hg, since MLT is followed by a series of tales which have no links at beginning and end. If MLP was not joined originally to MLT, then MLT would fall in with that series of linkless tales and that would account for its position in Hg and subsequent manuscripts. If so, it just happened to be the first of the linkless tales and so got joined with the free-standing link which became MLP. This view is more satisfactory than assuming that MLP was designed for either of the extant prose

2 Stevens 1979.

tales, both of which have introductory links, and was moved to MLT when TMel or PsT was given an alternative prologue. The alternative view that Chaucer did write MLP for MLT and was unconcerned about the anomalies which arose remains possible in view of the limited evidence we have available.

The other linkless tales were apparently arranged in a haphazard fashion. They were the tales of the Squire, the Merchant, the Franklin and the Nun. SqT may have been placed first in this group because it was incomplete, though it is evident that the scribe did not expect the rest of the tale to be found. He allowed a small gap after the tale, which was long enough for a link but certainly not long enough for an ending of the tale. For SqT concludes with the first two lines of part 3, and if there was to be only one more part we would expect the rest of the tale to contain at least a further three hundred lines, though the analogues indicate that the tale might have been longer even than that. The most satisfactory assumption is that Chaucer was working on this tale when he died and that the scribe was aware of this fact and so expected nothing further to appear. Although the end of CkT may have been lost and might turn up, this was not considered likely for SqT. No attempt was made to group the linkless tales thematically, for NnT which deals with a saint has more in common with MLT than with the other tales in the linkless group, but it is separated by the others from MLT.

Two interrelated matters arise concerning the grouping of the linkless tales in Hg: firstly the provision of links and secondly the allocation of tales to tellers. *The Canterbury Tales* consists of a sequence of tales in a pilgrimage frame. Generally, the tales are stories which do not reveal the identity of their teller and make no reference to other tales in the series. It is only from the frame, that is the links, and from the rubrics that one can identify the teller, though occasionally a tale may contain details like personal pronouns which may help to elucidate some feature, such as the sex, of the speaker. When the scribe of Hg arranged the linkless tales together, it is possible that he did not at first know who the tellers were. He had no links because he left gaps for them and he inserted the running heads and perhaps even the rubrics later. It would only be if his copytext contained some kind of rubric or marginal annotation identifying the teller that he would know who the speaker was going to be. This is a feature which may still be recognized in modern editions with regard to NnT. This tale follows either FkT or NPT in the manuscripts and in modern editions. In neither case is there a link to join NnT to the previous tale. There is nothing to introduce the speaker. In manuscripts and modern editions which contain CYPT, that tale follows NnT. CYP contains no reference to the previous teller; it refers only to the previous tale. In El, for example, CYP opens 'Whan toold was al the lyf of seinte Cecile'. In other words even today the identity of the teller of NnT is revealed only in the rubrics which accompany the tale. If Chaucer's original included no rubrics, and their diversity and even absence in the manuscripts suggest that this may well be the case, there would be no evidence to show that this tale was allocated to a pilgrim by Chaucer. Indeed in this case since the teller refers to himself as the 'vnworthy sone of Eue' (7:62), it is reasonable to suppose that Chaucer had envisaged the teller as male even though he had not determined precisely who it was. If this tale is anything to go by, then we might assume that the scribe of Hg had to deal with four (or possibly five if we include MLT) tales which had no links and had been allocated no tellers. To do this he left gaps between the tales for links and ultimately provided rubrics and running heads.

There are four gaps in Hg which needed filling: ML–Sq, Sq–Me, Me–Fk, and Fk–Nn. Only the two middle gaps were subsequently filled in Hg, though a link which would fit the ML–Sq gap is extant and was included in some later manuscripts. There is no extant link for the Fk–Nn gap in an early manuscript. It is widely assumed that the order found in El and reproduced in many modern editions is Chaucer's final order; so that Chaucer's ultimate arrangement for this part of his poem is the sequence MLT–section 2–ClT–MeT–SqT–FkT. It is also accepted by scholars who think along these lines that Chaucer wrote links for the MeT–SqT and SqT–FkT gaps which are those found in El and some other early manuscripts. These two links do appear in Hg where they serve as the SqT–MeT and MeT–FkT links respectively. It is usually argued that the El forms are Chaucerian and that the scribe of Hg adapted the MeT–SqT and SqT–FkT links to form his SqT–MeT and MeT–FkT links because he had already copied the tales in this order into his manuscript. This view presupposes that the tales were circulated before Chaucer died so that the Hg scribe did not have the tales in the correct order or even with all their parts. We have already noted that there are important arguments against the hypothesis of prior publication of the tales. If the tales were circulated by Chaucer, then we would have to assume that they were circulated without their links, for otherwise the Hg scribe would have acquired the links with the tales. This would not be so if the tales were circulating in two forms, one without the links and one with. Why one or two tales should circulate with links and what readers would make of such links is not easy to decide. Alternatively we could imagine that the Hg scribe first picked up the free-standing tales from among those that were circulating and then the links found only with the tales that were in Chaucer's possession when he died. If this were so, it would mean that some manuscripts like El which preserve these links preserve the real Chaucerian text and are not edited manuscripts as so commonly assumed. This view would not explain why the Hg scribe acquired some tales with links, such as the tales of section 1, and some without. If he had access to some genuine Chaucerian versions, why did he not have access to all of them?

Let us, however, assume for the moment that the El links are genuine and that they came to the Hg scribe in this form after he had written out the tales in a different order. How would he treat these links? The El MeT−SqT link consists of two parts [E2419-40 and F1-8], in the first of which the Host comments on the preceding tale and refers to his own talkative wife, and in the second he asks the Squire to tell his tale. The two parts are unconnected thematically, and their only connection is that they succeed each other in the link. If this link came to the scribe of Hg as a Me−Sq link, there seems no reason why he should not have cut it in half and attached the first part to the end of MeT and the second half to the beginning of SqT, which in his order preceded MeT. The second link in El is the Sq−Fk link which consists of three parts. In the first the Franklin compliments the Squire on his tale though he makes no reference to its unfinished state. In the second the Host asks the Franklin to tell a tale; and in the third the Franklin agrees. Although these three parts are clear, there are connections between them in that the Host picks up the word *gentillesse* used by the Franklin and the Franklin responds to what the Host had said. It may not have been so easy to divide up this link in the way the other one might be cut up. Nevertheless, there were gaps in Hg which could have been filled by breaking up these links into their various parts if they had come to him in the form they have in El. He did not do this, but it is suggested that he altered the names of the speakers. Since the Hg scribe is known to have been a conscientious copyist, this does not seem likely to be the way in which he would have behaved. We need also to remember that he did not fill the gap between MLT and SqT, even though a link for that gap is known to exist and would have fitted the space he left. If that link is genuine, then we would expect the Hg scribe to have acquired it when he acquired the other links which he is said to have adapted. He did not, but simply omitted to fill the gap he had left for a link. He could have behaved in the same way with the other two links. If their El forms are genuine and came to the Hg scribe in this way, we might have assumed he would leave them out as he did the ML−Sq link because he would realize his arrangement was faulty.

It seems more reasonable to accept an alternative hypothesis. The Hg scribe arranged certain linkless tales in a group with gaps for the links that were not among Chaucer's papers but which were to be provided by someone. Three links for these four gaps were provided, but only two were copied into Hg. The third was not copied in because during the course of copying the Hg scribe came up against the problem of WBPT which is referred to in MeT and ClT. He was forced to move the section with this tale earlier in his order, although he could not put it after MLT where he wanted it to go because he had provided no coincidence of tale and quire boundary at the end of MLT. He realized that in later manuscripts section 2 could be placed after section 3, and this would make his ML–Sq link redundant. He therefore did not bother to copy it in. He did, however, copy in what were his Sq–Me and Me–Fk links because he or his editor had not yet decided that moving section 2 after section 3 might also involve reversing the positions of SqT and MeT. We may assume that the ML–Sq link which had been written was left with the copytext papers. Similarly since the Sq–Me and Me–Fk links were written after Hg's order was determined we may assume that each was written as a unit on a separate piece of paper. These units would then be treated as indivisible by later scribes, and this would account for the fact that they were not broken up into parts but simply had the names of the pilgrims altered. This provides a satisfactory reason for the way the scribes treated these links as units – a reason which would not apply if the Hg scribe had come upon the links in a sequence of tale–link–tale in some other copy.

The other gap in Hg is that between FkT and NnT. As we saw earlier, NnT was not copied in the manuscript in its correct sequence for it was inserted at least after FkT and ClT were copied. The reasons for this are not clear, but it may have something to do with the inclusion of CYPT in later manuscripts. If this tale was being composed while Hg was being copied, then the scribe may have delayed copying NnT to see whether it would be ready in time. When CYPT was linked with NnT, it often led to the latter being moved from its Hg position to a later one because of a reference in CYPT to Blean. If this was known when Hg was copied, and the delay in copying NnT suggests that it may have been, then it may have been considered unnecessary to compose a FkT–NnT link at all since it would not be needed in subsequent copies of the poem.

For the moment it seems best to adopt the following hypothesis. The scribe of Hg arranged the linkless tales in a group leaving gaps for the links to join them. Three of these links were written by somebody, but only two were included in Hg because of the rearranged order which was envisaged for WBPT. All the new links were kept with the copytext, and each occupied a separate sheet of paper and was treated as a unit. The final acceptance of this hypothesis or not depends upon the order of tales in the various manuscripts. If Hg's order can be shown to form the basis of later orders, it would follow that its arrangement of these links was the original (though not Chaucerian) one and that the later manuscripts adapted them for different positions. The major argument against this hypothesis remains the familiarity to modern readers of the links in their El form and the universal acceptance by critics that the links fit more appropriately into the poem in this form. Regrettably critical approval does not prove Chaucerian authorship.

The latter half of Hg contained tales with links and they were arranged to give a sequence tale−link−tale without any apparent concern for geographical or temporal references which may have occurred in the links. There is little to be said about this arrangement except to call attention to its arbitrary and formal character. No attempt at thematic or narrative linking was made, for the guiding principle was simply the continuity of the parts. We may assume that Gamelyn and CYPT were either not available to the Hg scribe or not accepted as genuine parts of the poem. Gamelyn could have been inserted in the gap left at the end of CkT, where there was a coincidence of tale and quire boundary. CYPT may have been in the making, for as we saw there was a space left for NnT which was subsequently filled with the tale but nothing else. The late insertion of NnT may have been intended to allow time for the completion and inclusion of CYPT. The provision of CYPT may have been the reason behind the failure to provide a link for FkT−NnT since CYPT was in some manuscripts to pull NnT away from its position in Hg to later in the order.

As for the layout of the text in Hg it is accepted that the running heads were added later. It is improbable that there were any such heads in the copytext, particularly if that copytext was Chaucer's working draft. Doyle and Parkes suggest that 'The treatment of the headings, subheadings, and explicits and their wording and indentations for major and minor painted capitals must have been present in the exemplars, introduced therein by the director of the copying, or devised by the scribe in the course of the work in accordance with general instructions'.[3] It seems more likely that the rubrics were added in embryo by the 'director of copying' or even by individual scribes into the copytext. The diversity among these headings in the various manuscripts and even the variety within individual manuscripts such as Hg indicate that they were part of the *ordinatio* being superimposed on the text by the scribes. Since we do not have Chaucer's original we cannot tell how he would have presented the text, but we may note that Gower's *Confessio Amantis* does not provide headings or subdivisions of the tales within the text itself. There are Latin verses in the text at major divisions as well as marginal notes in Latin, which may well have

---

[3]Doyle and Parkes in Ruggiers 1979 p. xxxiii.

encouraged some copyists of *The Canterbury Tales* to introduce annotations and authorities in its margins. That the poem was left in a fragmentary state by Chaucer may also have encouraged scribes to introduce a system of headings and sub-headings since there would be the occasional hiatus in the poem which could be concealed through the use of rubrics. Chaucer himself may have thought of his poem as a seamless web in which there were perhaps occasional notes in the margins. In Hg we may detect the possible basis of this in that ReT has no heading, but simply *narrat* in the margin. KtT begins with a rubric in English, but then after 1:894 there is the heading *Incipit narracio* which is here in the text rather than in the margin. After ClT there is simply the word *Explicit* before the Host-stanza, which has no heading or concluding rubric, for ClT itself was said to end before the envoy. In some instances the marginal note *narrat* or *Incipit narracio* may have been accompanied in the copytext by the title or subject matter of the tale, for some rubrics in Hg (and also in later manuscripts) refer to the matter of the tale as well as to its teller. For example, PrT has the heading 'Here bigynneth the prioresse tale of *Alma redemptoris mater*'. If there were in the copytext marginal notes like *narrat* to announce the start of each tale, this might account for that division into prologue and tale of FkT and NnT which occurs in some later manuscripts. We may conclude then that there was no comprehensive system of headings in Chaucer's original papers, but there may have been occasional marginal notes indicating the beginning and end of a narrative or even a prologue. If they occurred, they were probably in Latin. It is, however, the scribes or their directors who were largely responsible for dividing the poem into parts and providing the appropriate rubrics to go with them. This was what a scribe was trained to do: he had to make his text presentable to its readers.

In Hg a system of rubrics, largely in English, has been introduced and allowance was made for headings when the manuscript was copied. This treatment is not reflected in some later manuscripts, and it may be an indication of the scribe's professionalism and experience. However, in some cases a rubric or part of it has had to be squeezed in, as is true of WBP and PdT; and this is hardly surprising for the scribe cannot have adopted a uniform system from the start. At first he had a set of rubrics which referred to prologue, tale and teller. The beginning of the prologue is indicated, but not its end by a rubric. In section 2 which follows, but which was probably written last, a similar system operates but in this section there is a rubric to end each prologue as well. Since this is the only section in which this concluding rubric for the prologues is found, it confirms that this section was written at the end. MLP is referred to as a 'prohemie' and MLT is introduced by

'Here bigynneth the tale' without the teller being mentioned. The concluding rubric refers to the Man of Law. SqT has an introductory rubric but no concluding one, because the tale is incomplete. MeT, FkT and NnT have rubrics to open and close them in the normal way. ClP, which was the next prologue to be written after MLP (for the intervening tales had no prologues at first) is also called a 'prohemie', and his tale like MLT is introduced without the name of the teller. The rubric ending ClT is placed before Chaucer's envoy. After PhT we get a series of rubrics which refer to the merry words of the Host, though some tales such as PdT may also have a prologue. The scribe was prepared to accept that the links between tales could consist of more than one part. His scheme was of link—tale rather than of prologue—tale. Nevertheless, it is interesting to note that the rubric of PdP read at first 'Here bigynneth the pardoners tale' as though the scribe expected the tale to follow on from the link. He then inserted above the line 'prologe of the' after 'bigynneth', perhaps when he came to fill in the rubric to the tale itself. The system of rubrics referring to the Host's merry words continues till MkT which reverts to the original prologue and tale formula. It may be recalled that MkT begins part III of the manuscript, and there may be some connection in this in that this part of the manuscript may have been written a little later than the other parts. The only change within the rubrics in the early part of section 10 is that the rubric to TTh—TMel link has 'Here the hoost stynteth Chaucer of his tale of Thopas and biddeth hym telle another tale'. The tales in sections 10 and 11 are often referred to by their subject matter as well as by the teller, though this does not apply to MkT. PsP has an introductory rubric in English, but has a Latin *Explicit prohemium* at the end. It can be seen that there is a changing pattern of rubrics in Hg, which was doubtless superimposed by the scribe. The changes reflect the stages in his copying, for it is not conceivable that Chaucer by coincidence varied his rubrics in a way that was to be reflected in the order of copying the tales in Hg.

In addition to the rubrics, the scribe reveals his experience in copying by the way he presented the tales. Those tales in stanzas are set out with a gap between the stanzas. TTh is written out with the third, sixth and ninth lines to the right of the other lines, and the rhymes are joined together by lines. Tales with subdivisions are normally provided with gaps so that the rubrics can be included within the text rather than in the margin. KtT, SqT, ClT and PsT are provided with subdivisions in Hg. Those in KtT are found only in Hg except for the subdivision indicating the beginning of the tale at 1:895. Since those manuscripts which have tale divisions in KtT have the divisions in other places, we may assume that the subdivision was scribal. It may be that the scribe started copying with the intention of subdividing the tales and abandoned this scheme after KtT. He then introduced subdivisions only with those tales which had them in the copytext. SqT has three parts, and this is fairly regular in most manuscripts, though some omit the third. ClT has only five parts, and this division is echoed in many early manuscripts. PsT is incomplete, but Hg has two parts and rubrics for the seven deadly sins. It does not have rubrics for the remedies of those sins. The scribe also provided the names of the pilgrims in the margin of Pro and the names of the tragic sufferers in the margin of MkT, though these were added later.

Hg contains marginal notes, though they occur erratically, and some words have an interlinear gloss in Latin or French. Of the latter the most important is the gloss *Qi la* to the merchant's 'Who ther' in ShT (10:214), since some later scribes were to incorporate this gloss into their text. The other marginal glosses occur erratically throughout the tales, and some may reflect the Latin word or phrase in the sources. Others explain who the person referred to is. The *me* at 10:694 is identified as Chaucer in the gloss. The majority of these glosses are repeated in manuscripts which have glosses and they may have appeared in the copytext. The marginal notes are of different types. Some like the interlinear glosses are Latin equivalents of what is provided in the text itself, and so fulfil much the same function. In KtT at 1:1166 where the text has 'That who shal yeue a louere any lawe?' the marginal note reads *Quis legem det amantibus*. Some notes provide more information than is given in the text so that 'Trophee' in MkT 10:2109 has the gloss *Ille vates Caldeorum Tropheus*. Others provide a reference to the authority being used at a particular point, and sometimes a reference to the work he wrote as well. Then there are marginal directions to the reader to pay attention to a passage such as *Nota* or *Argumentum*. Finally, there are marginal notes which may almost be described as sub-headings. These occur in Hg particularly in NnT and PsT, in the former in Latin and in the latter in English. The notes which are Latin equivalents of the text or source material are found particularly for the didactic and classical material. There are a large number in MLT, in January's initial monologue in MeT, and in ClT. They are also found, though rather infrequently, in FkT, NnT, PhT, PdT and TMel. Whether this type of annotation was in the copytext is uncertain, but it is possible. It was frequently added to by later scribes, and this may suggest that the scribes introduced the notes because they felt it would make the poem more learned and didactic. In many ways these notes reflect the attitude expressed in Rt that the moral tales are a matter for congratulation; for the annotations make these tales part of the learned didactic tradition of medieval tale-telling.

There are not many directions to the reader like *Nota* in Hg, and in this respect it differs from some later manuscripts. It is probable that such directions were inserted by the scribes as part of their presentation of the material. In KtT there are examples of *Nota* at 1:1776 which criticizes those lords who have no mercy, and at 1:2983, the first line of the passage on the First Mover of the fair chain of love. There is an *Argumentum* at 1:2839, which introduces Egeus's speech offering comfort for Arcite's death. In MiT there is a *Nota malum quid* at 1:3726 when Absolon kisses Alison's arse. In WBP there is a *questio* against 2:115 which asks for what reason genitals were made, and in WBT a *Nota bene* at 2:1083 in which the old hag discusses the nature of true *gentillesse*. In MeT there is a *Nota* against 5:217 in which January notes that, though old, he is still blooming. There are also in MeT three examples of *Auctor* to indicate passages of authorial comment, usually of a moral nature as is true of those at 5:539 and 813; the third at 5:625 is a passage where the author apostrophizes Damian and is introduced by 'I seye', where the *I* is the poet. There is a *Nota* in ShT at 10:176, where it is said that wives wish their husbands to have certain characteristics. There are also three examples in PsT which refer to moral sayings. These examples are perhaps too scattered and diverse to draw any conclusion from them. They are usually set against moral passages, particularly those in a rather high style, though there is a suggestion of interest in wider social issues.

As for the text in Hg there is not a great deal that needs to be said because this manuscript contains fewest additions. As we saw in the previous chapter the scribe left gaps where he could not read his copytext or where it was defective, and this suggests that he was conscientious in his copying and did not intend to edit his material. The only passage in Hg which is not found in later manuscripts is 1:253-4, and that is likely to have been in the copytext as we shall see later. The scribe omitted 1:639-40, almost certainly through eyeskip for 'Thanne wolde' is repeated at the beginning of 1:638 and 1:640. That the scribe did make occasional mistakes is indicated by the corrections he made. Several lines have been inserted in the margins after being omitted at first. One of these corrections is the couplet in KtT at 1:3023-4. Although this could be an addition inserted by the scribe, it is preferable to think of it as a correction of a scribal mistake. Other mistakes were corrected by inserting 'a' and 'b' to reverse the order of the parts in which the scribe had first copied them. Even in the prose tales, which caused other scribes trouble in copying, the scribe of Hg made few mistakes, though there is an example of eyeskip in PsT at 12:511. Otherwise, the text was copied accurately and we shall see in dealing with other manuscripts how it came to be developed. It may have been a sudden attack of modesty which caused him to insert '&c' for 'swyue' at 11:256, for he had copied the word many times before, though that may have been the reading of the copytext. The rhyme guaranteed that other scribes would have the correct word if '&c' was in the copytext.

From the foregoing we can deduce that the scribe of Hg was conscientious and experienced. If, as the palaeographers have suggested, his handwriting was somewhat old-fashioned by the turn of the century, this would simply confirm his experience. He imposed an order on the fragments and provided the parts of the poem with rubrics and running heads. He provided KtT and PsT with subdivisions to make the material more manageable; and he evidently found no difficulty in this type of work. He corrected many of his mistakes as he went along, though he made few to start with. He copied only what was in front of him and took no liberties with the text and did not seek to edit the contents. There are few omissions in his text. Passages which are not in Hg and which appear in later manuscripts·are consequently likely to have been introduced into the text after Hg was written. The scribe of Hg did not know the poem well before he started copying. How far he was responsible for the order in which the tales appear is difficult to say, but it is not likely that he composed the extra links which were copied late into his manuscript. The evidence suggests that the copytext he had to work from was not in a good condition for it contained gaps and it had not been put into a final form. Nevertheless he made an excellent job of presenting its material in a coherent and accurate text.

6

The Development of the Text 1: Corpus, Ha7334 and Lansdowne

In this chapter I shall deal with Ha7334, Corpus and Lansdowne, because there are clear signs of association among them, though they were allocated to different groups by Manly and Rickert. Ha7334 and Corpus were written by the same scribe; and Lansdowne and Corpus belong to the same Manly–Rickert group of manuscripts and the former was probably copied from the latter. Of these three Ha7334 and Corpus are the earliest and will be dealt with first and in most detail. It has been widely accepted hitherto that Ha7334 is earlier than Corpus, and this is why a longer description of it was included in the previous chapter. Yet in the account of Corpus certain details were pinpointed which could indicate that it was as early as, or even earlier than, Ha7334. In particular Corpus has fewer links and a more muddled system of rubrics than Ha7334. I accept that both are written by the same scribe, shared the same exemplar, and are probably not far separated in time. Even so the indications, slight as they are, that Corpus is the earlier manuscript encourage me to take that one first; I will assume that it is based on the same copytext as Hg.

The order of the tales in Corpus, and in all other early manuscripts for that matter, is sufficiently close to that in Hg to prove that there was continuity in the arrangement of tales. Certain tales, those of the Squire, Merchant, Franklin and Clerk, change their order frequently, but the others maintain a stability that is impressive. If the sections had been circulating independently we could not expect such uniformity to show up in the manuscripts, particularly as there were no clues to determine the order some sections should follow. Even in those sections which have references to geography or time, these seem to have been ignored by the scribes. Most significant in the order is the regular appearance of section 9 before section 10 in all manuscripts, because section 9 contains no references to time or place. The regularity of its position in the manuscripts cannot be accidental. Since Doyle and Parkes have proved that the scribes of the early manuscripts came from the London/Westminster area and co-operated in the production of other manuscrips, there is no problem in accepting that they collaborated in the matter of the order of tales in *The Canterbury Tales*. Indeed, it would be surprising if they had not.

The order in Corpus can readily be understood to be an adaptation of the order found in Hg. It starts with section 1 to which Gamelyn is now added, though this tale was not found in Hg. The tale has the marginal heading *Incipit fabula*, but no concluding rubric; it has not been worked into the fabric of the poem. This is perhaps not surprising since, as we shall see, there were few rubrics in this part of Corpus. The scribe arranged the tales as chapters of a book rather than in the link—tale formula found in Hg; and Gamelyn is regarded as part of the same chapter as CkT. It therefore did not merit any special introduction in the eyes of the scribe. Since Gamelyn starts on the same page as the incomplete CkT finishes, there are no signs of uncertainty in the order. The same applies to MLP which follows Gamelyn; it commences on the page on which Gamelyn finishes. The order had been determined in advance; and this is hardly surprising since Corpus has chapter numbers which were presumably incorporated in the copytext to guide the scribe. In the discussion of Hg in the last chapter it was suggested that its scribe wanted MLP to follow CkT, but disrupted that order late in the production of the manuscript because he had to move section 2 forward in the poem order and could accommodate it only between CkT and MLP. This position of section 2 was not his intended or preferred order. Hence by allowing MLP to follow Gamelyn, the scribe of Corpus was merely carrying out what had been the intention in Hg (apart that is from the inclusion of Gamelyn itself). The inclusion of Gamelyn may be attributed to the new organization imposed on the text by the scribe of Corpus. The poem in Corpus is divided into chapters, but CkT by itself would form a very small chapter and clearly needed filling out. One way of doing this was by including another tale to fill out the Cook's chapter. This would explain why Gamelyn was included and allocated to the Cook. It is only in Corpus that this situation would arise, and so it is likely that Gamelyn first appeared in the poem in that manuscript. A similar situation would not prevail with SqT, since that tale, though unfinished, was already quite extensive. MLP led naturally to MLT. This is followed by ML endlink, which can also be referred to as SqP in Corpus since it has the reading 'Esquier' at [B^{1}1179] and is followed by SqT. As we saw in the description of Hg, in that manuscript SqT follows MLT and a gap was left for a link passage which was never filled. It seems most reasonable to assume that a link for that gap was written, but not included in Hg because of potential changes in the order of the tales. If, however, the link was left with the copytext, then it would be perfectly natural for the scribe of Corpus to include it in his manuscript and to follow its lead by placing SqT after MLT. The reason why WBPT was moved to an earlier position in Hg was the occurrence of references to the Wife of Bath in MeT and ClT. These references would mean that MeT and ClT should follow WBPT, but do not mean that SqT should change its position. If there was a link indicating SqT's position, then it is no surprise that it should be found in that position. SqP is written on the same page as MLT finishes. Although SqT begins on the next page, as that is the verso of the recto on which SqP is written, there is no evidence of hesitation on the scribe's part.

When he finished SqT, he left a gap of about half a page blank after it. He added the last two lines which form the start of part 3 to part 2, whose conclusion is indicated by a marginal rubric. The gap may signal that he thought some conclusion to the tale would be provided. It does not appear to indicate hesitation about the order, for although WBP begins on the top of the following recto, that prologue commences within the same quire. The scribe was not providing an opportunity to include another tale or anything lengthy. He was simply uncertain what to do about the incomplete SqT. There was of course a link which was added in Hg to round off SqT, but that link provided for MeT to follow SqT. Since MeT had to come after section 2 and ClT, this link could not be used in Corpus. Even so its availability may have led him to leave a blank. It was the only blank he left. WBP introduces section 2 which proceeds as in Hg. SuT which ends section 2 is followed on the same page by ClP. This introduces ClT. In Hg ClT had been much further back in the order, but it is here brought forward because of the reference to the Wife of Bath at the end of ClT. ClT was put before MeT because this would disrupt the order found in Hg least. In Hg FkT followed MeT, and by placing ClT before MeT the scribe of Corpus could maintain that order. The unwillingness to disrupt Hg's order too much also helps to explain why SqT was left to follow MLT. ClT ends with the *lenvoye de Chaucere*, which is incomplete because a leaf is missing. It is not possible to be absolutely certain what was included on that leaf. MeT follows ClT. Now one page finishes at 8:1189 of ClT and the next begins at 5:49 of MeT. There are thus 48 lines missing from MeT. Normally a page of Corpus has 36 or 37 lines so that the missing leaf could have accommodated 72 or at most 74 lines of text; it is more likely to be no more than 72 since one or two rubrics may have been included as well. The conclusion of the envoy to ClT would occupy 23 lines of text, and this with the 48 lines of MeT makes 71 lines. One can therefore deduce with reasonable certainty that there was no link between ClT and MeT and with a high degree of probability that there was no Host-stanza either. The Host-stanza contains seven lines and could only have been incorporated if the lines on this missing leaf were crowded in, which would seem to be an unwarrantable assumption. It is not surprising that there is no Cl—Me link in Corpus since there was no such link in Hg because that manuscript had a different tale order. It is less easy to decide why the scribe eliminated the Host-stanza. There are several occasions in the manuscript where he changed the end of tales; we have already seen that he reorganized the last two lines of SqT. He left out the last lines of TTh and he omitted the last part of MeT. Since he arranged the tales as chapters, he may have decided that there was no room for an endlink, particularly as ClT has one conclusion in the form of Chaucer's envoy. It is equally possible that the Host-stanza was omitted through carelessness, for there are several signs of that in the manuscript in that pages are missing from MeT and TMel. As the Host-stanza is also missing in the other two manuscripts of group c, Lansdowne and Sloane 1686, we may accept that it was not in Corpus. As for MeT its conclusion was never copied into Corpus, possibly because the relevant leaves in the copytext were missing or mislaid. The scribe went straight from 5:1074 in MeT to the beginning of FkT (6:1) on the same page. He made no provision for a link between these tales. A link had been included in Hg and one might have expected it to appear in Corpus. As the end of MeT was never copied into Corpus, we may assume that the Me—Fk link of Hg was attached to the end of MeT in the original copytext and was omitted for the same reason when Corpus was copied. The reason for the absence of the end of MeT and the Me—Fk link may be either because part of the copytext was temporarily missing or because of carelessness on the scribe's part. In favour of the first solution is the change of ink in Hg at this point which suggests a new leaf beginning in the copytext; and in favour of the second are the marks of carelessness throughout Corpus. In FkT both 6:1 and 6:21 have illuminated initials, and the former lines has the rubric 'The prologe of the Frankeleyn' in the margin, though that may have been introduced later since there is no rubric or line space to introduce the tale itself at 6:21. NnT follows FkT as it had done in Hg. The end of FkT and the beginning of NnT are now missing, though it seems improbable that they were joined by a link. FkT finishes on one page at 6:867 and NnT commences on the next page at 7:37. There are thus 41 lines missing from FkT and 36 from NnT. The total of 77 missing lines is slightly more than one might anticipate. It proves that there was no link, but raises the possibility that a few lines at the end of FkT were not included. There are other omissions in FkT in Corpus and a few missing lines at the end of FkT in Lansdowne to support this view. NnT is followed on the same page by CYPT so although this may be the first time this tale was included in the poem there was no doubt as to where it belonged. The first line of CYP refers to the tale of St Cecilia, i.e. NnT. The running heads in Corpus refer to this tale as 'Cecile' and the final rubric refers also to 'Seint Ceciles Tale'. As the introductory rubric, if it ever existed, is missing, there is no evidence that this tale was allocated to a teller in Corpus. It is perhaps not surprising, therefore, that if it is the first manuscript in which CYPT appeared its prologue referred only to the tale of St Cecilia rather than to a teller. From CYPT the manuscript continues with the order of tales as in Hg, namely sections 9, 10, 11 and 12, without any apparent uncertainty or hesitation. In MkT a gap was left for the Adam stanza, although the stanza is not included. This stanza is not in Hg, though it occurs in most later manuscripts. Its absence in Corpus may be explained by the decision to include a stanza about Adam to complete the series of tragedies, for what could be more appropriate to the human tragedy than Adam's story. We may assume that the stanza was ordered but was not ready for inclusion when MkT was copied, and when it eventually appeared it was not copied into the space which had been provided for it. In MkT the Modern Instances are in the middle of the tale. The reason for this move may have been motivated by the Knight's remark which opens NPP 'namoore of this' (10:2759). This was taken to be a means of terminating the tale abruptly, which therefore had to be shown to be incomplete. By moving the Modern Instances to the middle of the tale, the chronology was disrupted and the stories in the tale made to appear random and incomplete. However, this move appears not to have had the blessing of the corrector who placed an 'a' by the tale of Nero and a 'b' by the first of the Modern Instances as though the latter group should follow the tales introduced by the former. The change in order may have been made by the scribe himself. If the change was made accidentally rather than deliberately, it would indicate that the copytext was of loose leaves whose order had become disrupted. This might be a further sign of lack of care on the scribe's part. The end of section 12 is missing and so it is not possible to decide whether Rt was originally part of the manuscript or not. If Corpus is the manuscript which followed Hg in the hierarchy, it would mean that the two earliest manuscripts were incomplete at the end, and that might cast greater doubt over the authenticity of Rt than has usually been the case.

The headings and rubrics in Corpus are irregular. The running heads commence only with WBP; none are found before then. When they do start they are imperfectly executed, although some have been cut off by the binder. The normal running head consists either of 'Prologus' or of the possessive form of the teller's name, e.g. 'Pardoneres', to indicate the tale; but the pattern is not regular. For instance, NnT has the running head 'Cecile'. Normally the heads occur on recto pages only, but FrT has 'Freres' on verso and 'tale' on recto. WBPT has simply 'Bathe' on the recto pages. The rubrics to the tales are equally erratic, as may be seen by those in section 1. The beginning of the manuscript is missing so it is impossible to say whether there was a general title to the poem, but it seems unlikely. KtT has no rubric at all, but it does contain the Latin quotation from Statius in the text. MiPT are treated as a single unit which has the rubric 'The Millewardes Tale' in the text in a one-line gap. MiT itself has an illuminated initial. RePT is also treated as a unit, but there is a two-line gap to introduce it which contains the two rubrics *Explicit fabula Molendinarij* and 'Here begynneth the Reeues tale'. ReT itself has, however, the rubric *fabula* in the margin together with an illuminated initial. CkP has no heading, but CkT is introduced with *Incipit fabula* in the text in a one-line gap. Gamelyn has *Incipit fabula* in the margin, but no rubrics within the tale. The somewhat erratic set of rubrics continues throughout the manuscript. MLP has no rubric to introduce or conclude it, but MLT has the marginal rubric *Incipit Fabula* to start it. At the end of MLT there is a marginal heading *explicit*. SqPT have no rubrics at all, though SqT has two parts with the second being introduced by the rubric 'The Stag of an Hert' in a one-line gap and the rubric *Explicit prima pars* in the margin. It is not clear where this rubric 'The Stag of an Hert' came from, but it occurs for the first time in Corpus. WBP is introduced by a marginal rubric *Prologus uxoris de Bathe C°vij°*. This prologue is said to finish after 2:802 where a one-line gap has the rubric 'Here endeth the prologe of the gode wife of Bathe'. The next part of the poem has no rubric; it contains the interruption by the Friar and the exchange among him, the Host and the Wife. Her tale begins at 2:831 after the rubric in a one-line gap '[Here begynneth] the goode wyues tale of bathe'. Her tale ends with the rubric in a one-line gap 'Here begynneth the prologe of the Frere', but at the end of WBT there is the marginal note *Explicit,* and at the start of FrP there is another marginal note *Incipit prologus fratris*. FrT itself has a marginal rubric 'Here begynneth the Freres tale'. At the end of the tale there is a rubric in a one-line gap 'Here endeth the Frere his tale', but there is also an *Explicit* in the margin. There is no rubric to introduce SuP, but SuT is introduced by a rubric in a one-line gap 'Here begynneth the Somnours tale'. At the end of SuT there is a two-line gap filled with the rubrics 'Here endeth the Somnours tale' and 'Here begenneth the prologe of the clerk of Oxenford'. The leaf containing the end of ClP and beginning of ClT is missing, as is that with the link between ClT and MeT. As we have seen the end of MeT was never copied, and it is possible that the link which went with it in Hg was omitted in the same way. No gaps were allowed for to introduce FkT, but there is the marginal heading 'The prologe of the Frankeleyn' against 6:1 and an illuminated initial at 6:21. The end of FkT and beginning of NnT are missing, though the latter was not divided into prologue and tale. There is however a rubric *Et lamentat* in a one-line gap after 7:207. CYPT follow on the same page as the end of NnT and there was a one-line gap included before it, into which the scribe included the two rubrics in a rather cramped fashion 'Here endeth Seint Ceciles Tale' and *Hic incipit fabula Canonici.* CYT has two large illuminated initials within it, but no rubrics. PhT starts on the same page as CYT ends, and in the one-line gap there is the rubric 'The doctour of phisik'. At the end of the tale there is no gap for a rubric, but there is the marginal heading *Prologus.* PdP when it commences has no gap for a rubric, and in the margin there simply occurs the heading 'C^m xvj^m'. There is no rubric for PdT itself, but there is an illuminated initial. At the end of PdT there is a marginal *Explicit,* but the one-line gap before ShT contains the rubric 'Here bygynneth the schipmannes tale'. After ShT there is a marginal *Explicit,* and the one-line gap before the link has the rubric 'Here endeth the schipmannes tale'. It is clear that the scribe or rubricator did not have any idea as to how to label linking passages such as the one which follows here. The two-line gap at the end of this link has the three rubrics 'Here begynneth the tale of Alma redemptoris the prioresses Tale', *Prologus* and *Domine Deus noster.* There is no rubric to end the prologue, but there is an illuminated initial at 10:488. Probably the whole tale was regarded as a unit at first, and the rubric *Prologus* was added later. There is no gap at the end of PrT, but there is an *explicit* in the margin. TTh is introduced by the rubric 'Here bygynneth the tale of Chaucer of sire Thopas' in a one-line gap. The last four lines of TTh were not copied, and there is no rubric or provision for one. The two-line gap at the end of the TTh and TMel link is filled with the rubric 'Here bygynneth Chauceres tale of Melibe and his wyf Prudence and his doughter Sapience'. This longer title may be designed to fill in the two-line gap left free, because the proceeding link had no title and so had no concluding rubric, though the supervisor may have intended one. The one-line gap at the end of TMel is filled with two rubrics 'Here endeth Chaucers tale of Mellibe' and *Prologus monachi.* The prologue has a marginal explicit at its end, and the one-line gap is filled with the rubric 'Here telleth the monk *De casibus virorum illustrium*'. MkT finishes with an *Explicit* in the margin and the one-line gap is filled with the rubric 'Here begynneth the prologe of the nonne prestes tale'. At the end of NPP there is an *Explicit* in the margin and the one-line gap has the rubric 'Here begynneth the nonnes prestes tale of the kokke and his vij hennes'. At the end of NPT the one-line gap contains the two rubrics in a very cramped manner 'Here endeth the Nonne prestes tale' and 'Here folweth the prologue of the maunciples tale'. The end of McP has the marginal heading *Explicit prologus Incipit fabula.* McT finishes with an explicit in the margin and the one-line gap has the rubric 'Here bygynneth the prologe of the person'. The beginning of PsT is missing, as is its end.

It is clear that the scribe or his supervisor did not have a firm plan as to presentation of the tales and their rubrics. It seems certain that the running heads and many of, it not all of, the rubrics were added when the manuscript was complete. Nevertheless, provision was made for some rubrics by the one or two-line blanks which are found sporadically. Although Corpus resembles Ha7334 in the provision of running heads only from WBP, the rubrics suggest that each manuscript had a different method of presenting the material. In Corpus the introduction of chapter numbers and the absence in the first part of the manuscript of any distinction between prologue and tale indicate that the scribe was trying to present each prologue and tale as a unit so that each unit could be presented as a chapter. He had thus moved away from the system of tale−link−tale found in Hg in order to impose a different organization on the text. However, this system was disrupted during the course of copying and a somewhat half-hearted attempt was made to revert to the system found in Hg. Tales may be provided with prologue and tale, but the system never achieved regularity. The rubrics themselves occur in a variety of languages and forms; and it is evident that considerable uncertainty was present as to how best to present the tales. The inconsistencies in Corpus almost certainly spring from this attempt to impose on the poem a different arrangement from that found in Hg and from its abandonment before it could be fully carried out. When it was abandoned, the scribe reverted to Hg's organizational principal without carrying it out systematically or coherently. It was this new textual arrangement designed for Corpus which led its scribe to be less concerned about linking passages between the tales.

If the scribe of Corpus had Hg's copytext, he should have had twelve sections and probably ML endlink, Sq−Me link and Me−Fk link on separate sheets. However, as he did not copy the end of MeT, it is likely that Me−Fk link was omitted for the same reason (whatever it was). He used ML endlink as a SqP, but he could not use Sq−Me link because he changed the order of tales which made that link redundant. In addition to what had been available to the scribe of Hg, he also had Gamelyn and CYPT, which both made their first appearance in Corpus. As we saw in an earlier chapter, CYPT may have been in the process of composition when Hg was being copied, but was not finished in time. Its emergence in Corpus is therefore hardly surprising. CYPT was clearly written to be incorporated in *The Canterbury Tales,* and since its inclusion in Corpus it has been included in copies of the poem almost regularly until recently. Gamelyn is different since it contains neither prologue nor any indication of teller or relationship with the rest of *The Canterbury Tales*. It is often suggested that it was found among Chaucer's papers and therefore included in the poem. This may be so, but since the number of possibilities is so large it is perhaps wiser not to speculate. It may have been included after CkT because a conclusion had been expected for that tale by the Hg scribe, and when one failed to materialize it was necessary to adopt a different solution to the problem. The brevity of CkT meant it needed supplementing to make a full chapter. Gamelyn was added without any attempt to insert it within the pilgrimage frame, but that is not surprising in view of the different organization the scribe of Corpus imposed on the poem. We may assume that links which are found in some later manuscripts were not available to the scribe of Corpus, because they had not yet been written. With respect to Gamelyn we may note that the Squire was never provided with another tale in the way that the Cook was. This we may attribute to the way the scribe of Hg set up the text. He allowed for a link to end the incomplete SqT and when that was written it effectively prevented any different solution to the incompleteness of SqT being proposed. He left CkT with a blank, but that blank was not filled in Hg. In Corpus it was filled with Gamelyn, and so later scribes were faced with the problem of how to assimilate this tale into the poem.

For a variety of reasons, not all of which are clear, the scribe of Corpus embarked on a process of editing the text which involved cutting out existing passages and including new ones. This editing follows different lines from that found in the group *a* manuscripts, though there is occasional overlap; but many omissions may be accidental rather than deliberate. In Pro Corpus omitted 1:253-4; and this couplet was not to be included in any of the other manuscripts. If it is original, then we must assume that the scribe deleted the couplet in the copytext which is why it was not found again. This couplet describes certain dubious activities of the friars which the scribe of Corpus may have preferred to suppress. There are no marginal rubrics of the names of the pilgrims in Pro, which proceeds in an uninterrupted way. In KtT the scribe includes two passages not in Hg. One couplet [A2681-2] describes the fickleness of women and may well have been added by the scribe of Corpus. The other passage of four lines [A2779-82] is spoken by Arcite on his deathbed and increases the pathos of the situation and could also have been added by the scribe of Corpus. Some of his other alterations reveal an interest in women and pathos. In they were added by this scribe he may have added them in the margin of the copytext as they occur in some other manuscripts. In the rest of section 1 and section 2 Corpus includes none of the extra lines found in group *a* manuscripts. When he copied MLT, ClT and NnT which are all in stanzas, he did not provide any gaps between the stanzas. Illuminated paragraph marks were added in the right-hand margin to indicate the beginning of some stanzas, though even this was not carried out systematically. These illuminated marks were added later. Hence these tales in stanzas were copied out as though they formed a continuous text, which may be a sign that the scribe was not used to this type of metre, though this feature may reflect what was in the copytext. It is hardly surprising that he should have made frequent mistakes in copying these tales, for on many occasions he probably forgot he was copying stanzas in rhyme royal and thought rather in terms of couplets and simpler stanzas. As it happens he copied out MLT without mishap, but he started to go wrong with ClT. On some occasions he omitted the fifth line of the stanza so that he produced stanzas rhyming more simply as ababcc. It is interesting to note that in ClP he added *Pausacio* in the margin as though to indicate stanzas of six lines each. But he failed to count the lines properly so that each 'stanza' has a varied number of lines. He gave up this means of marking stanzas before he came to the end of ClP. We shall see a similar series of mistakes in NnT to those in ClT.

In SuT he made two small changes. At 2:1705-6 he left out one line and included a new one in which the friar encourages the congregation to turn from sin and so avoid the pains of hell. This may be because he thought friars preached well on such topics and that the message to avoid hell needed to be reinforced. At 2:1846-8 he omitted two lines through eyeskip. Lines 1845-8 in Hg had been:

> And moore we seen of Cristes secree thynges
> Than burell folk althogh that they were kynges.
> We lyue in pouerte and in abstinence
> And burell folk in richesse and dispence.

The repetition of *burell folk* led him to omit the last half of 1846, all 1847, and the first half of 1848. But he changed *dispence* to *wynnynges* to provide a rhyme for *thynges*. This need for change did not lead him to question whether there was a mistake in his own text. In MeT he had an exemplar which had the incomplete couplet at 5:61-2 and he simply took the easy way out of omitting the half-line at 5:61 so that his text goes direct from 5:60 to 5:63. He omitted 5:403-4 in which January claims he will have heaven on earth — a claim which may have offended the scribe. At 5:533-4 he replaced the following couplet in Hg

> So sore hath Venus hurt hym with hir brond
> As that she baar it dauncyng in hir hond

with the new lines:

> As that sche bare daunsyng in hir hand
> So freisshe sche was and therto so likand.

The new couplet is clearly inspired by the old one and was probably designed to get rid of the reference to Venus. There seems no very obvious reason for the rearrangement at 5:571-4, though it emphasizes January's haste to go to bed with May. At 5:986 he supplies a line which is missing in Hg so that the new couplet reads:

> Folwyng his wyf the queene proserpyna
> Which that he rauyssched out of Proserpyna.

The new line is the second one. We may note the repetition of *Proserpyna,* the lack of sense in the couplet, and the indication that his knowledge of classical mythology was limited. As we saw earlier the end of MeT is missing in Corpus. We may suggest in view of the other alterations that the possibility that he left it out deliberately because of its indelicate subject matter is one that should not be ruled out too hastily.

FkT shows considerable editorial activity. The order of 6:21-2 is reversed, perhaps because it was felt the tale started more fittingly with the words 'Ther was a knight'. It shows that scribes paid quite close attention to minor details. Much of the other editorial activity in FkT consists of omission. Usually this consists of the elimination of a couplet, a fact which strengthens the theory that in Pro 1:253-4 was omitted as part of a general tidying up. Corpus omits 6:439-40, which reduces the list of marvels that *tregettours* perform. It omits 6:483-8, which reduces the miracles performed by the clerk of Orleans. It omits 6:715-16 and 6:725-7, both of which contain reference to suicide; the omission may have been intended to play down the use of suicide by these unfortunate ladies. The spurious line which follows the last of the omitted couplets also changes a reference to suicide to something less painful. The rearrangement of 6:813-14 eliminates the reference to the shame which Arveragus was willing to suffer, and emphasizes only his truth. The rearrangement of 6:840-2 introduces the idea that Aurelius is now totally destroyed ('I am forlorn') and was probably intended to emphasize the moral that someone who intended to do evil would end up in a bad way. This is accentuated by the omission of 6:851-2 in which Aurelius decides to offer to pay the clerk of Orleans' debt gradually by paying a small sum each year. A simple solution is not available to the wicked. It was noted earlier that the missing page in Corpus might not have contained all of FkT as found in Hg. In fact Lansdowne, which echoes Corpus, omits 7:879-86 and we may assume these lines were first omitted in Corpus. They eliminate Arveragus's acceptance of shame rather than that Dorigen should be false to her word. We can see in these omissions and rearrangements that certain things in FkT offended the scribe's sense of decorum. He did not like references to suicide, magic and breaches of the marriage code, and he would not accept that people who planned such wicked actions as Aurelius did could be virtuous.

In NnT which is in stanzas he omits several passages. Two or three of these can be attributed to eyeskip, such as 7:213-14, 7:389-90 and 7:432. The other passages may have been omitted deliberately, though that is difficult to prove: 7:73-4 refers to earthly lust; 7:156-9 refers to the need to avoid lust in marriage; and 7:326-37 refers to Christ's message about the next world. Although there are references to lust which might have motivated some omissions, this reason does not apply to all passages. Probably carelessness is a more likely cause of the omissions. In section 9 there are changes in Ph—Pd link. At 9:291-2 he replaces a couplet which refers to misfortune befalling all judges and their clerks with a general denunciation which refers only to the wicked characters in PhT. He inserts a new couplet after 9:296 which refers to Virginia's beauty as the cause of her death, and so emphasizes the pathos of the story. This caused a rewriting of 9:299, in which it is said that the theme of beauty causing death will not be followed up now. In PdT he inserts a couple of spurious lines, the second being determined by the first. In Hg the couplet 9:485-6 reads:

So dronke he was he nyste what he wroghte.
Herodes, whoso wel the stories soghte.

This is changed into:

So drunke he was he nyste what he wrought
And therfore sore repente him oughte
Heroudes who so wole the stories seche
Ther may ye lerne and by ensample teche.

The intention is to drive home the message of the need to repent — a message which echoes the addition in SuT to avoid the pains of hell. This theme was clearly close to the scribe's heart. He also omits 9:601-2 which contains a reference to Stilbon the philosopher. This may be accidental; if deliberate, it would probably be to avoid too many classical references.

In section 10 we may note that Corpus in ShT introduces the reading *Qi la*, a marginal annotation in Hg, into the text at 10:214 — a decision which affected many later scribes and editors. TTh is not written in stanza form, and so it is not surprising that there are omissions in the text. These include 10:852-4 and 10:915-18, the final lines of the poem. TMel which follows is notable for its many omissions. The majority of these are caused by eyeskip, a fact which suggests that the scribe may well have been inexperienced. Or else we may assume he was not very familiar with copying prose. A couple of examples must suffice as illustration. The passages are quoted from Hg, with the words omitted in Corpus being underlined:

10:1463-4 to do thee a newe vileynye. *And also for my suffrance men wolden do me so muchil vileynye* that I myghte neither bere it . . .

10:1506-7 stire yow to pacience. *Forthermoore ye sholde enforce yow to haue pacience* considerynge that the tribulacions . . .

There are at least twenty examples in TMel where passages have been omitted through eyeskip. In addition the scribe omitted one long passage (10:1138-72) which can be attributed only to carelessness. It is possible that this passage was the equivalent of a page of the copytext. It seems unlikely that the page was missing, though that is possible. Perhaps the omission of this page and the end of MeT are the result of inattention. There are one or two other smaller omissions in TMel which may be accidental or deliberate. At 10:1320 where Hg reads 'For Senek seith that the wise man that dredeth harmes escheweth harmes', Corpus has 'For as saith the wise man', which seems more like a rewriting to avoid a reference to Seneca than a simple omission. Other possible deliberate changes occur at 10:1329 and 10:1335-6. In MkT, which is written continuously, there are five omissions of single lines, three of which commence stanzas. These omissions may be put down to carelessness. However, omissions in NPT may be more deliberate. At 10:2894 he omits the claim that dreams are mere vanity and so not to be believed. This obliges him to leave out 10:2896 and to allow 10:2895 to rhyme with 10:2893. This treatment of the text is very similar to how the scribe operated in changing PdT. His omission of 10:3015-20 would appear to have been caused by mere carelessness. There are no significant changes in section 11. As much of PsT is missing now in Corpus it will not be treated here; it will suffice to say that it contains many omissions through eyeskip in much the same way as found in TMel.

The scribe omitted many of the marginal annotations found in Hg. At first he copied almost all those found in KtT, MLT and SqT, particularly in MLT. But after that he decided not to copy any more and he proceeded in this way until he came to PdT. He started to copy the annotations in PdT, but after the first three he gave up once more. In TMel he did not copy the few annotations found in Hg, but he introduced many of his own. These were usually the names of the authors quoted in the text, like Cato or Seneca. They appear erratically, but frequently. He was clearly influenced by material of a religious or didactic nature to introduce annotations; even the few examples of *Nota* he added to WBP exhibit an interest in sentential remarks.

The picture we can build up of the scribe of Corpus is of someone relatively inexperienced. In many respects he might be called provincial. It has been shown from studies of his spelling system that he was not a native Londoner, and it is possible he had not been long in London. Doyle and Parkes date his London activity from the late 1390s. He shows none of the conscientiousness and experience of the scribe of Hg. He found certain types of stanza difficult to copy, and he made many mistakes in the prose. He lacked the sophistication of London and so altered Chaucer's text to make it more traditional in a religious sense. He was moral and perhaps easily offended by attacks on religious and professional people, as well as by the bawdiness of some of the fabliau tales. His ability at composition of Chaucerian verse was limited and he tended to cut out rather than to include passages in the text. This may well be why the Adam stanza was being written by someone else. The scribe's inexperience may also account for the fact that his text was gone through so carefully by a corrector or supervisor. The scribe certainly took liberties with the text, which may in some cases be the result of carelessness. He repositioned the Modern Instances, he left out the end of MeT, and he omitted a section of TMel. He tampered with the text as he saw fit. Unfortunately his knowledge of Chaucer's framework of reference was not very extensive. His addition at 5:986 is matched by his copying of Epicurus at 1:338 as *Opiournes*. It is perhaps unfortunate that he should have been employed as the next scribe of the poem after the scribe of Hg. If this scribe had recently arrived in London, it may account for the fact that he was free to copy so many texts of *Confessio Amantis* and *The Canterbury Tales*. He was employed again, probably not long after copying Corpus, to make another copy of *The Canterbury Tales,* Ha7334.

For the purposes of this chapter I shall assume that Ha7334 was the next copy of the poem to be made after Corpus. When we come to examine the manuscripts of group *a*, this assumption may have to be reconsidered. However, Ha7334 may be taken to be a later manuscript than Corpus, and it is likely that the scribe used the same copytext although when copying Ha7334 he may also have had access to Corpus. The reasons for the priority of Corpus will emerge during the discussion which follows. It may, however, be suggested that there are elements in the spelling system which support this chain of copying.[1] The scribe came from outside London, and some features of his original system such as the use of *yogh* are more prominent in Corpus than Ha7334. It appears as though he assimilated some London elements as he went along.

The order in Ha7334 may best be understood to arise from that in Corpus but adapted to meet the needs of a different arrangement. As we have just seen, Corpus imposed a system of chapters on the poem, which made the need for links less important. However, this system was abandoned before it was completed in favour of the tale–link formula of Hg, though it was never applied to the whole of Corpus. Hg's arrangement made different demands in that it called for the provision of links between the tales, which the chapter system did not. Hence the tales had to be provided with links if possible. It is this demand for links which created problems for the scribe when he copied Ha7334 and led to the marks of uncertainty which can be traced from his failure to achieve regular quiring in it. The lapses involve Gamelyn and SqT, and each has something important things to tell us about the way in which the manuscript was put together. We may assume that the scribe, who was the same person who had copied Corpus, had the same copytext which had been marked up with numbers in the chaptering system found there. This numbering system would have imposed an order on the poem in which Gamelyn is part of CkT and SqT follows MLT. However, if each tale is to be separated by a link, Gamelyn would present a problem because it is not linked to CkT in any way and it had no link with MLT, though MLP could be said to fill the needs of a linking passage. When the manuscript was copied, Gamelyn was held back in order that a linking passage with CkT could be provided. It may be that it was going to be allocated to a different pilgrim or it may have been intended to link it in some way to the unfinished CkT as part of the Cook's storytelling. The scribe simply arranged his quires in such a way that he could include Gamelyn when the link was ready. It was for this reason that the included 1:4406 on the same line as 1:4405 at the foot of the last page of the quire (for the two lines make a couplet). He then omitted the last eight lines of CkT to be included on the first page of the next quire when Gamelyn was ready to be copied. However, when it was finally decided that Gamelyn for some reason could not be provided with a link, it was copied on a quire and the quire was inserted in the manuscript. The scribe had, however, forgotten by then that he had left eight lines of CkT to be copied, and so they were never included in Ha7334. It is clear from the way in which the scribe made provision for this extra quire that

[1]However, Professor M.L. Samuels has informed me privately that he regards the spelling system of Ha7334 as earlier than that of Corpus.

Gamelyn was known of when he copied CkT. The delay was caused by some reason other than the absence of Gamelyn; and the best solution seems to be that outlined above. This handling of Gamelyn has important bearings on its non-appearance in other manuscripts.

SqT introduced different complications for the scribe. If we assume that the scribe of Ha7334 had the same copytext he used for copying Corpus, he would have had Hg's twelve sections, Gamelyn, CYPT and the three links, ML endlink (used as SqP), Sq—Me link and Me—Fk link. SqT had a position which was clearly marked in the order of the tales and it had a preceding and a following link. Unfortunately one of these links did not match the order in Corpus because both had been provided for the order in Hg. When Corpus was copied, this did not matter, since the arrangement in chapters meant that links were not so important and could be abandoned if not suitable. This was no longer an option when Ha7334 was copied, since its organizational system demanded links between the tales. As we shall see shortly new links were provided, as in the case of the Cl—Me link. As there were spare links available, Hg's Sq—Me and Me—Fk links, the solution adopted was to adapt these links to a different order and to convert them respectively into a Sq—Fk and a Me—Sq link. This solution can have been adopted only after the manuscript had been started, and it resulted in the confusion surrounding SqT. It also had the knock-on effect of making ML endlink (which had been SqP in Corpus) redundant or at least inappropriately placed. It was treated in the same way as the other links; it was adapted to the new order. Unfortunately that order has WBP following MLT, and Wife of Bath is a name that would not fit in a line of verse as a replacement for Squire. Hence the scribe did the next best thing; he chose the next pilgrim in the order whose name began with S. That was the Summoner. Before going on to consider the order more closely, we may note that the treatment of Hg's Sq—Me and Me—Fk links as indivisible units indicates that they were each written on a separate leaf and added to the copytext. The links were not broken up into two parts, as could easily have been done.

Ha7334 starts like Corpus with section 1, to which Gamelyn was added, and section 3. At the end of section 3 he started to include ML endlink which in Corpus was SqP. It must have been at this stage that the problems of the links became manifest, and this resulted in the confusion attending this link. The scribe copied [B^{1}1163-74] and then left a one-line gap. He finally copied [B^{1}1176-83], at which point he broke off in the middle of a sentence and a couplet. He thus had two incomplete couplets in his last passage of this link. At [B^{1}1179] he inserted 'sompnour' as the teller of the next tale, and he added a rubric 'Here endith the man of lawe his tale'. In this way he avoided calling this link a prologue, a function it could clearly no longer fulfil, since the next teller was to be the Wife of Bath. It was probably when he had got to this point that he copied SqT or at least its first part on a separate quire which he put on one side. It was now designed to go later in the sequence of tales. Although he signed off ML endlink with a rubric, he later added to that on the same page a supplementary rubric (now in red ink) introducing WBP. Once SqT was put back, the order MLT–WBPT became inevitable and completed the movement of tales which was foreshadowed in Hg.

WBPT is followed by the rest of section 2. The section ends with SuT which is followed by ClPT, as it had been in Corpus. Apart from Gamelyn, the sequence of prologue–tale is thus maintained, except there is an extra link at the end of MLT. ClT ends with the *Lenvoye de Chaucer* which is followed by an *Explicit* as in Hg. The Host-stanza, as we saw, was almost certainly missing in Corpus, and it is not found in Ha7334 either. Instead the link to MeT is provided by a new link which was written for this position, namely [E1213-44]. As Corpus did not have the Host-stanza, if the composer of this link was relying on that manuscript for his linking passage, it is hardly surprising that he should have let the start of his new link echo the last line of the envoy since that was the conclusion of the tale in Corpus. It seems as though the composer was not aware of the Host-stanza, and his use of Corpus to work from provides the best reason for that fact. In view of the short-comings of the scribe of Corpus and Ha7334 as a composer of verse, we may assume that this new link was not his. As this link was made to fit an order which arose only at this stage in the development of the text, it is clear that its author cannot have been Chaucer. This new link introduces MeT which finishes on the bottom of a page. On the verso of the same page we find the rubric concluding MeT, and the whole of Hg's Me–Fk link adapted as Me–Sq link, though it has no rubric. This link is spread out over the page because it was not long enough to fill a normal page of Ha7334; and the leaf itself is the final one in a short quire of only six leaves. It is clear that this quire has been truncated to allow SqT which had already been written (or at least started) to follow next and that the adaptation of Hg's Me–Fk link into a Me–Sq link was an impromptu solution designed to fill a gap in the linking sequence. The *ordinatio* of SqT resembles that of the first part of the manuscript and so cannot have been written in the sequence in which it appears in the manuscript. A quire is missing here now which contained the end of SqT and beginning of FkT. Since with the Hg Sq–Me link adapted to the Sq–Fk link, there are 608 lines of text missing, there must have been a quire of eight leaves with 38 lines per page as normal. It is probable that this quire was written after MeT was finished; in other words only the first part of SqT was written immediately after MLT. As ClT had been moved earlier in the order in Corpus, NnT follows FkT but there is no link to join it to the previous tale. The attempt to provide new links appears to have died out about here, and this may explain why no link was forthcoming for Gamelyn. As in Corpus CYPT follows NnT, which is now definitely allocated to the Second Nun. CYPT is followed by sections 9, 10, 11 and 12 as in Corpus and Hg. Once again there is no link to join PhT with CYPT. This perhaps need not surprise us too much. The tales of the Clerk, Merchant, Squire and Franklin change their order in the manuscripts and were provided with links which did not fit a different order. Clearly the first problem was to order these tales and provide new links or adapt existing ones. When that had been done, time might well have run out so that further links were not composed. That they were intended is suggested by the treatment of Gamelyn; and that they were set in hand is suggested by their occurrence in later manuscripts. An extended link was provided in NPP which in Ha7334 includes [B^{1}3961-80] for the first time. This extra passage may have been added to link up with the move of the Modern Instances to the middle of MkT, a move which occurred first in Corpus. There are echoes in these extra lines with the tale of Croesus which concludes MkT in Corpus (as we saw in an earlier chapter) and these echoes suggest that the extra lines were added after the Modern Instances were moved. Perhaps what is interesting about Ha7334 is the evidence that its scribe was working within certain constraints, namely the order of the tales in Corpus, the need to provide links, and the presence of some links handed down from the Hg order.

Ha7334 resembles Corpus in that it has running heads only from WBP. They are also missing in SqT, because that was written before WBP, and in a couple of other later quires. Similarly the rubrics change at WBP, for before that prologue they are in black ink and after that in red ink. There are no rubrics to Pro or KtT, which does not even have the quotation from Statius to introduce it. KtT has no internal divisions. After KtT we get a rubric in English announcing the end of that tale and the beginning of the next prologue, though the two are crowded in on a single line as though added afterwards. There are similar rubrics till the end of ReT, for CkT and Gamelyn have none. MLP has no introductory rubric, but at its end both *Explicit prologus* and *Incipit fabula* appear in the margin. There is the English rubric at the end of ML endlink already mentioned. From WBP onwards two-line spaces are left for the rubrics which now have a different pattern. This pattern consists of a rubric in English for the prologue, a *narrat* for the beginning of the tale often in the margin, and a rubric in English to announce the end of the tale. Occasionally other headings are inserted in the margin. In WBP the Friar's interruption is noted with the marginal heading 'Here makith the frere an interpretation of the wyfes tale' (2:803). Since in Corpus the Wife's prologue finished at this point and left the following 'link' without a rubric, it is not surprising that the scribe supplied one here since rubrics were now in order. ClPT has a different pattern of rubrics. The prologue is introduced by an English rubric, but it has a concluding *Explicit prohemium*; the tale is introduced *Incipit narrare*. The envoy has its usual French rubric and is followed by *Explicit*. SqT has the same style of rubric found in the early part of the manuscript. NnT is not divided into prologue and tale and so the introductory rubric refers to the tale alone, not to the prologue. CYPT has a slightly different style of rubric. Corpus started CYPT with a Latin rubric introducing the tale, and there were no further rubrics in it. Ha7334 has at the beginning 'And here bygynneth the tale of the Chanouns Yeman' which is followed by a cramped *Prologus*, as though this was an afterthought. A *narrat* occurs at [G720]. This means that CYPT is now made more regular with a prologue and tale. The normal pattern commences again with PhT, but is broken in ShT which has no concluding rubric. This absence of rubrics continues till TMel which contains a concluding rubric and a rubric to introduce MkP. In MkT there is no *narrat* and no concluding rubric, though the appearance again of the Modern Instances in the middle of the tale may have caused some confusion. NPPT have rubrics which resemble those at the beginning of the manuscript, and that to NPP refers to the subject matter of the tale '& here bygynneth the prologe of the Nonne prestes tale of the kok and the hen'; Corpus had a similar rubric for the tale. McP has a rubric, and McT is introduced by *narrat*. The tale concludes 'Here endith the tale of the crowe'. PsP has an introductory rubric, but PsT has no rubric at beginning or end. After a small gap at the end of PsT there is the rubric *Preces de Chauceres* which introduces Rt which has no concluding rubric. The rubrics are generally in English, though *narrat* and other Latin formulas occur. They are varied in style and in rubrication, as though a format was aimed at but never achieved successfully.

In textual matters Ha7334 shows many similarities with Corpus. It differs in writing numbers in the text out in full instead of keeping the Roman figures, and it is the first manuscript to do this. It has no headings in the margin for the pilgrims in Pro, but each description is introduced with an illuminated initial. Ha7334 omits 1:253-4 as Corpus had done. Perhaps the scribe had scratched out the lines in the copytext, as that was the first change he made in the text. He did not treat other omissions in this way later and so they are not repeated necessarily in Ha7334. In KtT a major omission occurs at the foot of a page which seems to have been caused by eyeskip. What in Hg had been an eight-line passage (1:2013-20) is reduced to the couplet.

> I saugh woundes laughyng in here rage
> The hunt strangled with wilde bores corage.

The two lines of the couplet represent the first and last lines of the text in Hg, and the last line has been adapted from Hg's 'The hunte strangled with the wilde beres' to complete the rhyme. It seems as though the other lines were omitted because of the repetition of 'yet saugh I' in 1:2013 and 1:2019, even though the scribe of Ha7334 changed it to 'I saugh'. The method is exactly the same we have seen in Corpus: omission of lines with consequent adjustment of the rhyming word. A couple of other lines are omitted in KtT probably through carelessness. One, 1:2042, occurs where some manuscripts begin a new part of the tale; and the other, 1:2954, was the result of eyeskip. Ha7334 does, however, contain the six extra lines found in Corpus but not in Hg, namely [A2681-2, 2779-82]. In MiP the scribe includes [A3155-6] in praise of good wives and this reflects the appreciation of virtue he showed in Corpus. In CkP he omits 1:4347, probably deliberately for its suggests one can be truthful in game. He was consequently forced to adjust the rhyme of 1:4349 to match 1:4348 and to omit 1:4350. This is again exactly how he had behaved in Corpus: an occasional line which offended him is omitted and the consequent adjustments are made. In CkT he omitted 1:4367-8, in which the prentice is said to dance at every wedding, and 1:4407-14, the last lines, which were omitted as already noted for technical reasons.

In MLT the stanzas are written continuously as they had been in Corpus, and this applies to all the other tales written in stanza form. However, the scribe made fewer mistakes when copying these tales in Ha7334 than he had done in Corpus; presumably he had become more familiar with this type of arrangement. He was certainly no more careful, as his omissions in KtT indicate. There are no part divisions in MLT, though there is a large initial at 3:197. WBPT show no changes, but a small change occurs in FrPT. In FrP the Summoner makes some disparaging remarks about friars. In this passage the scribe removed the couplet.

> And eek of many another cryme
> Which needith not to reherse at this tyme (2:1269-70)

and placed it in FrT after 2:1282, which is a passage describing the crimes punished by the archdeacon. In this way a couplet that had been critical of the friars is neutralized. We should perhaps remember here that the same scribe had removed 1:253-4 from Pro, a couplet which was also very damaging to the friars. Clearly friars were not so reprehensible in the eyes of this scribe. In SuT the scribe added four couplets and they represent his major addition to the text. It may not be an accident that they occur in the friar's sermon, for that unites two of the scribe's interests, friars and morality. Of these four additions two deal with anger, in each of which it is treated metaphorically; one emphasizes that women are incomprehensible; and the fourth less happily inserts potential narrative in the middle of the judge's verdict. The next major inclusion is the Cl−Me link, which shows some familiarity with both tales. In MeT itself the scribe did not in Ha7334, as he had in Corpus, omit the halfline 5:61. Instead he completed the couplet in this way:

> And if that thou take a wif be war
> Of oon peril which declare I ne dar.

The couplet does not fit in well, but the scribe has tried to improve it by modifying the next couplet (5:63-4) to

> This entent and an hundrid sithe wors
> Writith this Masther god his bones curs.

Equally at 5:986 the scribe provided the line which had been missing in Hg but which was completed in a different way in Corpus. In Ha7334 the couplet reads:

> Folwyng his wif the queene preserpine
> Ech after other as right as a lyne

This new line seems no better than that in Corpus. Both these passages are significant, though, in showing that in copying Ha7334 the scribe did not use Corpus, but he used the copytext which he had earlier employed in making Corpus. Later in MeT the scribe omitted a couplet (5:1112-13) through eyeskip caused by the repetition of *his sighte* in 5:1111 and 5:1113.

In SqT there are two parts, but the second does not have the rubric 'The Stag of an Hert'. At the end of 4:583 he wrongly copied 'for his honour' which are the first words of 4:584. Instead of correcting his mistake, he invented a new line as 4:584 'Wher for I wold not ben ayein his honour'. It will be seen how he repeats 'honour' in each line as the rhyme word, which is exactly parallel to what he had done in MeT in Corpus when he added a new line at 5:986. Some of FkT is now missing, but in what is left there are no omissions. The concern he felt at some of its statements when he copied Corpus had evidently been replaced by a greater sophistication. In NnT the scribe omitted 7:155 and 7:210-16, the latter of these being caused by eyeskip resulting from the repetition of *where*. The other line occurs at the beginning of a stanza. In CYPT he omitted [G1282-3] at the bottom of a page, a mistake which he did not notice since the rhyme was not corrected. In the Ph–Pd link he follows Corpus, but also develops what he had done there. He includes the Corpus version of 9:291-2 and the extra couplet [C297-8]. The couplet which follows [C297-8] had been rearranged in Corpus, but in Ha7334 it is now eliminated entirely. He also went on to eliminate 9:303-4

> And eek thyne vrynals and thy iurdones,
> Thyn ypocras and eek thy galyones.

This may have been caused by eyeskip of *And* at 9:305 or by the scribe's distaste. In PdT he omitted 9:476-7, two lines which occur in the middle of four with the same rhyme. Whether he was affected by that or the subject matter, which deals with wicked women who haunt taverns, is uncertain. He did not include the changes made in Corpus at 9:486. At 9:715-16 the scribe appears to have embarked on an addition which he did not complete. In Hg this couplet reads:

> Answerde agayn: 'What, carl with sory grace,
> Why artow al forwrapped saue thy face?'

The scribe of Ha7334 changed 'with sory grace' to 'with meschaunce' and left a line free after each line of the couplet, presumably to make new couplets rhyming *-aunce* and *-ace* respectively. The new lines never appeared, but the method is that we have seen elsewhere in Corpus and Ha7334.

In section 10 there are few mistakes till TMel. In ShT he omitted 10:165 'Neither abedde ne in noon oother place', but as there is no adjustment of rhyme this may have been a mistake, though its content may have upset him. He omitted 10:186-9 through eyeskip of the rhyme word *praye*, which left the resulting couplet with a perfect rhyme, but indifferent sense. In PrT and TTh the stanzas are not separated and there are no omissions except the last incomplete line of TTh (10:918) is left out. In TMel there are many omisions through eyeskip, but they are not so numerous as in Corpus. They are also different examples, and it is clear that when copying Ha7334 the scribe did not use Corpus. This can be seen by comparing a passage (10:1254-5) in Hg, Corpus and Ha7334.

Hg   Ye han erred also for ye ne han nat examyned youre
conseil in the forseyde manere ne in due manere as the
cas requyreth. Ye han erred also for ye han maked no
diuision bitwixe youre conseilours; this is to seyn bytwixe
youre trewe freendes and youre feyned conseilours.

Corpus   Ye han herd also for ye han herd nought youre counsel
in the forseyde manere ne in dewe manere as the cas
requyreth. Ye haue herd also for ye haue maad no
dyuysion betwixe youre trewe frendes and youre feyned
counselours.

Ha7334 Ye have erred also For ye haue maked no diuisioun
bytwixe youre counsailours this is to seyn bitwix youre
frendes and youre feyned counseilours.

Corpus and Ha7334 have both omitted passages through eyeskip, but the passages are different in each case, and both must have used a copytext which had a reading like that found in Hg. In MkT the scribe omitted a whole stanza concerning Sampson (10:2015-22), two lines which come last in their stanzas (10:2166 and 2238) and one that is the penultimate line (10:2557). None of these are attributable to eyeskip. In NPT he omitted 10:2918-19, two lines which occur in a set of four with the same rhyme; this omission resembles that in PdT. He also omitted 10:3261-2, probably through carelessness.

In section 12 he failed to complete two lines in PsP. Both of these (12:4 and 9) concern measurements with reference to the sun's position. As noted earlier Ha7334 is probably the first manuscript in which the Roman numerals have been written out in full. It may well be that while he was thinking about this transfer of numbers to letters, he decided that the figures were wrong and left them out. He made a similar alteration in NPT, though in that case he did complete a change (10:3162). In PsT there are numerous omissions, about fifty, caused by eyeskip as well as others which may be accidental or deliberate. These are not the same as those found in Corpus (or, where Corpus is missing, in Lansdowne). They are more numerous than in Corpus. It may be that as he got to the end of his task he speeded up and so made far more mistakes.

When he copied Corpus the scribe omitted many of the marginal annotations found in Hg. When he copied Ha7334 he omitted even more. He started including them at the beginning of PdT, TMel and PsT, but quickly gave up in each case. He included four examples of *Nota* and one *Auctor* in WBP and MeT, none of which correspond with notes in Corpus and were presumably introduced in Ha7334 for the first time. They occur at 2:333 and 336, where although the reference is sexual the main message is that those who have enough ought not to complain, and at 5:309, 625 (*Auctor*), and 813. The last two examples often drew a scribal note for they are authorial apostrophes; the first is a proverbial utterance. In other words, the scribe's additional comments are largely made to mark sentential expressions; the motivation was probably moral and pedagogical.

What we have learned of the scribe from Ha7334 merely reinforces the picture of him that we gained from Corpus. He exhibits a lack of experience and certain prejudices in copying the text. More importantly, the evidence supports the contention that Ha7334 does follow Corpus in the hierarchy, for many of the features in Ha7334 are explicable only on the assumption that Corpus came earlier. Although the fact that both exhibit different methods of organization could be taken to suggest that either manuscript has precedence, the way in which the chapter arrangement gives way to the link–tale arrangement within Corpus confirms that it must have preceded Ha7334 in which the different method of organization is more fully carried out as though it was developing what had started in Corpus. Other developments in Ha7334 from Corpus have been noted, and their combined evidence is impressive.

Lansdowne is an interesting manuscript because it is essentially a copy of Corpus. Manly and Rickert described it as a manuscript from the same shop as Corpus, and one can understand their reason. Lansdowne contains many links not found in Corpus. Apart from these links, however, Lansdowne is identical with Corpus except that there are further mistakes and omissions in it. All the omissions found in Corpus are reflected in Lansdowne; nevertheless we cannot imagine that these omissions were in a shared copytext, for Corpus's copytext was also used by Ha7334. All we need to assume is that the scribe of Lansdowne was told to copy Corpus, but to refer to additional material in the link passages which may not have been taken direct from Corpus. This would account for the fact that many omissions in Corpus which presumably appeared only in that manuscript because they were caused by the inexperience of the scribe are repeated in Lansdowne. Particularly significant are the omissions in both Corpus and Lansdowne of the end of MeT and an extensive passage, equivalent to one page, in TMel. In addition almost all the omissions in Corpus which were caused by the scribe's carelessness are repeated in Lansdowne. Only in two instances are there gaps in Corpus which are filled in Lansdowne. The first occurs in KtT at 1:3041. The line is found in Ha7334 and in Hg, and it is also in Lansdowne, though it was missed out in Corpus. It forms the first line of a couplet, and so the scribe may have noticed its absence and checked it against another copy such as Ha7334. Clearly other material relating to the poem was available since the scribe could turn to it for the links. The second passage occurs in TMel at 10:1777. This passage is slightly different, as the quotations from Hg, Corpus (which is identical here with Ha7334) and Lansdowne show:

Hg   And he seith in another place: . . . that hath shame of his synne and knowelicheth it. (The dots represent a gap in the manuscript).

Corpus   And he saith in another place he that hath schame for his synne and knowlecheth it.

Lansdowne And the wiseman seithe in another place he that hath schame of his sinne & knowleche it is worthi haue merci.

Since Hg had a gap it is clear that the copytext also had a gap here. The scribe of Corpus and Ha7334 simply ignored the gap, but the result is clumsy and unintelligible English. The scribe of Lansdowne understood that something was missing, probably because his copytext made no sense. He decided to complete the omission and took his cue from the sentence which precedes the one quoted above, for that indicates that forgiveness follows confession. Instead of including some words where the gap occurred in Hg at the beginning of the clause, he decided to put some extra words at the end of the sentence; but the result is perfectly satisfactory. The insertion shows that the scribe of Lansdowne could read the text carefully and make alterations to it, especially if he was prompted by his copytext; however, he did not act in this way very often.

The scribe of Lansdowne carried the arrangement of the poem found in Ha7334 a step further, partly by adding further links and partly by regularizing the rubrics. He intended to give each tale a prologue, and both were to be introduced with rubrics in Latin. Other, intermediate rubrics were discarded. The system breaks down at ReT, where the rubrics are in English. Generally the system of rubrics refers only to the teller. NnT is introduced in Latin as the Second Nun's Tale, but it concludes *Explicit vita sancte Cecilie,* which is a Latin form of the ending in Corpus. The introductory rubric of MkT refers to *De casibus virorum,* as Corpus had also done, and not to the Monk. NPT does not have an introductory rubric.

The attempt in Lansdowne to regularize the rubrics shows that it was expected that each tale would have a prologue and tale, and this meant that extra links had to be provided. The poem commences with section 1 as normal, to which Gamelyn is added. But now Gamelyn, which is still allocated to the Cook, is introduced by a four-line link which says that CkT was too bawdy and so the teller will fall back on a different tale. From here Lansdowne proceeds to section 3, to which ML endlink (here serving as SqP as in Corpus) is added. Naturally Lansdowne reads

'sqyere' at [B¹1179]. SqT follows this prologue. The last two lines
of SqT, which had been added to part 2 in Corpus, are omitted and
SqT is followed by a new Sq–WB link of twelve lines. This
introduces section 2 which proceeds as normal, and it is followed
by ClP and ClT. At the end of ClT there is the envoy, but no Host-
stanza or other link with MeT, the next tale. This reflects the
position in Corpus. The end of MeT is missing in Lansdowne as it
had been in Corpus, and similarly there is no Me–Fk link in either
manuscript. FkT is now divided into a prologue (6:1-20) and tale
(6:21ff). This leads to NnT, which has no link from the pilgrimage
frame to attach it to FkT, but the tale is also divided up into a
prologue (7:1-119) and tale (7:120ff). NnT leads straight on to
CYPT, which are divided into prologue [G554-719] and tale
[G720ff] as in Ha7334 and thus made to harmonize with the pattern
of the rest of the poem. After CYT there is a new sixteen-line link
acting as prologue of PhT, which introduces section 9. At the end
of this section there is a new six-line Pd–Sh link acting as prologue
to ShT. ShT introduces section 10 which proceeds as normal. The
linking passages are here referred to as prologues as elsewhere in
the manuscript, and so there was no need to divide PrT into a
prologue and tale. The long form of NPP found in Ha7334 is
included in Lansdowne. After section 10, there follow sections 11
and 12 as normal. Rt is included in section 12 with the rubric
Composito huius libri hic capit licenciam suam.

A puzzling feature of Lansdowne is the breakdown of the
prologue–tale formula in the sequence ClT–MeT–FkT. This can,
I think, be explained only by accepting that Lansdowne was copied
from Corpus. When the scribe of Lansdowne was given Corpus to
copy, he was also given those links which it was thought were not in
Corpus because they had not been ready in time: Ck–Gamelyn,
Sq–WB, CY–Ph, Pd–Sh and the longer version of NPP (in
addition to the Adam stanza). He may also have been instructed to
divide NnT into prologue and tale. These extra passages he would
include because he was given them. But it may have been assumed
that he had a Cl–Me link, which appears in Ha7334 and so
available earlier, and the Me–Fk link, which had been added to Hg
and ought to have been with the copytext but was omitted in
Corpus along with the end of MeT. It was the failure on the part of
the Corpus scribe to include these which led to their absence in
Lansdowne, because it was assumed that his copytext, i.e. Corpus,
had them. Only the new material was given to him separately. The
aim of a complete poem was frustrated in Lansdowne simply
because of the incompetence of the Corpus scribe. It may be added
that the scribe of Lansdowne omitted almost all the marginal
annotations found in Corpus. Some tales have an odd one or two to
start with, and then the rest are missing. Even MLT has only three,

though the third was included in a gap between stanzas rather than in the margin. It may be the uncertainty where to place them that led the scribe to omit them. Another interesting feature of Lansdowne is that it is derived from Corpus rather than from Ha7334, which in the scheme outlined here is later than Corpus. It is not easy to decide why this should have happened, but a solution along the following lines is possible. When Corpus was written, an order in chapter form was imposed on the poem. When it was decided during the course of copying that each tale should have a prologue, arrangements were set in hand to have the missing links composed. Not all of these were ready when Ha7334 was copied and so the scribe or supervisor had to resort to impromptu arrangements to overcome the immediate problems which arose. But the resulting mess of ML endlink, which was a kind of false prologue to SuT, cannot have recommended itself as a model. In any case as the links ordered for the order in Corpus became available, it would naturally suggest that its order should be copied in the new manuscript.

Although the scribe of Lansdowne had occasional bursts of conscientiousness, he was not otherwise a very good scribe. He introduced further omissions into the text. However, his manuscript represents the culmination of a particular development of the text. This development concentrated on the order and its attendant links and rubrics. It did not bother so much about the layout of the individual tales. Pro never achieved in this development the names of the pilgrims as marginal headings. Similarly the tales were not divided into parts unless that part division, as in SqT and ClT, was already found in the copytext. There was an increase in the amount of marginal annotation and glossing, but even by Lansdowne it had not got very far. The marginal notes appear most frequently in MLT. These aspects of text presentation were more important in the other development which we must now consider.

7

The Development of the Text 2: Dd 4.24, Gg 4.27 and El

The three manuscripts in this chapter all belong to Manly and Rickert's group *a* and they represent a different line of development from Corpus and Ha7334. This·is not, however, to say that this line is independent of the other development. Taking our cue from the production of Lansdowne, we can suggest that the scribes of these manuscripts knew of the developments that were going on in the link passages elsewhere, but they did not follow the changes within the tales found there. Hence Dd 4.24, which we shall consider first, repeats many of the developments in presentation and order which we saw in Ha7334 and Lansdowne, but it does not repeat any of the omissions and additions within the text found in Corpus. It would, therefore, be possible to assume that its scribe made use of the original copytext while also having available many of the additional links found in Ha7334. It does not have the new links found in Lansdowne, so it must represent a different answer to the problem of text presentation from that found in that manuscript. It is natural to suppose that this manuscript dates from the same time as Ha7334 or a little later. The question of priority may have to wait until we have discussed all the manuscripts in this group. Dd 4.24 I shall take first in this chapter because it is clearly earlier than El which is an edited text and probably earlier than Gg 4.27, though that manuscript is difficult to argue about since so many of its leaves joining tales together have been vandalized. First it may be best to outline how the text in Dd 4.24 was arranged and how it developed the pattern already established in the manuscripts discussed in the previous chapter.

As compared with Corpus and Ha7334, Dd 4.24 shows two major differences in the order and arrangement of tales. It does not include Gamelyn and it has moved NnT and CYPT from before section 9 to after section 10. This latter change may be considered as a development of the position of these two tales found in Corpus and Ha7334. It is easy enough to understand why if CYPT had originally been placed before section 9 it was subsequently moved later in the order. When CYPT was added in Corpus it was naturally inserted immediately after NnT, because its opening line refers to the Tale of St Cecilia. NnT remained in Corpus in the position it had occupied in Hg, and so CYPT joined it before section 9. However, besides referring to the tale of Cecilia CYP also refers to Boughton under Blean, which is mentioned in McP, and so it is understandable that as the text became more familiar to the scribes it was felt that CYPT should be moved to a position in front of section 11. This meant that NnT would have to go with it since CYP also refers to NnT. If, however, Dd 4.24 was considered to be earlier than Corpus and if CYPT (with NnT) had been placed before section 11 as soon as they were introduced into the poem, there would be no reason to explain why these two tales subsequently were moved by a later scribe forward in the order to a position before section 9. NnT has no prologue and so there is no indication in it as to where in the order it might come. The only possible reason that could be adduced for putting it earlier is that, as NnT had an earlier position in the order in Hg, some later scribe who knew this felt that it ought to be put in an earlier position and should take CYPT with it. This seems, to say the least, unlikely. Hence we may conclude that the position of NnT and CYPT in Dd 4.24 is developed from that in Corpus and not the other way round.

The omission of Gamelyn, on the other hand, would seem to argue for the priority of Dd 4.24 since once this tale was incorporated in the text it would seem strange to omit it without good reason. It is here that the evidence from Ha7334 is so important. Gamelyn was probably included in Corpus for the first time in the poem because Corpus's arrangement of the text into chapters meant that CkT needed expanding to make it into a full chapter. When Ha7334 was copied Gamelyn was not included at first because the method of organization was based not on chapters but on a prologue and tale system. Gamelyn had to be worked into the framework now imposed on the poem through the provision of some link with CkT. It was left on one side at first for this link to be produced, but when it failed to materialize the tale was included without one. It subsequently got one in Lansdowne. It is not difficult to understand that in Dd 4.24 a similar situation to that in Ha7334 prevailed: Gamelyn was left on one side because it had no link to the previous tale. Unlike Ha7334, however, Gamelyn was never included in Dd 4.24 because the linking passage or whatever other device was envisaged for the tale never materialized. The solution adopted in Dd 4.24 is a perfectly rational one, which reveals that the omission of material does not in itself prove priority of a particular manuscript. That other manuscripts in the *a* group were prepared to include Gamelyn if the necessary links were provided is suggested by the blanks which occur in some manuscripts after CkT.

Dd 4.24 is now incomplete because it lacks its beginning and end as well as various leaves internally. It starts with section 1 (though Pro and some of KtT are now missing). When he finished copying CkT on fol.53^v he left the rest of the page blank and commenced MLP at the top of fol.54^r. Although this leaf does not start a new quire, it would have been possible to insert new material such as Gamelyn. After section 1 Dd 4.24 has section 3, as had now become standard. Instead of having ML endlink after MLT, Dd 4.24 has WBP. It thus exhibits the same decision arrived at in Ha7334 but without any of the indecision found in that manuscript. Ha7334 had included ML endlink in a truncated form and adapted it into a false SuP. This was clearly an impromptu decision which was quite unsatisfactory, and the scribe of Dd 4.24 adopted the sensible solution of simply omitting ML endlink. The endlink had no role to play and so was left out; its availability did not mean that it would be included automatically.

This decision, to omit material which was not assimilated to the organizational system adopted in the manuscript, is quite in harmony with the omission of Gamelyn. Section 2 proceeds normally and is followed by ClP and ClT, as in Corpus and Ha7334. Unlike these manuscripts Dd 4.24 includes not only the envoy, but also the Host-stanza at the end of ClT. Even so, it also includes Cl–Me˙ link, which had made its first appearance in Ha7334. Corpus had neither the Host-stanza nor the Cl–Me link; Ha7334 had the latter, but not the former. The link echoes words in the envoy and was no doubt written when the Host-stanza was not part of the text, as in Corpus. Its inclusion again in Dd 4.24 may be attributed to its scribe's use of the original copytext together with additional material for the links. MeT follows Cl–Me link, and is followed by the Me–Sq link [E2419-40, F1-8], which is the adapted version of Hg's Me–Fk link. This link had appeared in its new, adapted, form for the first time in Ha7334, and we may assume Dd 4.24 had taken it over from there. It is interesting to note how this link has changed in one or two particulars. In the link added to Hg, the earliest version, the Host's words to the next speaker [F1-3] are:

> 'Sire frankeleyn, com neer if it your wille be
> And sey vs a tale, for certes ye
> Konnen theron as muche as any man.'

When this passage was adapted in Ha7334 to the Squire's tale which follows, it became:

> Sir Squier com forth if that your wille be
> And say vs a tale for certes ye
> Connen ther on as moche as ony man.

This passage was further developed in Dd 4.24 to make it even more suitable to this new speaker, the Squire:

> Squyere come ner if it youre wylle be
> And seye som what of loue for certes ye
> Konen ther oon as meche as any man.

First the passage is adapted to the Squire, and then it is made to refer to love, which is the subject of the tale to be told by him. One may also note that in Ha7334 when the link was included it was given no introductory rubric; in Dd 4.24 it was included with a rubric announcing it to be SqP. The link as a whole was designated as SqP, and the modern division of the link, consisting of partly an endlink and partly a prologue, is not reflected in the manuscripts.

After this Me−Sq link there comes SqT, which is incomplete as in all manuscripts. The last two lines of the tale, which formed the beginning of part 3, are omitted and the scribe added the rubric *Explicit secunda pars* at the end of part 2. He then added another note 'Here endith the Squyeres tale as meche as Chaucer made' and left the rest of the page and the whole of its verso blank. Unfortunately the following leaf which contained the beginning of FkT is missing, so the reason for the blank here is more difficult to assess. It may of course reflect a similar blank in Ha7334, though the relevant quire is missing in that manuscript. Although the lines on each page of Dd 4.24 are irregular in number, the leaf which follows the one missing at this point contains 88 lines. There are 45 lines of FkT missing at the beginning of the tale. As the Sq−Fk link (adapted from Hg's Sq−Me link) contains 36 lines, that together with the 45 lines of FkT and with gaps for rubrics would add up to an average leaf in Dd 4.24. So we may assume that the missing leaf contained the adapted Sq−Fk link and the opening of FkT. In other words the blank page and a half at the end of SqT were not intended for a link. They can have been intended only for some continuation of SqT. It may well be that the scribe thought that as there were two lines of part 3 in the copytext, this meant there was a continuation of the story which he had not got, but which he might expect to get. He therefore omitted these two lines until the rest of part three materialized. The copytext used by the scribes of Hg and Corpus did not lead them to expect a continuation, whereas that used by Dd 4.24 did, unless of course this scribe ignored the signs interpreted differently by the others. It might nevertheless be sensible to acknowledge the possibility of an intermediate text between Dd 4.24 and the original copytext. This possibility will be taken up again later.

From SqT the scribe went on to FkT. That tale was followed in Dd 4.24 by section 9 because NnT and CYPT had been moved from the position they had occupied in earlier manuscripts. Section 9 proceeds as normal and is followed by section 10. At the end of PdT he left part of fol.150^r and all of fol.150^v blank. There can be no doubt that this blank was designed for a prologue to ShT, though it never materialized. This hypothesis is confirmed by the rubric which was added to ShT, which commences section 10. Here the scribe wrote 'Here bigynneth the Shipmans tale next folwyng the Pardoner', a rubric which was intended to emphasize that one should ignore the blank and that the order of the tales was intended to be the one which occurs in the manuscript. Section 10 proceeds normally, but it leads to NnT in Dd 4.24 and not to section 11 as hitherto. This new arrangement created a problem for the scribe of Dd 4.24 since there is no link to join NPT and NnT; indeed, how could there be since this was the first occasion on which these two tales had been associated in the order of tales. When he finished NPT he left a blank, which extended from the bottom of one page to about two-thirds down the next. This blank was designed for a prologue for NnT. However, what materialized was not so much a prologue for NnT as an epilogue for NPT; it is now referred to as NP endlink [B^{2}4637-52]. Not only was this not acceptable as a prologue, it was also not long enough to fill the blank provided. The scribe had to make the best of a bad job. He included the endlink, after which he added the rubric 'Heere endeth the Tale of the Nonnes Preest'. The space which could not be filled by this endlink was left empty, and NnT was given the rubric '& bigynneth the Secund Nonnes Tale of Seynt Cecile withoute a Prologe'. NnT, as can be seen, is definitely allocated to the Second Nun, though reference is still made to the subject matter. After NnT the scribe included CYPT. The end of the manuscript is missing from the middle of CYPT onwards, though there is no reason to doubt that it was followed by sections 11 and 12. It is likely that Rt was included, for so many features in Dd 4.24 suggest a position after Ha7334 in which Rt is extant for the first time.

Dd 4.24 has arranged the poem in the same way as in Ha7334; its scribe has sought to impose a pattern of prologue–tale–prologue–tale on the poem. It is important to emphasize that this is not a pattern now of link–tale, but of prologue–tale. It is this pattern which created some difficulties for both scribes. When in Ha7334 it was decided not to include SqT after MLT, the ML endlink which had served in Corpus as SqP had no role to play because WBT had its own prologue. The scribe therefore had to conclude MLT after his truncated version of ML endlink. It is not surprising that the scribe of Dd 4.24 should have omitted this link, for it had no function in this arrangement. In the same way when the scribe of Dd 4.24 left a gap between NPT and NnT he was expecting to be provided with a prologue which would be suitable for NnT. He got instead a link which referred back to NPT and made no mention of the following tale or teller. Whoever provided this passage, it was evidently not the scribe of Dd 4.24 himself. He therefore had to conclude NPT after NP endlink, just as in Ha7334 MLT is said to finish after ML endlink. In Dd 4.24 ML endlink is eliminated because it had no function in the prologue–tale system adopted by the scribe; and it will hardly surprise us if later manuscripts drop NP endlink because it too has no function in such a system. Hence the absence of NP endlink in other manuscripts will not necessarily prove that they are earlier than Dd 4.24 in the hierarchy of manuscripts. The reverse may well be true.

The imposition of this organization on the poem is made clear by the rubrics which occur in Dd 4.24. Spaces are left within the text for rubrics to begin and end each prologue and tale, though not all of them have been provided with one. Intermediate headings are relegated to the margin so that the overall effect of the prologue and tale headings is not minimized. There are many of these marginal headings and comments, which I shall deal with in a minute. There are no running heads. In section 1 the rubrics for the prologue and tales are generally in English, though they fall into no consistent pattern. KtT, whose beginning is missing, has no concluding rubric but only 'Amen quod Wyttoun'. The conclusion of the prologues is not indicated by a rubric, but the start of the tales is. This pattern continues until the end of CkT, which has a concluding rubric in Latin. From here Latin is used in the rubrics which occur both to introduce and conclude prologues as well as tales. The rubric at the end of FrP is missing. In ClT there are no rubrics to introduce Chaucer's envoy or the Host-stanza, for the scribe was clearly determined to make each tale into a single unit without subdivision. MeP is introduced as *& incipit prologus of the Marchant*. Probably it originally read at first only *& incipit prologus*, as is true of several other prologues, and then the words in English were added subsequently. It is not necessary to read anything into this 'improvement'. SqT has a concluding rubric in English which was quoted above, and the fact that it is in English suggests that it, like 'of the Marchant', was added later. However, FkT, whose start is missing, has a concluding rubric in English; the same applies to the introductory rubric to PhT. But that rubric as we saw was added later as allowance was made for a prologue to PhT which never arrived. Perhaps both these rubrics were added later. From here onwards the rubrics continue in English. The Ph–Pd link is described in its rubric as 'the prologue of the Pardonere' at the beginning, though there is no rubric at the end. It is followed by what the scribe labels 'The Perdoners owyn Prologe' at 9:327 and then at 9:461 he has the Latin rubric *Et nunc narrat* *fabulam suam*, which is a kind of pendant to 'The Perdoners owyn Prologe'. PdT has no concluding rubric, and ShT is introduced after the blank with the rubric in English quoted above. The Sh – Pr link is missing and it is not clear how the scribe tackled that link since PrT is divided into a prologue and tale. The tale itself which commences at 10:487 has the rubric in English 'Here bigynneth the Prioresse hire Tale'. As a result of missing pages the next rubric to occur should be that to conclude TTh, but it is missing, as is the one to introduce the prologue to TMel. However, that prologue concludes with the rubric 'Here endeth Chaucers tale of Thopas & the Prologe of Melibeus'. The titles continue in English. That to MkT reads '& bigynneth the Monkes tale that is titled de casibus virorum Illustrium', which echoes the title found in Corpus. The rubrics continue in English to the end of the manuscript, as now extant. CYT has the introductory rubric 'and bygynneth his tale of Multiplicacion'.

From some of the clues in these rubrics it is possible to suggest that some, if not all, of the rubrics in English were written later. It is, however, an interesting feature of them that they should turn to Latin in the middle part of the poem. It is interesting because this is a pattern that is reflected in other manuscripts, as we have seen. Relative regularity is achieved only in Lansdowne where the rubrics are for the most part in Latin. Earlier in Hg there had been regularity in English. But Corpus, Ha7334 and Dd 4.24 all show some change which occurs either at or shortly after the end of section 1.

As noted above, Dd 4.24 does not normally repeat the omissions and additions found in Corpus. It is, therefore, unfortunate that its opening leaves are missing, because we cannot tell whether it included 1:253-4 or not. As the couplet is missing from Gg 4.27 and El, it is likely to have been missing from Dd 4.24. It is also impossible to tell whether it included 1:639-40, which are missing in Hg, but found in the other early manuscripts. It is probable that Dd 4.24 had this couplet. In KtT Dd 4.24 omits [A2681-2], a couplet introduced by the Corpus scribe. This couplet was not to appear in the *a* group manuscripts. It omits also 1:2754-7, which is one of the scribe's few copying mistakes; it arose because the rhyme sound was the same in 1:2757-8 as in 1:2753-4. Hence the omission of the four lines did not disturb the rhyme, though it played havoc with the sense. Dd 4.24 also omitted [A2779-82] which had been introduced in Corpus, although these two couplets were to appear in both Gg 4.27 and El. The lines had not been in Hg. In MiP the additional couplet [A3155-6] is found for the first time in Ha7334. It is not found in Hg, Corpus or Dd 4.24; but it was to appear in Gg 4.27 and El. In MiT a couplet which was to appear only in El, [A3721-2], is not in Dd 4.24 or any other early manuscript. There are no further alterations of note to the text until WBP. But this prologue shows a marked difference from all those manuscripts considered so far because it includes five extra passages, namely [D44a-f, 575-84, 609-12, 619-26 and 717-20]. The addition of these passages is very much associated with group *a* manuscripts. But El omits [D44a-f] (the relevant leaf is missing in Gg 4.27), and Gg 4.27 omits [D717-20]. The omission of the last passage in Gg 4.27 is not surprising since it is more religious in tone, for it emphasizes that a woman, Eve, caused the fall of man. It is different from the other four additions which all refer to the Wife of Bath and her sexual character. They all increase the portrayal of sexual aggression found in the Wife. It seems probable that these passages were added by the scribe of Dd 4.24 − a view which receives support from the signs of correction or composition which occur in [D44c-f]. It is not easy to disentagle precisely what the scribe wrote first, but it may have been:

> Diuerse scoles / maken diuerse werkes
> And diuerse practyk / in many a sondry werkes
> Maken / the perfyt man / sekirly.
> Of fyue husbondes scoleiyng / am I.

In [D44c] *diuerse werkes* was underdotted and replaced by *perfyt clerkes*; in [D44d] the *a* was underdotted; and in [D44e] *man* was underdotted and replaced by *werkman* before *perfyt*. The result is that the lines read in their corrected version:

> Diuerse scoles / maken perfyt clerkes
> And diuerse practyk / in many sondry werkes
> Maken / the werkman perfyt / sekirly
> Of fyue husbondes scoleiyng / am I.

There is no comparable passage of correction in this manuscript, and so it is difficult to escape the conclusion that its scribe had some hand in the composition of these additional pieces. The second version certainly makes more sense than the first. The reason for the inclusion of these passages will be discussed shortly.

No further alterations to the text are found in Dd 4.24 till MeT, for the additions made to SuT in Ha7334 are not found there. In MeT Dd 4.24 had the first halfline of the couplet 5:61-2 in its copytext, for it completed it in a different way from those we have already met. Its solution was:

> And if thow take a wyf of heye lynage
> She shal be hauteyn and of gret costage.

However, when the scribe reached 5:986, which had been blank in the copytext and filled with two separate readings in Corpus and Ha7334, he had access to the reading in Ha7334 for he repeated that to give the couplet:

> Folwyng his wyf / the Quene of Proserpyne
> Ech after other / as right as a lyne,

though the *of* occurs here for the first time and suggests ignorance of the name Proserpina. In SqT the scribe of Dd 4.24 omitted four lines, 4:61-4, in which it is said that in Cambiuskan's country there is a food which is valued highly though it is not rated of any worth in this country. This omission may be a mistake, though it may have been left out deliberately because the scribe thought the lines added nothing. In FkT Dd 4.24 shows none of the editorial activity found in Corpus and the manuscripts dependent on it. It does not have the couplets at 6:209-10 and 6:557-8 reversed, as is true of Corpus, Lansdowne and Petworth. It does contain 6:439-40, 6:483-8 and 6:725-6, which were missing in those three manuscripts. On the other hand, Dd 4.24 does not include [F1455-6], which had not appeared in any manuscript so far, but was to be included in El. It is not possible to make any comment on the rest of the tale, which is mostly missing in Dd 4.24, except to say that it is not likely to have included any changes found in Corpus.

Similarly in section 9 the scribe of Dd 4.24 did not introduce any of the changes found in Corpus. The Ph–Pd link is the same in Dd 4.24 as it is in Hg. In PdP he did, however, introduce a change of his own. The couplet which had appeared in Hg after 9:330 is moved a few lines later so that it follows 9:344, which is also changed from 'And for to stire hem to deuocion' to 'In euery village and in euery toun'. The reason for the change can readily be understood, if I quote the passage in Dd 4.24 in full.

> And in latyn speke I / wordes fewe
> To saffron with / my predicacioun
> In euery village / and in euery toun
> This is my Teme / and shal / and euere was
> Radix malorum / est Cupiditas.

The last two lines are those which have been moved and the last line has now been made to refer to the Pardoner's use of a few words of Latin to spice his sermons. This passage then continues with the Pardoner showing forth his relics and in this way the scribe of Dd 4.24 has made the activities of the Pardoner progress in a logical way. He commences his text and then shows his relics. The placing of the couplet later caused the change not only to 9:344, but also to the first line of the couplet itself. This editing indicates that the scribe read his text with some care. The alteration introduced in Corpus in PdT after 9:486 is not repeated in Dd 4.24.

In ShT at 10:214 Dd 4.24 has 'Who ther' in the text with *qy la* in the margin, as had been found in Hg. The Sh–Pr link is missing, but it would appear that Dd 4.24 divided PrT into a prologue and tale, since the rubric introducing the tale occurs at 10:488, as in Hg. Dd 4.24 is the only early manuscript to include a reading at 10:805 in TTh; it is likely that the line was invented and included by the scribe. It shows that he was reading his text carefully as he went along and realized a line in the stanza was missing. The line makes good sense and has usually been adopted in modern editions. There are no omissions in TTh. In TMel there are about half a dozen omissions, the majority of which have been caused by eyeskip, though none is extensive. One or two of these overlap with similar omissions in Corpus, but they are never identical. An interesting omission occurs at 10:1777, where Hg reads 'And he seith in another place: . . . that hath shame of his synne and knowelicheth it', where the dots represent a gap. The scribe of Lansdowne added a piece after 'knowelicheth it' to complete the sense. In Dd 4.24 the passage as a whole was omitted, for its scribe evidently took a different way out. He saw the passage was incomplete, and instead of trying to complete it like the other scribe he left it out altogether. The scribes of Corpus, Ha7334, Lansdowne and Dd 4.24 responded to an incomplete sentence in the copytext in different ways: two kept it as it was; the third omitted the whole sentence; and the fourth added something at the end. In MkT the Adam stanza is included. As we saw its future appearance was signalled in Corpus, and after that it appeared in Ha7334 and Lansdowne. It had evidently become attached to the copytext papers. More interestingly the Modern Instances are at the end, but the colour of the ink suggests that they were copied in after the rest of the tale and NPP had been copied, for the ink is of a different colouring from that which precedes and follows the Modern Instances. In other words the scribe knew of a manuscript or manuscripts in which the Modern Instances were placed in the middle, and so he was hesitant whether to place them at the end which is where they occurred in the copytext or in the middle where they had been placed by other scribes. This suggests that Dd 4.24 is later than Corpus and probably later than Ha7334. Because Dd 4.24 also has the long form of NPP, it must come after some manuscripts in which the Modern Instances were in the middle of MkT so that the extra lines in NPP could echo the tale of Croesus, which was the last story in the tale when the Modern Instances were moved. The scribe of Dd 4.24 may not have recognized that there were echoes between these two passages and so he was content to keep the extra lines in NPP even though he placed the Modern Instances at the end. Dd 4.24

omits one line, 10:2656, in MkT, though he left a blank for it. This line occurs in the Modern Instances, but it is difficult to explain its omission. In NPT the scribe omitted four lines, 10:3135-8, in which Chantecleer misinterprets the Latin *Mulier est hominis confusio*. It is possible the omission is deliberate, for there seems no other cause for the absence of the lines. We may also note that at 10:3162 the scribe included a marginal note *id est secundo die Maii* (i.e. May 2nd), since the line in question had been changed by the scribe of Ha7334 to make this date clear.

NnT is not divided into prologue and tale, because the scribe had anticipated getting a prologue from the pilgrimage frame. NnT is followed by CYPT in which the scribe reversed the order of the couplets [G562-3] and [G564-5], and he omitted [G711]. The former was no doubt thought to improve the sense; the latter was probably accidental.

A notable feature of Dd 4.24 is that it contains far more marginal annotation than Hg or any other early manuscript, and it is worth considering this feature in greater detail. As Pro is missing in Dd 4.24 we may consider KtT first to illustrate some of the changes in annotation. Hg had some interlinear glosses, one Latin translation, one *argumentum* and two examples of *nota* in this tale. In Dd 4.24 the interlinear glosses are mostly kept as is the single *argumentum*. Hg's Latin version of 1:1166 may have been in Dd 4.24 but that leaf is missing. Dd 4.24 does not have Hg's two examples of *nota*, but it has introduced many new ones. In two cases the marginal note reads *verum est*; both are philosophical and moral in import. One (1:1468) concerns the inevitability of destiny and the other (1:2760) states that death will follow if a sick man does not have the benefit of the healing power of nature. The catalogue of trees at 1:2917 has the marginal note *Arbores*, which could be understood as a kind of sub-heading. Otherwise, there are seven examples of *nota* or *nota bene*. Two refer to the battle scene: one for the sound of the trumpets and the other for the description of the battle itself. Three deal generally with age and the human condition: one reinforces Hg's *argumentum* that life and death are inevitable; another notes that even the mightiest of oaks will die in the end; and a third draws attention to the claim that age has many advantages. The last two are concerned with love: one is placed against Palamon's wish expressed in the temple of Venus to have total possession of Emily and to die in Venus's service; the other against Arcite's claim that he has suffered 'peynes stronge' (1:2771) for Emily for a long time. These examples do not seem too strange, since they cover traditional moral and sentential utterances as well as more literary references to passion. One could well deduce from them that the scribe's interests lay in old age, death and love.

This picture changes somewhat as the manuscript proceeds. Hg had two notes to MiT, one a source and the other a *nota malum quid* against the line where Absolon kisses Alison's arse. Both are repeated in Dd 4.24. However, it has a number of other notes. One is a Latin translation of a moral saying, and another, reading *quia pro*, explains the *For for* of the line stating that the maid could not get any answer from Nicholas (1:3411). There is one example of *Auctor* (1:3605) against the passage commenting on the power of imagination. There are four examples of *nota*, including one in MiP, all of which are concerned with relations between the sexes. One emphasizes that husbands should not be too inquisitive about what their wives get up to, but should accept God's bounty (1:3157); the second draws attention to the description of Alison (1:3227); the third is placed against Nicholas's rather vigorous flirtation with Alison (1:3297); and the fourth refers to the way Absolon prepared himself to meet Alison at night (1:3686). The annotations in this tale suggest an interest in the way each sex tries to outwit and outdo the other. The single *nota bene* of ReP refers to the four sins of old age, and it recalls the concern with age in the notes of KtT. There are no further notes till MLT, in which tale the scribe of Dd 4.24 simply reproduced the annotations found already in Hg and Corpus. However, WBP and WBT which together had only two notes in Hg have a large number in Dd 4.24. One of these (2:1083) is repeated in Dd 4.24 as are two other examples not in Hg but found in Corpus (2:633 and 1151). The scribe of Dd 4.24 includes two examples of *verum est*: one against the claim that no man can lie like a woman (2:228) and the second against the claim that women cannot keep a secret (2:954). He provided a Latin translation of 2:180-1 to the effect that if a man refuses to accept advice from others he will come to act as a warning to other people. This sentence occurs in the context of tyranny in marriage and should be understood to refer to the consideration a man should exercise before getting married. Other examples of *nota* in WBP occur at 2:509 (the Wife's fifth husband could talk flatteringly to her when he wanted sex); 2:519 (women want whatever they are forbidden to have); 2:598 (the Wife had the best pudendum); and 2:754 (women are wicked and contrary). It repeats the *nota* found in Corpus at 2:635 (men ought to be hanged who allow their wives to go on pilgrimage). In WBT the notes refer to true nobility and the dictates of poverty. There is also a note against the example of Midas's wife who could not contain herself with his secret. The import of the annotations in WBPT reinforces that found in MiT, namely that the scribe had an obsessive interest with the relation between the sexes.

In ClT the scribe of Dd 4.24 repeats the marginal annotations found in Hg, but again he adds a few more. Two examples of *nota* mark out the claims that married men know no moderation (8:622) and no man can be as humble as a woman (8:937). In addition he inserts *Auctor* against the passages where the author addresses first the fickle people (8:995) and secondly noble wives who should not let humility shackle their tongues (8:1183). In MeT he again keeps the notes found in Hg, but he adds several new ones. One is in the form of a possible alternative reading. At 5:98 the tale reads in Hg 'If he be poure she helpeth hym to swynke', but the scribe adds in the margin the variant 'or to drynke'. With this reading a wife would be a rather different helpmate to a man. There are two examples of *verum*: one at 5:73 which notes that a wife will endure far longer than you might wish: and the other at 5:1022 where Proserpina indicates that she will give May a sufficient answer if Pluto gives January back his sight. There are four examples of *nota* or *nota bene*: one at 5:43 against the claim that no-one can be as obedient as a wife; the second at 5:357 against the passage where January imagines to himself the beauty which he attributes to May; the third at 5:511 where January thought how sad it was that May must be deflowered that night by him; and the fourth at 5:1026 where Proserpina claims that women will be able to outface whoever accuses them of wrong. The scribe added no notes not found in Hg until TMel, where he included *nota* in the margin against the names of many authorities quoted in the text. It is difficult to determine any pattern in these, though the authorities are naturally recommending different forms of moral behaviour. A few additional notes are added to NPT, though these are either explanatory or act rather as subtitles.

In general it may be seen that the scribe of Dd 4.24 annotated certain tales carefully, particularly those which deal with love and the relationship between the sexes. In many instances he marked off those passages which are critical of women either explicitly or ironically. One is tempted to imagine from the range of his annotations that the scribe was probably old and had had difficulties with his wife, though many of the passages marked are very conventional. Certainly the kind of things he annotates is very different from that marked as noteworthy by any of the other early scribes. His concerns were not so much pedagogical and moral as social and sexual. This is a matter of some importance for in Dd 4.24 we come across the additional passages in WBP for the first time. These additions tend to increase the tyrannical and sexual qualities of the Wife of Bath. As we saw there are indications that [D44a-f] were composed by this scribe. The implication of the annotations in Dd 4.24 is that this scribe was sufficiently interested in the Wife and in the relationship between the sexes to make these additions. At all events the tone of these additional passages matches what we know of the scribe from the annotations he introduced into the text, and so it is not unreasonable to attribute the additions to him.

Gg 4.27 is a difficult manuscript to analyse because many of its pages have been torn out. It contained illustrations of the pilgrims and it is these pages in particular which are now missing. Because these illustrations were allowed for, gaps were left at the bottom of pages so that the illustrations could be placed at the beginning of the prologue or tale in question. Hence it is not easy to calculate what may have been found on a leaf no longer extant. The scribe used an East Anglian spelling system, though it seems possible that he copied the manuscript in London. Since Gg 4.27 contains the additional passages in WBP found in Dd 4.24 it is reasonable to assume that it is later than that manuscript. It is not certain whether it is later or earlier than El, though it does not contain certain additional passages found in El. As we saw when discussing Dd 4.24, there is a possibility that another copy lies between it and the original. It may be that Gg 4.27 also made use of this intermediate copytext rather than the original. At all events it reflects the order of the tales found in Dd 4.24, though it does not contain all its additional passages. Its order is section 1, but without Gamelyn added, section 3, but without ML endlink [B^{1}1163-90], section 2, section 8 which is followed by the Host-stanza and the Cl–Me link [E1213-44], section 5, whose end is missing but it probably included the adapted Me–Sq link [E2419-40 F1-8], section 4, whose end is missing but it probably included the adapted Sq–Fk link [F673-708], section 6, section 9, whose beginning is missing but it probably did not contain a PhP, section 10, whose beginning and end are missing, but it probably did not contain a ShP or the NP endlink [B^{2}4637-52], section 7 with CYPT, section 11 and section 12, to which Rt was appended though it is now missing. Since NPP is missing it is not possible to tell whether Gg 4.27 included [B^{2}3961-80], but it seems probable. In other words, Gg 4.27 contained the order and links found in Dd 4.24 with the probable exception of NP endlink. It is not possible to say whether the scribe had any difficulties in arranging the tales in this order, for although the quiring is erratic, the reason behind this situation cannot now be determined on account of the manuscript's incompleteness. As it is usually dated by palaeographers rather later than Dd 4.24, it is likely that the scribe followed an established order and that the erratic nature of his quiring should be explained in some other way.

The text and organization of Gg 4.27 show some significant differences from Dd 4.24. In Pro it omits 1:253-4 and also 1:292, though the scribe left a space in the text for this line. In KtT a line was omitted at 1:2062 and then filled incorrectly by a later hand as 'That shynyth in the hevyn from yow so ferre'. Like Dd 4.24 it omits [A2681-2], a couplet found in Corpus and Ha7334, but unlike Dd 4.24 it does include the two couplets [A2779-82] which are also found in Corpus and Ha7334. The scribe omitted 1:3059 by mistake, though he inserted it at the bottom of the page. This is an interesting omission because it suggests that as he had a regular number of lines per page which ended with the last line of a couplet, he realized he was a line short at the bottom of the page and inserted it with the necessary marks to indicate its right place. He did not need to insert it in the margin. In MiP the scribe included [A3155-6] which had been found up till now only in Ha7334, though it was also to appear in El. In MiT he does not have [A3721-2], an addition to be made in El. There are no textual matters of note in MLPT. As WBP begins only at 2:77 after a missing page, it is not possible to say whether [D44a-f] were included. Of the other four additions in WBP found in Dd 4.24, Gg 4.27 has the first three but not the last one. As this is different in tone, it may well have been omitted by the scribe as unnecessary. This would have been possible if the additions had been noted in the margin of the copy-text. In FrT he omitted 2:1465-6, which refers to Job. The omission may have been caused by carelessness, though eyeskip is not the reason. It does, however, explain the omission of 2:1499b-1501a where 'I holde' is repeated. In both cases the effect is the loss of a couplet, which the scribe did not notice when he got to the bottom of each page. In SuT the scribe omitted six lines through eyeskip. The lines are 2:1881-6 and were omitted through the repetition of 'we freres' in 2:1880 and 1886, though in the former line most manuscripts read 'we sely freres'.

The next point of textual interest is in MeT at 5:61-2 where Gg 4.27 reads

> And yif thow take a wyf on to thyn hold
> Ful lyghtely mayst thou been a coukewold.

This is the reading inserted by a later hand in Hg, and it was also to be included in El. The scribe omitted 5:240, but the omission was noted and a line left blank at the bottom of the page, though the line was not inserted there. At 5:986 Gg 4.27 has the reading 'Eche aftyr othir right as ony lyne', which was now becoming the standard reading for it had appeared in Ha7334 and Dd 4.24. In FkT the scribe made a couple of alterations. At 6:401-4 Hg reads:

> Vnder his brist he baar it moore secree
> Than euere dide Panfilus for Galathee.
> His brist was hool withoute for to sene,
> But in his herte ay was the arwe kene.

The scribe of Gg 4.27 inserted an extra line and had three lines rhyming on -ene. He arrived at this reading:

> Vndyr his brest he bar it sore
> And so fer forth it greuede hym the moore
> Than euere dede Pamplius or Galatheene
> His brest was sor withoutyn for to sene
> But in his herte ay was the arwe kene.

Apart from the fact that the scribe was ignorant of the story in *Pamphilus de amore*, it is not clear why he wanted to change this reading which should have left him a line out at the bottom of the page. This did not happen because he reorganized another passage a few lines later. What in Hg had been at 6:421-4:

> Which book spak muchel of the operaciouns
> Touchyng the xxviij mansiouns
> That longen to the moone and swich folye
> As in oure dayes is nat worth a flye,

became in Gg 4.27 a passage of three lines only, for the fourth line was omitted. Gg 4.27 did not include in FkT the two passages [F1455-6 and 1493-8] that were to appear in El. It also omits 6:763-4 in which Arveragus advises his wife to keep her word. The omission was not caused by eyeskip and may have been deliberate. In PdT, however, he omitted 9:741-2 as a result of eyeskip; equally in ShT the omission of 10:114-19 was also the result of eyeskip. In TTh he did not include 10:805 which is found only in Dd 4.24 of the early manuscripts. In TMel there are about a dozen omissions caused by eyeskip and one or two others which have different causes. At 10:1777 he omits the whole sentence as Dd 4.24 had done. In MkT the Adam stanza is included and the Modern Instances are at the end of the tale. In NnT the scribe omitted 7:158, but left a double space at the end of the stanza so that the look of the page was not impaired. There is no sign indicating an omission. In CYT he omitted [G1046-7], and the second half of [G1121] has been scratched out. In McT he omitted 11:215-16, presumably in error since it makes a nonsense of the passage. In PsT the scribe omitted a large number of passages through eyeskip; and in this he resembles many of the other early scribes. This scribe made more mistakes in the prose than in the verse, but he is always prone to make mistakes through eyeskip. On occasions it appears that he may have made changes deliberately, though there are few convincing cases.

Because so many illuminated leaves were torn out of the manuscript, many of the rubrics are also missing. Those that survive are in English, and we may assume that this was the regular pattern. The first extant rubric occurs before MiT, where it has been crowded in on a one-line gap. It reads 'here endith the prologe & here begynnyth the tale.'. This is not the usual pattern of rubric, for prologues normally do not have a concluding rubric to start with. There is little doubt that this one was inserted later. ReP has no concluding rubric, and the tale is introduced 'Here begynnyth the Reue his tale'. CkP has no introductory or concluding rubric, but his tale is introduced by 'Here begynnyst the kok of lundene hi tale' [*sic*]. The tale itself is missing. The pattern continues in this way. WBP is the first prologue to have a concluding rubric which was allowed for by the scribe. Once again you notice a change in *ordinatio* at this point in the poem. In ClT the rubric ending ClT occurs after the envoy, which has its own title. The Host-stanza, which is included, has no rubric at beginning or end. It is followed by the rubric announcing the prologue of MeT. Although the rubrics to PdP are missing, the rubric announcing PdT occurs before 9:461. In section 10 there is a rubric ending PrT which is followed by 'Byhold the myrie talkynge of the Hoost to Chaucer'. TTh is introduced as 'Heere begynnyth Chaucers tale of sere Thopas'. MkT is introduced simply as 'Here begynnyth the Monk his tale' and there is no reference to *De casibus*. There is no concluding rubric to NnT, and any introductory rubric, if it existed, is now missing. As there are no running heads in the manuscript, it is not possible to say to whom the tale was allocated. At the end of NnT occurs the rubric 'Here folwyn the mery wordys of chauncer and of the Host And the prologe of the chanounys man'. This is a different type of rubric from the one normally found here and suggests that the tale was now being further assimilated to the poem and given a type of rubric which occurs elsewhere in this manuscript. After CYT there occurs the double rubric 'here is endit the chanounnys manys tale. Heryth the merye wordys of the Host to the cok of lundene'. McP is thus given a rubric which is unparalleled among the other early manuscripts; McT itself is introduced 'Here begynnyth the manciple his tale'. At the end of McT we find another double rubric which reads 'Here is endit the Mauncipell tale. And here folwyn the wordys of chaucer to the host'. At the end of PsT there is the rubric 'Here takyt the makere of this bok his leue'. It is clear from these rubrics that the scribe of Gg 4.27 was not motivated by the same principle of organization as the scribe of Dd 4.24, for the former was not influenced by the latter's rigid application of the prologue—tale formula. The scribe of Gg 4.27 was quite happy not to have what was called a prologue before a tale and to have more than one linking passage between tales. Hence his rubrics are freer and more diverse than those found in Dd 4.24. The evidence suggests that the order of tales was relatively established when he wrote his manuscript and he simply introduced those rubrics which he thought acceptable. Of the other early scribes he resembles the one who copied Hg and El most in his use of rubrics.

He is unlike that scribe in the way he divides the tales up for he shows no signs of adding further subdivisions. KtT has no subdivisions or parts; and MLT has no subdivisions. Even ClT, which had had subdivisions in all manuscripts up till then, has no parts. There is, however, a rubric to introduce part 2 of SqT, which reads quite simply *Secunda pars*. It does not appear that FkT was divided into a separate tale at 6:21, though there is a large initial. It is not possible to tell, because of missing leaves, whether PrT and NnT were divided into prologue and tale. There is no subdivision within CYT. PsT, however, does have a number of subdivisions. The three parts of penitence are each introduced by a rubric as are the seven deadly sins and their remedies, though not all the rubrics survive today. Although MLT and ClT have no subdivisions, there are indications that the manuscript was copied from a copytext which had subdivisions in ClT, for there is provision for large initials to introduce parts 2 and 5. In MLT there are directions to the rubricator to insert *Explicit* after 3:322 and 3:952, but there is no provision for large initials, and so this instruction may have been made by the corrector. The tales which are in stanzas have been copied out with gaps between them, and TTh is copied with the third line of each group on the right-hand side of the page. In Gg 4.27 there are a few marginal annotations which have clearly been added later, but whether they are by the main scribe or not is difficult to determine since he uses a variety of scripts. The names of the pilgrims are inserted in the margin in Pro and of the tragic figures in MkT. In KtT there are a number of marginal notes which are more in the nature of subtitles. A few others occur in ClT and MeT, but they rarely agree with the annotations found in the other early manuscripts already dealt with. Mostly they consist of a single word or two: either the name of an authority, *Auctor* or a Latin gloss.

El is the best-known manuscript and so it may need less attention than the others, though modern editions do not represent the state of El with any exactness. Its status as an edited text is clear, but the problems associated with the order of the tales have not been finally solved in it. Its order is that found in Dd 4.24 and Gg 4.27, though in the presentation of the text it is more like the latter than the former. It commences with section 1 which progresses in its normal order. Gamelyn is not included, but at the end of CkT the scribe left one and a half pages blank. He started MLP on the next recto. This in fact was the first leaf of the second half of the quire so that if the scribe had wanted to include Gamelyn he could have done so by adding pages in the middle of the quire. There is no concluding rubric to CkT, which is unusual in this manuscript, and so the scribe evidently considered including Gamelyn or something else to finish off CkT. The reasons for not including Gamelyn cannot now be decided, though we should remember that it is in a semi-alliterative rhymed metre and that it was not fully assimilated into the poem before Lansdowne, a manuscript which may be later than El. After section 1, the scribe included section 2 without ML endlink; section 8, which has both the envoy and the Host-stanza and which is followed by the Cl−Me link [E1213-44]; section 5 which is followed by the adapted Me−Sq link [E2419-40 and F1-8]; and section 4 which is followed by the adapted Sq−Fk link [F673-708]. A gap at the end of the page was left at the end of SqT and again there is no rubric to conclude SqT. There is evidence again here of a little uncertainty on the scribe's part. The link begins on the next recto which is the first leaf of the second half of the quire. But as the rubric which follows refers to the Squire, the only addition (if there was to be one) could have been a conclusion to SqT. After that the scribe included section 6; section 9 which has no introductory link; section 10 including the long version of NPP; section 7 with CYPT; section 11; and section 12 with Rt.

From a textual point of view El contains several omissions and additions. In Pro it omits 1:253-4, but it contains 1:639-40. In KtT it does not include [A2681-2] which were included in Corpus and Ha7334. It does include [A2779-82] which are found in Corpus, Ha7334 and Gg 4.27, but not in Hg and Dd 4.24. In MiP it includes [A3155-6] which had been found previously in Ha7334 and Gg 4.27 only. In MiT it includes the couplet [A3721-2] and is the only early manuscript to do so. The text reads perfectly well without the lines, which cannot have been omitted in the other manuscripts through eyeskip or any other technical reason. It is likely that the lines were inserted by the scribe of El and the couplet serves merely to increase the humour of the passage and the heartlessness of Alison. In WBP El contains the last four of the additional five passages found in Dd 4.24, but not the first passage [D44a-f]. It is possible that he knew of this addition, but decided not to include it. In SuT the scribe does not include the extra passages found in Ha7334; but he does include a unique reading at 2:2198. Where other manuscripts read 'Who sholde make a demonstracioun', El has 'Certes it was a shrewed conclusion' − a change which like some others in El seems to point the moral. In MeT the scribe included what had become the traditional reading at 5:61-2:

> And if thou take a wyf vnto thyn hoold
> Ful lightly maystow been a Cokewold.

He omitted 5:113-16 through eyeskip. At 5:986 the scribe included the reading which had become traditional 'Ech after oother right as a lyne'. In FkT there are two passages found in El and in no other manuscript, and they may almost certainly be ascribed to its scribe.

The first passage is the couplet [F1455-6] which increases the examples of unfortunate women in Dorigen's complaint:

> The same thyng I seye of Bilyea
> Of Rodogone and eek Valeria.

As we shall see the scribe was learned and interested in academic exempla of this kind. The second passage occurs shortly afterwards [F1493-8], and the author addresses the audience about Arveragus's decision to allow Dorigen to keep her word to Aurelius:

> Parauenture an heep of yow ywis
> Wol holden hym a lewed man in this
> That he wol putte his wyf in Iupartie
> Herkneth the tale er ye vp on hir crie
> She may haue bettre Fortune than yow semeth
> And whan that ye han herd the tale demeth.

There is no reason why other scribes should have omitted this passage. It is interesting to note that the scribe of El usually introduces *Auctor* in the margin against passages like this, but he did not do so here. Perhaps as it was his own addition he overlooked the need for his marginal note.

In PhT the scribe omitted 9:103-4 in which the poet says that one example is sufficient. The passage was not omitted through eyeskip and may have been left out deliberately since this scribe seems to have appreciated exempla. In TTh the scribe omits 10:805, which was evidently absent in the original. In TMel the scribe omitted six passages, largely on account of eyeskip. One of these, 10:1000, it shares with Hg, but the others it does not. It does not share these omissions with Dd 4.24 or Gg 4.27, except that Gg 4.27 omits more of 10:1556-7 than El does. In 10:1777 El agrees with Dd 4.24 and Gg 4.27 in omitting the whole of a sentence, part of which was kept in Hg, Corpus and Ha7334. In MkP the scribe omitted 10:1957-8 through eyeskip. In MkT the Adam stanza is included and the Modern Instances are at the end. In PsT there are several omissions in El which are caused by eyeskip. Some of these it shares with Hg and with other manuscripts, though there is no pattern in the portion for which Hg is extant. At 12:168 El shares a possible omission with Hg and Gg 4.27, but the passage is in Ha7334; but at 12:273 El shares another possible omission with Hg and Ha7334, but the passage is in Gg 4.27, and this pattern of congruence is repeated at 12:511. After the end of the extant passage in Hg, El continues to share omissions with other manuscripts, though the pattern is far from uniform. In this section of the text the majority of agreements in omission are between El and Gg 4.27, but El shares some omissions with Ha7334. Unfortunately as the tale is missing in whole or in part from several manuscripts, it is not possible to detect any pattern in El's relationship with other manuscripts. It needs also to be remembered that most scribes made many omissions through eyeskip in PsT, the last tale, and so it is not surprising that many of these omissions should be identical.

When the scribe of El had copied Hg he had shown his experience through laying out the text in a comprehensible way; he did the same in El. The tales in stanzas are written with gaps between them and TTh has the third line of each group on the right-hand side of the page. In ClP the marginal note *Pausacio* has been added in the margin against 8:6, 14, 20, 30, 38, 46 and 54 to make the prologue harmonize more with the tale. In this El resembles Corpus. Many of the tales have been provided with subdivisions and there is a regular series of rubrics. The names of the pilgrims in Pro and of the tragic figures in MkP have been added in the margin.

The rubrics commence with the title of the poem, which is the same as that in Hg. KtT is introduced 'Heere bigynneth the knyghtes tale' with the Latin quotation from Statius preceding it. At 1:895 there is the marginal note *Narrat*, which is equivalent to that found in Hg. But in El the Latin headings have been largely eliminated and most tales have a prologue to precede them. It is the existence of Pro which prevented the development of 1:861-94 from becoming the prologue to KtT, though this is foreshadowed in El. KtT itself is divided up into four parts, which begin respectively at 1:895, 1357, 1883 and 2485. In Hg the tale was divided into three parts only, and Hg and El are the only early manuscripts to provide subdivisions for it. The inference is plain: this scribe was an inveterate subdivider. In his opinion this kind of material needed to be arranged in smaller units. As we shall see, he accomplished this more fully in El than he had done in Hg; and he did so partly through the rubrics and partly through marginal annotations. At the end of KtT the rubric reads 'Heere is ended the knyghtes tale', and MiP is introduced 'Heere folwen the wordes bitwene the hoost and the Millere'. This rubric is unusual since most tales have a prologue, though that is not true as such of KtT. The scribe did not insist on having only the prologue dividing one tale from another, but he did normally provide one where possible. This rubric is similar to others which occur later in the manuscript, though they normally occur together with prologues. It seems likely that at the start of the text, no regularity had been achieved. We may recall that a similar position appeared to exist in Gg 4.27 which has a cramped rubric to introduce MiT. MiP has no concluding rubric, and this was standard at the beginning of the manuscript. MiT is introduced 'Heere bigynneth the Miller his tale'. From now on the pattern which emerges is an introductory rubric to the prologue, which states baldly 'The prologe of the Reues tale' for example. There is no concluding rubric to the prologue. The tale is introduced by the formula 'Heere bigynneth the Reues tale' and it is concluded by the formula 'Heere is ended the Reues tale'. This formula is carried out throughout the early part of the manuscript with a few exceptions. There is no concluding rubric to CkT, as we have seen. What had been MLP in earlier manuscripts is now introduced as 'The wordes of the Hoost to the compaignye', a rubric which emphasizes the new start to the proceedings which MLP gave after the incomplete CkT. A new MLP is formed in El out of MLT. That prologue is introduced according to the standard formula and extends from 3:99 to 3:133. The tale is divided into three parts which have Latin rubrics for the divisions; the parts start at 3:134, 386 and 876. This division had occurred in Dd 4.24 where the subheadings were in the margin; in El they are centred. Another break to the pattern of rubrics occurs in WBP. At 2:803 there is the rubric 'Biholde the wordes bitwene the Somonour and the Frere'. This heading is anticipated in Ha7334 and Dd 4.24, though in those manuscripts the subheading had been in the margin. At 2:831 the scribe has a concluding rubric to WBP and an opening rubric to WBT in one: 'Heere endeth the Wyf of Bathe hir Prologe And bigynneth hir tale'. The standard rubrics continue again until the middle of SuT, for at 2:2217 El has the rubric 'The wordes of the lordes Squier and his keruere for departynge of the fart on twelue'. This heading is not found in any other manuscript.

ClT is divided into five parts as usual. The envoy has the title *Lenuoy de Chaucer*, though no concluding rubric, and the Host-stanza which follows is introduced by 'Bihoold the murye wordes of the Hoost'. At the end of the Host-stanza the rubric to conclude the whole tale reads 'Heere endeth the tale of the Clerk of Oxenford'. This is a different solution to the one found in Hg, where the tale ends at 8:1176, with an *Explicit* after the envoy and nothing to introduce or conclude the Host-stanza. The solution adopted in El is modelled on that found in Dd 4.24, but with intermediate rubrics inserted for the envoy and the Host-stanza. The solution is not ideal, since the Host-stanza is hardly part of the tale proper, for it belongs to the pilgrimage frame. One can, however, easily understand how the scribe came to adopt this position. MeT also provides an exception to the standard pattern in so far as the concluding rubric refers to the subjectmatter of the tale. It reads, as it did in Hg, 'Heere is ended the Marchantes tale of Ianuarie'. SqT is divided into three parts as normal. At its end, the formula of rubrics continues though with the adapted Sq–Fk link being introduced as 'Heere folwen the wordes of the Frankelyn to the Squier and the wordes of the hoost to the Frankelyn'. FkT is now divided into prologue and tale, with the prologue occupying 6:1-20. The solution adopted here is identical with that used in MLPT.

With PhT the scribe was faced with a difficulty since it had no prologue. He altered his normal formula to introduce it with 'Heere folweth the Phisiciens tale'. The Ph—Pd linking passage is introduced by 'The wordes of the Hoost to the Phisicien and the Pardoner', and PdP itself is introduced by 'Heere folweth the Prologe of the Pardoners tale' with *Radix malorum est Cupiditas Ad Timotheum 6º* on a line underneath. He then reverts to his normal pattern but ShT has the concluding rubric 'Heere endeth' instead of 'Heere is ended'. The Sh—Pr link is introduced 'Bihoold the murie wordes of the Hoost to the Shipman and to the lady Prioresse' and it ends with an *Explicit*. From now on every link and prologue has the concluding rubric *Explicit*. The Prioress has a prologue (10:453-87) and tale (10:488-690). TTh has no prologue but the link is introduced as 'Bihoold the murye wordes of the Hoost to Chaucer', and the Th—Mel link is introduced 'Heere the Hoost stynteth Chaucer of his tale of Thopas'. The opening rubric to TMel refers to Melibee, as does its concluding one which reads 'Heere is ended Chaucers tale of Melibee and of Dame Prudence. MkP is not described as a prologue, but has the rubric 'The murye wordes of the Hoost to the Monk'. His tale refers to the subject matter in the manner of Dd 4.24 for it reads 'Heere bigynneth the Monkes tale *de casibus virorum Illustrium*'. MkT has a concluding set of rubrics which are different from the pattern. They read '*Explicit Tragedia*. Heere stynteth the knyght the Monk of his tale'. The rubric is clearly modelled on that to TTh, and it acknowledges for the first time what had been implicit in the rearrangements at the end of this tale and in NPP. The rubric introducing NPT refers to Chauntecleer and Pertelote. NnT is given to the Second Nun, and her introductory rubric also refers to the 'lyf of Seinte Cecile'. Her tale is divided into a prologue (7:1-119) and tale (7:120-553). CYP has a rubric to end it as well as to introduce it. CYT is divided into two parts, the second of which commences at [G972]. McP is introduced by the rubric 'Heere folweth the Prologe of the Maunciples tale' and there is no reference to the Cook; there is no *Explicit* at its end. Both introductory and concluding rubric to McT refer to the 'tale of the Crowe'. PsP has a concluding rubric *Explicit prohemium*. PsT has no concluding rubric, but there is a rubric to introduce Rt which reads 'Heere taketh the makere of this book his leue'. It is concluded by 'Heere is ended the book of the tales of Caunterbury compiled by Geffrey Chaucer of whos soule Ihesu crist haue mercy Amen.'

The rubrics in El show considerable uniformity but not perfect regularity. The scribe did not embrace the concept that each tale must have only a prologue to accompany it; he was prepared to have more than one link between each tale. The pattern of his rubrics changes in the middle of the manuscript, but a feature that is noticeable is the attempt to make the rubrics informative. Instead, as in Hg, of referring only to the words of the Host, the links in El also include to whom the words are addressed. It is doubtless for this reason that he included the rubric referring to the Knight's interruption of the Monk. The rubrics are generally in English, but a few in Latin have been retained, possibly from the copytext. This scribe has divided up some tales into prologue and tale to provide each tale with a prologue as far as possible, but he did not include spurious prologues to PhT or ShT, which are therefore without a link from the pilgrimage frame beforehand. There is clearly an attempt in El to make the text as coherent as possible and to help the reader as much as possible; this is why the scribe introduced more rubrics and made them as full as he could.

In addition to the rubrics El contains a large number of marginal annotations. These fall into different categories: some are subtitles, some are glosses, some are sources, some are Latin translations, and some simply draw attention to some feature in the text. It is characteristic of El that the sidenote *Nota* which had appeared in so many other early manuscripts is not used to a significant degree. The scribe preferred to use more informative annotations so that *Nota* itself often appears together with some further comment. When Arcite falls from his horse (1:2689), an annotation reads *nota periculum*. It may be best to consider the subtitles first since they tie up with the rubrics which have just been discussed. Many of the tales have quite extensive series of these subtitles. Thus KtT has a series when Palamon, Arcite and Emily go to the temples before the battle in the lists. These include 'The preyere of Palamoun to Venus goddesse of loue' (1:2223); 'The preyere of Emelye to dyane goddesse of Maydens' (1:2299); 'The answere of Dyane to Emelye' (1:2350); and 'The orisoun of Arcite to Mars god of Armes' (1:2375). In WBP there is another series, which includes 'Bihoold how this goode wyf serued hir iij firste housbondes whiche were goode olde men' (2:193); 'Of the condicioun of the fourthe housbonde of this goode wyf And how she serued hym' (2:453); and 'Of the fifthe housbonde of this wyf and hou she bar hire ayens hym' (2:503). Other tales have their own series. In TMel the names Prudence and Melibeus are entered in the margin to indicate where each of them starts to speak. In PsT there are subtitles for the various types of penitence in part 1 of the tale. In Hg these had appeared in an embryonic form, but in El they are explained and made into a complete series. These subtitles complement the rubrics in providing a means to break down the text into smaller units.

In addition to these subtitles which form a series in certain tales, there are also the notes which fulfil much the same function though they are not part of a series. These include *Auctor, Argumentum* and *Exemplum*. These occur much more commonly than they had in earlier manuscripts and were no doubt designed to make the reader's task easier by directing his attention to features in the text. Thus in KtT *Exemplum* is inserted in the margin at 1:3013 and 3017. Some of these annotations repeat what had occurred in earlier manuscripts, though in El this kind of annotation is more frequent than previously. The glosses reflect what had appeared in previous manuscripts for the most part. But we may note that a few which are new are glosses in English rather than Latin. In ClT *wrye* is glossed '.i. couere' (8:887) and in NPT *mette* is glossed '.i. dremed' (10:2974). In ShT the text reads 'Who ther' and the gloss *qi la* appears in the margin, as in Hg and the manuscripts of group *a* at 10:214.

The source annotations are also more extensive in El than elsewhere, though those annotations which had appeared in earlier manuscripts like those in MLT are reproduced in El. El contains extensive source material which had not appeared in other manuscripts in WBPT and FkT, and those appearing in other tales are often increased in number. These additions are usually learned. Hence the glossing of WBP in El, for example, is very different in nature from that in Dd 4.24, for El's scribe was interested in providing the academic background. In addition to source material which is quoted in Latin, the names of authorities are often noted in the margin where they had also been quoted in the text. In some cases the scribe reveals he knows the source which is alluded to rather than specifically quoted in the poem. In FkT at 6:402 Chaucer refers to Pamphilus and Galathea, of whom as we saw the scribe of Gg 4.27 was completely ignorant. The scribe of El introduced the annotation *Pamphilus ad Galatheam vulneror & clausum porto sub pectore telum & cetera* which indicates he was aware of the original poem to which Chaucer refers. It provides a further indication of the scribe's background and experience.

Overall this scribe was not as interested in making the work a uniform text divided into prologues and tales as the scribe of Dd 4.24 had been. He wanted to arrange it as a unified poem, but he presented it as consisting of various parts which could be taken in isolation and arranged to make a larger moral and intellectual whole. He makes the reader's task easier by arranging the material in these smaller units, and by providing the background material. We see in El the culmination of what was started in Hg. In Hg we found a little sub-division of tales and a few annotations; in El we find both carried through consistently and comprehensively. This behaviour may make us reconsider whether any of the annotations or rubrics were in the original. This scribe was an inveterate annotator and arranger, and as he was the first scribe to tackle *The*

Canterbury Tales, he may well have started the habit of adding rubrics and annotations. It may well be that the original had no annotations, and perhaps no rubrics either, though the occasional *narrat* and *explicit* as marginal headings may have appeared. Equally importantly, this scribe shows through El that although he was a careful copyist he could make mistakes through eyeskip and he did make a few additions. But those additions are either learned like [F1455-6] or help the development of the narrative like [A3721-2]. These indications confirm that Hg's omission of 1:639-40 was accidental and that the lines were in the original, but that it is not likely that the scribe added 1:253-4 which must therefore have been in the original as well. The scribe of Hg and El shows through his annotations an interest in order and learning; he does not show any of the interest in social and sexual relations we find in Dd 4.24. Hence it is most improbable that he could be responsible for that type of addition in WBP and elsewhere, which must have entered the scribal tradition before El was written. El came at the end of the first phase of the development of the text of *The Canterbury Tales* and its contents cannot be considered as reliably Chaucerian as has been assumed by so many editors.

In discussing Dd 4.24 I raised the possibility that it did not come direct from the original copytext used for Hg and other early manuscripts, but that there was one intervening manuscript. If so, that manuscript would have been used by the scribes of other group *a* manuscripts, which share certain features against the other early manuscripts. This remains a possibility, but the evidence is far from conclusive. Although these manuscripts share certain features among themselves, each manuscript in group *a* shares features which appear in the other early manuscripts but not necessarily otherwise in group *a*. It is likely that there was another early manuscript in the group *a* class, for the Merthyr fragment is claimed to exhibit certain textual features which link it with group *a*. This could be a manuscript which descended radially from the original copytext like the other group *a* manuscripts rather than acted as intermediary between that original and other group *a* manuscripts. All one can say is that if the group *a* manuscripts descend from an intermediate text rather than direct from the original, their scribes must nevertheless have been familiar with textual developments occurring in the other set of manuscripts. How this might have occurred we shall have to consider in a later chapter. At all events, we may conclude that Dd 4.24 is the earliest extant *a* group manuscript and that it was in that manuscript that the additional passages in WBP were introduced into the text. As these additions are not found in Corpus or Ha7334, it may be that Dd 4.24 was slightly later than those two copies. Whether Gg 4.27 or El comes next in group *a* is difficult to decide. Palaeography would favour the latter, but the textual evidence is less clear. They may be regarded as separate texts of about the same time, but with rather different attitudes towards the poem. Unfortunately the mutilation of Gg 4.27 prevents a full understanding of how its scribe operated.

8

Other Developments in the Text

Petworth is the only early manuscript not considered so far; it belongs to group *d*. It also needs to be remembered that no group *b* manuscript is classified among the early ones. Yet together these two groups account for perhaps half the total number of extant manuscripts, and they thus represent important fifteenth-century groupings in the text though modern editors have not considered them of much value in constructing their editions. From what was noted about Petworth in Chapter 4 and from what has been written by earlier scholars,[1] it is clear that groups *d* and *b* are affiliated to group *c* rather than to group *a*. In other words there is a major line of textual development which runs from Hg through Corpus and group *c* to the majority of fifteenth-century manuscripts which belong to either group *d* or group *b*. Group *a* forms a sub-group in the development of the text, which is in many respects independent of the major development. Characteristic of group *a* manuscripts are the extra passages in WBP, the placing of section 7 with CYPT after section 10, the occurrence of NP endlink (except in El and Gg 4.27), and the regular sequence of ClT−MeT−SqT with the consequent omission of ML endlink (which normally in other groups functions as SqP). Although some manuscripts outside group *a* may have the order ClT−MeT−SqT, this is not normally caused by the influence of group *a* manuscripts, for a feature of the textual tradition of *The Canterbury Tales* is that although group *a* manuscripts are influenced by those in other groups, they do not have much influence on those other manuscripts. Hence group *a* is a specialized, essentially non-productive, stage in the textual hierarchy. Its difference from the major tradition has been recognized in the scholarly labels 'All England' and 'Oxford', 'Private' and 'Commercial', and 'Original' and 'Revised'.[2]

Petworth may be the earliest extant manuscript in group *d*, though it may not represent the earliest stage in the development of that group. One feature which it contains is not reproduced in all

[1]See particularly Dempster 1948a and 1949.
[2]See, for example, Brusendorff 1925, Manly and Rickert 1940, and Benson 1981.

other manuscripts in the group and Petworth may through this feature represent, as suggested by Manly and Rickert, a minor development within group *d*: it places ShT and PrT after Gamelyn. Petworth is not the only manuscript to do this in the group, though other manuscripts also include MkT with ShT and PrT after Gamelyn. Several of the manuscripts in the group do not break up section 10 in this way, but keep it as a unit towards the end of the poem. That this was the intended position for ShT and PrT in Petworth as well is indicated by the presence in that manuscript of a prologue to ShT which is meant to join that tale to PdT. The confusion which allowed this break-up of section 10 to occur may be attributed to the copytext of the group, and this raises the question as to what this copytext was like that made this break-up possible. Since some manuscripts put ShT and PrT after Gamelyn, while others put ShT, PrT and MkT after Gamelyn, the copytext must have had at least some, and probably all, of the tales in section 10 in separate units for this rearrangement to be credible. Manly and Rickert thought that the group *c* copytext was a later copy of the original, though as manuscripts made in the fifteenth century had no juncture of tale and quire boundary it seems unlikely that a special archetype for group *d* would have been written in a way that allowed for the text to be broken up, for we may assume that the order of the tales in Petworth is unintentional. The only copy of the poem which is likely to have had breaks between the tales is the original copytext, particularly if it were Chaucer's working copy. There is, therefore, some reason to think that at least some group *d* manuscripts go back to the original copytext. This view receives support from Ha7334. As noted in an earlier chapter, the *ordinatio* of that manuscript fell into two separate categories, the first consisting of the early quires, quire 20 (which contained SqT which was ultimately repositioned in the order) and quire 26 (with part of ShT). This difference in *ordinatio* may indicate a potential misplacement of the first part of section 10; and although that misplacement did not occur in Ha7334, it did in Petworth. If so, Ha7334 and Petworth used the same copytext – namely, the original copytext. We shall see in a moment that this hypothesis is supported by group *b* manuscripts as well.

That Petworth did make use of the original copytext is suggested also by its close textual association with Corpus. It has many of the same omissions found in Corpus as well as many of the rearrangements; it also shares many aspects of its order. It does, however, contain many lines which were omitted accidentally in Corpus, particularly in TMel and the end of MeT, and so it probably did not use Corpus itself as a copytext. Or if it did, it was like Lansdowne in having access to a further set of material with which to supplement Corpus. However, the close textual connection which exists between Lansdowne and Corpus is not reproduced in the relationship between Petworth and Corpus, and so the same explanation of textual transmission need not apply to both Lansdowne and Petworth. It should, though, be remembered that Petworth, like Corpus, has some chapter numbers. It would not be difficult to imagine that the numbers were introduced onto the original copytext by Corpus's scribe or his supervisor, for this would account for the occasional appearance of the numbers in manuscripts belonging to the major textual development.

The order of tales in Petworth is as follows. Section 1 commences as normal. At the end of CkT there is a two-line link to Gamelyn:

> But here of I wil pas as nowe
> And of yonge Gamelyn I wil telle you.

Gamelyn is thus made part of CkT by this device, and the rubric at the end of Gamelyn refers to the ending of the 'tale of the Coke'. The last page of Gamelyn has more lines than usual as though the scribe tried to crowd it all in to prevent it spilling on to another page, but as ShT commences on the verso of the same leaf there is no apparent sign of uncertainty in the order. ShT and PrT follow at this point; but they are not inserted later. Their position is clearly intended to be here for they follow on without a break from Gamelyn, and MLP follows PrT on the same page. If the copytext was disturbed in its order, this did not produce any misgivings in the scribe of Petworth as far as we can now tell. MLPT follows PrT and is concluded by ML endlink, which is introduced as SqP and has the reading 'Sqwier' at [B^{1}1179]. There is no concluding rubric to SqP, and SqT begins at the top of the verso of the same leaf; it does have a rubric. SqT is divided into only two parts for the two extant lines of part 3 are included in part 2, but they are marked for omission by the marginal note *vacat*. There is a rubric concluding SqT after the rubric ending part 2; it is followed by Sq–Me link which commences on the same page. This is the Sq–Me link which had made its first appearance in Hg, where it was added later in the yellowish ink. It had been adapted as a Sq–Fk link or omitted in intermediate manuscripts. Its reappearance here as the Sq–Me link provides a connection between Petworth and Hg. More importantly it suggests a different approach to the development of the text. After Hg other scribes had rearranged the order of the tales to achieve particular ends, one of the most important of which was the establishment through the order of tales of the association between WBP on the one hand and ClT and MeT on the other. The need to achieve this aim had led to the invention of new links and to the adaptation of existing ones as the order changed. In Petworth we have a different approach in that the existence of links indicated an order to the scribe. Instead of a new order influencing the links, existing links were in this case affecting the order. Hg's order had led to the creation of ML−Sq and Sq−Me links which had probably been left with the copytext itself. Later scribes now used these links as guides to how they should arrange the tales. It was evidently less important to the group *d* scribes that MeT preceded WBP, even though the former referred to the latter, than that the links should be followed in the order.

MeT is followed by section 2 in its usual order. The only change here is that the final part of SuT is omitted and a couple of new lines introduced to conclude the tale. After 2:2132 the tale ends with

> He ne had nat ellis for his sermon
> To parten amonge his brethren when he come home
> And thus is this tale ydon
> For we were almost at the ton.

Since the last two lines echo the genuine ending of the tale, the omission was deliberate. It may have been felt that the humiliation of the Friar had gone far enough. It is an interesting aspect of many manuscripts of the poem that their scribes reduced the satire and attacks directed at the friars. Although we today often assume from such attacks that the friars were hated and despised at the time, the evidence of the manuscripts of *The Canterbury Tales* suggests rather the reverse. SuT is followed by ClT, introduced by ClP. At the end of ClT the final stanza, which contains the reference to the Wife of Bath (8:1170-6), is omitted. This is part of a wider reorganization which has taken place at the end of ClT, for the stanzas in the envoy are reordered. Its fourth stanza (8:1195-1200) has been put at the end following 8:1212. This final stanza refers to the resistance which the author urges all wives to make to their husbands. ClT has thus lost its particular reference to the Wife of Bath, and is used instead as a prelude to an envoy in which wives are generally asked to resist their husbands in the ways they know best. This rearrangement may have been prompted by the occurrence of the following link. For Petworth does not include the Host-stanza here, but it contains Hg's Me−Fk link adapted as a Cl−Fk link. This is introduced in Petworth as FkP, as it had been in Hg. The reasons for the introduction of the link here must wait until we consider the position in group *b* manuscripts.

In some manuscripts of group *d* there are different developments of the Cl−Fk link. These manuscripts include the Host-stanza and then rewrite Petworth's Cl−Fk link (which had been Hg's Me−Fk link) as two seven-line stanzas through a fairly drastic pruning of the passage. There can be no doubt that these two stanzas are designed to make the link harmonize with the metre of the Host-stanza. The question arises whether the Petworth link or the stanza version is the earlier. Dempster took the view that the stanzaic form was earlier, though this seems unlikely, for it would be difficult to understand why the Petworth scribe later eliminated the Host-stanza and reverted to the form of the link in Hg.[3] If Petworth is based on Corpus or a text like it, it would be natural for it to supply a link at this point which was missing in Corpus by introducing Hg's Me−Fk link adapted as a Cl−Fk link. Later, a different scribe who wished to include the Host-stanza (which may have been omitted by the Petworth scribe precisely because it was in a different metre) decided that this could be done if the rest of the link was adapted. Since the link as it stood in Petworth did not form a very satisfactory conclusion to ClT because it refers to wicked wives, the need to emend Petworth's link may have caused this scribe no qualms. Hence the Petworth version may not be a development within group *d*, but rather it represents the original group *d* version from which other manuscripts in it developed. A scribe who revised this link could easily also have re-established the original order of the tales in section 10.

FkT follows the adapted Cl−Fk link which acts as FkP. It is followed in turn by NnT. This has no link from the pilgrimage frame to introduce it, but the first 119 lines of the tale are marked off as the prologue. Prologue and tale are allocated to the Second Nun. NnT is followed by CYPT. PhT which comes next is introduced by a fourteen-line link, which is different from the link which is found in Lansdowne of sixteen lines. The link refers to CYT and contains the Host's comments on it and his request to the Physician to tell his tale. Section 9 then follows with its normal order. After PdT we find the prologue to TTh because the two first tales of section 10 appeared earlier. This introduces the second half of section 10 which is completed in the standard form. The Modern Instances in MkT are in the middle. Petworth has the short form of NPP without [B²3961-80]. Section 10 is followed by sections 11 and 12 with their normal contents, and section 12 includes Rt.

Apart from the mistaken position of ShT and PrT, the order in Petworth can be understood to have developed ultimately from that found in Corpus influenced by the use of links available in Hg which are used or adapted in Petworth. Like the scribe of Lansdowne, the scribe of Petworth was motivated by the desire to have a complete poem in which the tales were joined by links, designated as prologues. However, the scribe of Petworth was ignorant of the links used in Lansdowne and so he had to invent his own where he could find none in existence already. The rubrics are

---

[3]Dempster 1948a.

also designed to create a feeling of completeness for they indicate a regular progression of prologue–tale. Each prologue has an introductory and concluding rubric as does each tale. There is no general title for the poem as a whole, but Pro does have a concluding rubric. Despite this series of regular rubrics, there are marginal rubrics as well which are often in Latin and repeat in an abbreviated form what is stated in the English rubric. The effect produced is that the poem is complete and its form established.

In textual matters and in glosses Petworth is very close to Corpus, but it cannot depend upon the earlier manuscript entirely since it includes passages which are not found there. As a general rule, however, it may be stated that Petworth imitates Corpus textually except where there are major omissions and adaptations in Corpus. For much of the poem Manly and Rickert regarded the *c* and *d* group as textually indistinguishable. The same applies to the glosses, where those in Petworth almost always echo those found in Corpus. The scribe of Petworth does not seem to have interfered deliberately in the text to make alterations; he was satisfied with producing a text which was as complete as he could make it and which gave the appearance of a finished whole. In this aim he was successful.

I have dealt with group *d* before group *b* because Petworth, a group *d* manuscript, is classified as one of the early manuscripts and because earlier scholars have claimed that group *b* is a development from group *d*. Most group *b* manuscripts are late fifteenth century, and Cx76 is the best known example of this group. Nevertheless, the evidence for the priority of group *d* over group *b* is not as clear as previous scholars have imagined, for there are examples of early manuscripts in group *b*. For example, Helmingham, the manuscript which Manly and Rickert put at the top of group *b*, consists partly of vellum and partly of paper. The vellum part has been dated to the end of the first quarter of the fifteenth century, about the same date as Petworth, and the paper part which is much later was added to the manuscript to complete it presumably after the rest of the original vellum manuscript was lost. So it is quite possible to imagine that there was a group *b* manuscript in existence at the same time as, if not earlier than, the earliest group *d* manuscript.

The order of tales in Helmingham was probably as follows, though it lacks some leaves at beginning and end. It starts with section 1, though there is no Gamelyn after CkT. CkT is followed by section 2, which is then succeeded by ML endlink acting as SqP. This introduces SqT. Then comes what had been Ha7334's Cl–Me link, which here acts as MeP. This is then followed by MeT. Then comes section 2 in its normal sequence. This is followed by section 8, which contains ClP, ClT with envoy and the Host-stanza. FkT and NnT follow. Though neither has a prologue from the pilgrimage frame, each has a prologue made out of the tale itself. NnT does not have CYPT after it in Helmingham, though several manuscripts in group *b* do include this prologue and tale here; in Helmingham CYPT is missing entirely. So NnT is followed by sections 9, 10, 11 and 12 in their normal order, except that ShT is missing in section 10. It is, however, found in its usual position in many manuscripts in group *b*. As the manuscript is incomplete, it is not certain whether Rt was originally included in Helmingham, though it seems probable that it was. It occurs in all complete manuscripts of group *b*. The original vellum begins in the middle of TMel at 10:1395 and continues to the end of the manuscript. The text of the preceding part has been adapted to fit in with the vellum for the previous quire before the extant vellum has a truncated version of TMel.

There are two important points of contact between Helmingham and group *d*. The first is the order, for the order in Helmingham reflects that in group *d* except that Helmingham is not as full as group *d*. It does not contain Gamelyn, CYPT or Hg's Me−Fk link which in Petworth was adapted as the Cl−Fk link. That Helmingham has a less complete text than Petworth might suggest that it was the earlier version. The second is that in the part of section 10 which is on vellum in Helmingham there is evidence to suggest that the individual tales were copied separately rather than as part of a constant group. This is indicated by the rubrics in another hand and by the gaps at the foot of the pages which contain the ends of MkP and NPP. Although the links clearly indicate the order in which the tales should be placed, these gaps do indicate that the tales were not copied continuously, but as separate units perhaps at different times. This nature of section 10 in Helmingham links with the displacement of the tales within section 10 in group *d* manuscripts, for if both used the same copytext it would be easy to see how the tales in section 10 became misplaced in Petworth and associated manuscripts. It is likely that both groups used the same copytext, and that is likely to have been the original one used by the scribes of Hg and Corpus. However, textually Helmingham differs considerably from Corpus and Petworth, and so it cannot be closely linked with them other than in the order.

At this point in the discussion we are presented with a problem for the manuscripts allocated to group *b* by Manly and Rickert show marked divergences. Whereas Helmingham and other manuscripts like it contain the Cl−Me link [E1213-44] as a Sq−Me link, other manuscripts in the group like Lincoln have at this point Hg's Sq−Me link [F673-708]. There are other differences as well in that Helmingham and its associated manuscripts contain many extra additional passages in the text including the extra obscene lines in

MeT quoted in Chapter 1. These additional passages are not in Lincoln and its sub-group. The question arises as to which of these two sub-groups within *b* is the earlier. The answer is almost certainly Lincoln, for it is difficult to see how the additional passages in Helmingham would have been deleted later if they had been found in the copytext. We may, therefore, work on the assumption that group *b* originally had Hg's Sq−Me link to join MeT to SqT. Neither of the group *b* sub-groups have Hg's Me−Fk link as a means of joining FkT to ClT, though some have interesting and significant features. Lincoln itself has the last eight lines of this link [F1-8] inserted in the margin. It might therefore be possible to suggest that the group *b* ancestor had Hg's Sq−Me link as MeP, and that this accounts for the order found there. At a subsequent date, this link was replaced by the Cl−Me link adapted as a Sq−Me link. This may have happened only when this Cl−Me link became available, and may be attributable to the influence of Ha7334 or group *a* manuscripts since there are other points in which group *b* was influenced by these. Some manuscripts in group *b*, for example, contain the reading Summoner in ML endlink at [B¹1179] even though in these manuscripts it is SqT which follows and the reading Squire would be more appropriate. The influence of group *a* is seen in some group *b* manuscripts in the occurrence of the extra passages in WBP, but it is doubtful whether these passages occurred in the original group *b* manuscript since they are not found in manuscripts like Lincoln.

Although Helmingham is a useful manuscript to have available because its vellum part provides an early date for group *b*, it does not represent what was the group *b* archetype satisfactorily. This is better represented by Lincoln and its sub-group, and it may be remembered that Lincoln is itself a manuscript from the second quarter of the fifteenth century, and so it is not very much later than Helmingham. The main points of difference are that Helmingham has been influenced by group *a* to introduce the extra passages in WBP and some extra lines elsewhere such as [A3721-2] and that there are differences where SqT and MeT on the one hand and ClT and FkT on the other are joined. Lincoln ends ClT after the envoy and has the Host-stanza as FkP, though as we saw [F1-8] are included in the margin, as though there was some influence from Hg's original Me−Fk link. The problem associated with group *b*, and indeed with group *d*, is why FkT is placed after Clt rather than after MeT which is where the Hg link would suggest it should appear. Group *d* manuscripts include Hg's Me−Fk link adapted as a Cl−Fk link. If this link was available and if group *d* is earlier than group *b*, then one might have expected the link to produce the order MeT−FkT−section 2−ClT rather than MeT−section 2−ClT−FkT. The introduction of the link in group *d* would suggest that group *d* is later than group *b*, and that the available link was added to an existing order, namely that found in group *b*.

It is clear that there was a lot of experimentation in groups *b* and *d* with the link between ClT and FkT. The solutions are as follows. Lincoln ends ClT after the envoy and has the Host-stanza as FkP. The addition of [F1-8] in the margin suggests that this solution was not entirely satisfactory, and attempts were made to modify it. Helmingham has the Host-stanza in ClT and breaks up FkT into a prologue and tale at 6:21, a solution it may have borrowed from group *a*. Petworth abandoned the Host-stanza altogether and included Hg's Me–Fk link adapted as a Cl–Fk link. Other group *d* manuscripts kept the Host-stanza and adapted Hg's Me–Fk link into two stanzas to make it harmonize metrically with the Host-stanza. Everything seems to depend on the presence or absence of the Host-stanza, and one may suggest tht the form in Lincoln represents the earliest attempt in groups *b* and *d* to solve this problem. The constraints which encouraged this solution in the archetype are not too difficult to understand, if we assume that it comes later than Corpus and therefore also than Hg. Corpus had introduced numbers into the tales, which were probably copied on to the copytext for the numbers keep recurring sporadically in later manuscripts. There was, therefore, a numbering system which would encourage the scribe of the group *b* ancestor to keep to a particular order. But he was also influenced by the idea that each tale should be introduced by a prologue, and he had the prologues written for the Hg order available. FkT differed from MeT and SqT because it could be divided into a prologue and tale within itself. Corpus had indeed put a rubric indicating a FkP in the margin at 6:1. But MeT and SqT had no introductory parts which could be separated off as prologues, and hence they had to have prologues from outside the tales. These were provided by the prologues written for Hg, though Me endlink acting as SqP had not actually been included in Hg. The use of these prologues dictated the order MLT–SqT–MeT, even though the latter contradicted the numbering system in the copytext. But FkT could remain where it was in the numbering system for it had a potential prologue within the tale. Furthermore, the Host-stanza could also be adapted as a prologue. We may assume then that this is the earliest stage of group *b* development at this stage. Helmingham rejected this solution by including the Host-stanza in ClT and by breaking up FkT into prologue and tale; but this solution may have been influenced by group *a* manuscripts. Petworth and other group *d* scribes also rejected this group *b* solution, because they wished to incorporate the Hg Me–Fk link which was available. They tried to do this in two ways, though both involved rewriting the envoy to CIT. This solution means that group *d* is later than group *b*, or rather that its order is developed from it.

It may seem difficult to some readers to accept that the earliest group *b* manuscript precedes those in group *d*, since group *b* manuscripts are usually late fifteenth-century and have always been considered to be a late development, for no group *b* manuscript is included in the earliest eight manuscripts of the poem. It cannot be denied that there was at least one early group *b* manuscript for the vellum part of Helmingham dates from the same time as, or earlier than, Petworth. Equally the relationship of groups *b* and *d* has been hampered by the hypothesis that they do exist as two identifiable groups. The existence of group *d* has been questioned, and it now seems appropriate to discard it. It has been shown that the manuscripts allocated to group *d* descend from the original copytext individually and not through a linear descent. The earliest group *b* manuscript also descends from the same copytext. Hence there is little to separate the two groups, for it would be possible to say that the group *b* archetype is the earliest group *d* manuscript, if by group *d* one meant a series of manuscripts which were produced from the original copytext probably within the same editorial framework. Group *b* itself should not be considered as an entity, for it consists of two sub-groups which are markedly different in that the Helmingham sub-group has been strongly influenced by a group *a* manuscript. It is better to think of groups *b* and *d* as forming a large grouping of manuscripts which were largely produced in the same editorial environment. Some of these manuscripts were copied later in the fifteenth century to produce sub-groups. But many of them were produced from the same copytext which was the original copytext used by Hg and Corpus. However, whoever was responsible for the editorial work changed his mind about certain decisions and continued to make improvements in the text. The Helmingham sub-group was probably copied from a group *b* manuscript rather than from the original copytext, though this is a matter that needs further investigation. The important point about this loose grouping of manuscripts is the continuity in editorial development which it exhibits and the availability of the original copytext perhaps as late as the second quarter of the fifteenth century. This latter fact has considerable implications for the whole editorial tradition.

Textually it might be thought that group *b* manuscripts were bad, though this in fact applies only to the Helmingham sub-group. The Lincoln sub-group is textually much better, and although it has some links with Corpus, its text has none of the major omissions found in that manuscript. There are occasional omissions in Lincoln caused by eyeskip and carelessness, though they are not frequent. In section 1 Lincoln omits [A3155-6 and 3721-2]. It does not contain Gamelyn at the end, and this may reflect that the original *b* scribe was influenced by the same principles motivating Ha7334 and the *a* group. In part the lack of any linking mechanism was no doubt a factor in the omission of Gamelyn. In SqT the last two lines are omitted, and there is a clear link here with Petworth. In MeT Lincoln omits 5:61-2, and reads 'Whiche that he rauisshid out of Proserpina' at 5:986, two readings which suggest a link with Corpus. In FkT it omits [F1455-6 and 1493-8]. In Ph−Pd link it omits [C297-8]. In MkT the Adam stanza is found in Lincoln, though it is missing from the Helmingham sub-group and may have been absent in the *b* archetype. Lincoln has the Modern Instances at the end of MkT, though Helmingham has them in the middle; again Helmingham may reflect the *b* archetype, though in this case the position is less clear. The revision of the position of the Modern Instances may result from the influence of the *a* group on Helmingham. In NPP Lincoln has the long form of the prologue, but Helmingham has the short form. Clearly these two sub-groups had difficulty with MkT and NPP and seem to have come forward with different solutions to each problem. As we saw Petworth has the Adam stanza, has the Modern Instances in the middle and has the short form of NPP. It is clear that in this *bd* grouping there was frequent adjustment of the text at this point. One is tempted to think that the archetype had no Adam stanza, had the Modern Instances at the end and had the short form of NPP, though it does not seem capable of proof. Lincoln, like Helmingham, has lost some folios at the end and so it is not possible to say whether Rt was included in the *b* archetype, though as it is found in many *bd* manuscripts it was added fairly early if it was not there originally.

Lincoln does not contain any divisions into parts within the tales, and in this it no doubt reflects its archetype. It does have capitals in ClT where the parts begin in other manuscripts, and it evidently comes from a source which had some kind of part divisions. This does not apply to the other tales, for even SqT is without any part divisions. Lincoln seems to be moving to a system of prologue and tale only, but it has not achieved it, and it has not introduced spurious prologues for those tales which did not have them. A system of rubrics which refer to prologues and tales was undertaken, but not completed. Some tales have only a tale rubric, though some have both. We can perhaps see here the beginnings of the prologue−tale scheme which was to be executed more fully in other manuscripts like Petworth, Lansdowne and Dd 4.24. Even in Helmingham we can see that this schematization has been carried further for the rubrics are more regularly introduced. It was an inevitable consequence of this desire to have a prologue−tale scheme, that those tales without a prologue should be provided with one. This meant either dividing the tale into prologue and tale as with NnT or creating a new prologue.

Important questions which emerge from this reconstruction of the *b* group and its archetype are the date of the earliest *b* manuscript, which probably is no longer extant, its position in the textual hierarchy, and the overall development of what I have called the *bd* grouping of manuscripts. Earlier in this book I suggested that Hg is the first manuscript to arrange the tales in an order. It was followed by Corpus, in which a different principle of organization was employed. This method was abandoned and led to new attempts to arrange the tales in a framework. That new framework gradually emerged as a prologue–link scheme, though it was not introduced immediately – or at least its implications were not worked out fully at once. This new method can be seen in Ha7334 and Dd 4.24, which may be regarded as the earliest group *a* manuscript. The *bd* archetype seems to fit in the textual hierarchy at this stage. It has links with Dd 4.24 in that it omits Gamelyn, which is foreshadowed in Ha7334, and is motivated by the need to have a prologue–tale arrangement. The *bd* archetype also has links with Ha7334 and the manuscripts of the *c* group in that it includes ML endlink which appears as SqP with the consequent ordering of SqT after MLT. It may, therefore, be suggested that Ha7334, the *bd* archetype and Dd 4.24 (or its ancestor) all date from about the same time and reflect attempts to reorder the poem after the fiasco of Corpus whose arrangement was accepted as unsatisfactory. The difference is that Dd 4.24 represents a development which became standardized to a large extent and which formed a manuscript group which was largely independent of the others. It had an influence only on the Helmingham sub-group of manuscripts, though that influence was probably exerted later in the fifteenth century after the first phase of manuscript production had ended. The manuscripts in the *a* group may have been copied from a separate copytext and were less influenced by the original copytext which remained with the editor(s) of the *bcd* manuscripts. Characteristic of this grouping is the continued use of the original copytext, probably much marked by a succession of editors, and by the continued urge to seek a final solution to the problem of tale-order and presentation of the poem. Rather than dividing these manuscripts into the big Manly–Rickert groups, it is better to regard them as falling into certain sub-groups which share many features but which also witness to the wish to produce the definitive version. The constant, but varied, series of associated readings found in these manuscripts is attributable to the use of the same copytext which had itself undergone considerable editorial intervention and suggestion.

That there was some continuity in attitude towards the editorial development is indicated by the spurious link between MeT and WBP which occurs in some group *d* manuscripts. This link consists of sixteen lines and was made for the order found only in the *bd* grouping. In Royal 18 C II it reads:

> Oure oost gan to loke vp anon
> Gode men quod he herkeneth euerichon
> As euere mote I drynk wyn or ale
> This marchande hath I-tolde a mery tale
> How Ianuarie hadde a lither iape
> His wyf put in his hood an ape
> But hereof I wil leue as now
> Dame wyf of Bathe quod he I pray yow
> Telle vs a tale now next after this
> Sire oost quod she so god my soule blis
> As I fully therto wil consente
> And also it is myn hole entente
> To done yow alle disporte as that I can
> But holde me excused I am a woman
> I can not reherse as these clerkes kune
> And right anon she hath hir tale bygune.

This link occurs in only three of the group *d* manuscripts. Dempster noted that many of the expressions found in this link echo those found in other links found in many group *d* manuscripts such as the CY–Ph and Pd–Sh links. She, therefore, claimed that the links must have been written by the same person, and that is a reasonable hypothesis. However, since following Manly and Rickert she accepted a group *d* whose manuscripts all descended from a common source, she had to assume that that source contained this link – and indeed all the links written by this person. However, that seems unlikely for it is difficult under those circumstances to know why the link was omitted in so many of the manuscripts which form the Manly–Rickert group *d*. If we accept that there is no reality to group *d* other than that the manuscripts were copied from the same original at different times, we do not have to assume that one manuscript contained all the additions to start with and that the scribes decided which ones they would include. It is more reasonable to assume that there was a gradual development of the text, for various links were added at different times by the same person just as other influences were assimilated into the text. That one person kept on adding links is no problem if we accept that the manuscripts are copies of the original copytext which was kept in one place or at least under one person's supervision.

The basic order of these *bd* manuscripts is that found in the *b* archetype: section 1 without Gamelyn; section 3 with ML endlink as SqP leading to section 4; Hg's Sq–Me acting as MeP introduced section 5; section 2 in its normal order followed by section 8; sections 6 and 7 follow, though section 7 has CYPT attached to it;

then sections 9, 10, 11 and 12 follow in their Hg order. Whether Rt was part of the first manuscript we cannot tell, though if not it appeared very shortly afterwards. It is possible that this manuscript included the extra passages in WBP, but was otherwise relatively uninfluenced by the developments characteristic of group *a* manuscripts. This order is understandable if one assumes that the editor was coming to terms with the order in Hg, the links made for Hg, and the additions found in Corpus within the framework of an order which arranged the poem in a sequence of prologue–tale. The only gaps in the sequence are the absence of prologues to PhT and ShT, gaps which we have noted caused problems to other early scribes. Characteristic of the copytext at this time was the disorder in section 10. It is apparent that the tales which make up section 10 had become separated so that the scribes did not always copy them in the right order. This suggests that each tale and each link was a self-contained unit and that hitherto these units had been pinned together in some way. This was no longer true at this stage. For the disruption of section 10 is characteristic of manuscripts allocated to both group *b* and group *d*. The disruption occurs haphazardly in both groups and indicates that the copytext was sent out on an *ad hoc* basis to scribes who did not always get the parts of section 10 in the right order or did not trouble to make sure they remained in the correct order.

From this beginning various influences operated on the editor in charge of the copytext. He sometimes responded to new developments elsewhere such as the introduction of the Cl–Me link and the reading 'Summoner' in the ML endlink. He also restored Gamelyn to the poem because of its re-appearance in Ha7334. He also introduced new links in different stages. He introduced a Cl–Fk link and then revised it at a later stage. He introduced new links to introduce WBP, PhT and ShT, though these were not necessarily introduced at the same time. At an even later date FkT was moved in some manuscripts to a position after MeT and before WBP, and then new links were created or existing links adapted for this change. Because the original copytext was the basis of these manuscripts, one may understand why they were so popular and so common. What is surprising perhaps is that there should have been a continuous process of experimentation to improve the poem. But once the idea that the poem should be improved had taken hold, there was no reason why this process should not continue. The very existence of variant readings in and alternative links with the copytext may well have encouraged this sense of experimentation. In this way the manuscripts of this *bd* group differ sharply from those in group *a*. This is because manuscripts of group *a* may come from a separate copytext which split off from the major tradition at a fairly early stage. This particular sub-group maintained a degree of cohesion in its textual transmission because it was not influenced in the same way by the process of experimentation which characterized the production of manuscripts from the original copytext. This relative cohesion should not be taken to imply any superiority in the text for group *a*; it merely reflects a different process of transmission.

It is not possible to determine how long the original copytext remained available for copying. Individual manuscripts, which form sub-groups in the Manly–Rickert groupings, may have been copied from a copy rather than from the original. Certainly the manuscripts which they allocate to group *b* are descended from copies rather than from the original copytext. But the process of experimentation continued well into the fifteenth century – and even beyond. Ultimately the variety in the orders generated its own momentum. This picture contrasts very sharply with the position that has applied for the last hundred years, in which a fairly well-established text has been handed down from one editor to the next with very little change except in small details. Whereas the *bd* manuscripts are all motivated by the same order and attitude to the text, later scribes were still experimenting with the order. A manuscript like Holkham, which dates perhaps from the middle of the fifteenth century, exhibits certain novel solutions to the problem of tale order. It omits CkT in section 1, presumably because of its incompleteness, and follows ReT with NnT and CYPT. This was probably motivated by the fact that the Canon's Yeoman joined the party late. If you ignore the geographical reference, which many scribes did, you could easily assume that when the Canon's Yeoman joined the pilgrimage 'Er we hadde riden fully fyue mile' [G555], this meant after the rest of the pilgrims had ridden five miles from the Tabard Inn. It is a neat solution to the introduction of additional pilgrims, and it is surprising that other scribes did not think of it. That they did not is a reflection of the hold that the order handed down by earlier scribes had. The same applies to another solution adopted by the Holkham scribe. He is the only one to break up section 2. As we saw earlier, one principle motivating the editors in the order was to link ClT and MeT with WBPT, but they could not be placed immediately after WBPT because it occurred in a constant section. However, the Holkham scribe broke up section 2 in order to place ClT and MeT immediately after WBT. Again this is quite a sensible solution, but one which comes after the time when scribes felt constrained by the order of the constant sections in the original copytext. Editorial intervention in the text was not restricted to the early fifteenth century.

9

A Matter of Copytexts

In the previous chapters the question of what copytexts were used by the individual scribes has not been discussed in detail, though it has been assumed that the majority of early scribes had access to a single copytext which was Chaucer's own working copy. It is time now to consider this matter in greater detail for it is a hypothesis which has not won universal support in recent discussions of the manuscript tradition of *The Canterbury Tales*, and if there is a single copytext, it will also be important to examine its nature. Although many scholars have recently not been in favour of a single copytext, some have continued to propose solutions to textual problems as though there was an authorial copytext available, for they have suggested that some textual variations arose in the tradition because of authorial additions to or deletions on that copytext.

As we saw earlier, since the Manly–Rickert edition it has been common to think that there were many copytexts for the poem because they proposed that Chaucer issued the tales individually as they were completed. Each tale had a different textual tradition, and sometimes in copying a tale the scribe might have drawn on more than one copytext. However, the evidence available does not suggest that this was likely. For example, the tales which make up constant sections are found together in early manuscripts and this indicates that each section was treated as a unit in whatever copytext the scribe was using. If the tales had been circulating independently, one would not expect them to be gathered so regularly into constant sections. The only possible exception to this procedure is section 10, which occurs as two separate parts in Hg and whose tales are divided in Petworth. But section 10 contains a prose tale which needed separate lineation and so it is not surprising that a break in the manuscripts sometimes occurred at TMel, as is true of Hg. Nevertheless, the breaking up of the tales in section 10 in Petworth and the different *ordinatio* found in this section in some other manuscripts opens up the possibility that the tales in this section were only loosely joined together in the copytext and that they could be copied separately. Indeed, if the copytext was

Chaucer's draft this would not be unexpected, for we would naturally imagine that Chaucer wrote individual tales first and then linked them together in a sequence by providing links. Hence the original copytext might well have consisted of individual tales which were distinct physical units that had been joined together by some fastening. As section 10 is the largest one, it is possible that the fastening became loose so that the units were no longer joined together securely. On the other hand, it could be argued that each section was copied out for Chaucer as a complete unit; but this view seems difficult to justify. Why should he have parts of a poem on which he was still working written out as though they were self-sufficient units? The very fact that some parts of individual tales are missing altogether, such as the end of CkT, and others are missing in some manuscripts, such as the end of MeT, indicates that a solution along these lines is less probable. If the copytext was Chaucer's copy, it is likely to have been no more than a draft.

In the previous chapters I have shown that it is possible to follow a textual development from Hg through the other early manuscripts and to understand the reasons which led scribes or editors to make the changes they did. The similarity in the orders of the tales in the manuscripts and their clear interrelationship prove that there was a continuous approach to the poem which presupposes on the part of the scribes or editors a knowledge of what had gone before. From the editorial and textual point of view there is no need to posit pre-publication, particularly in its form of the circulation of tales independently. By the same token there is little need to posit a host of lost exemplars as is usually done, though naturally there may have been copies of the poem which have failed to survive. The extant manuscripts do present a picture of how the text developed from a single copytext. Some developments may be missing because manuscripts are now lost, but apart from the original copytext it is not necessary to posit lost manuscripts which were central to the textual hierarchy.

All the manuscripts of *The Canterbury Tales* extant date from after 1400, that is after Chaucer's death. It is natural to suppose from this fact that the development of the manuscript tradition in extant manuscripts is scribal: it reflects an attempt on the part of scribes and editors to impose some order on the fragments left by Chaucer at his death. This view has not always been accepted by previous scholars because they have decided that some passages in the poem are genuine even though they are not in the earliest manuscripts. It is not made clear how one can tell which passages are Chaucerian, but as a rule those which are regarded as of high literary merit are classified as Chaucerian no matter at what stage they appear in the manuscript tradition. This had led scholars to suggest that Chaucer revised individual tales by altering his draft either by cancelling passages or by adding extra lines in the margin. It is not usually made clear what the motive for these alterations was or why some scribes should have ignored them, apart that is from the assumption that scribes are inherently stupid and the author can do no wrong. On the other side, in this book I have tried to explain why certain changes in tales and their order were made and how scribes responded to the textual situation as it developed. I have worked on the basis that scribes and editors were in general intelligent people who were used to handling written material and who tried to find reasonable solutions to the problems they faced in the text. One cannot assume that scribes or editors made the changes or arrangements that Chaucer would have made, had he lived, though it remains conceivable that if there was a literary editor who took over Chaucer's draft manuscript he might have discussed with Chaucer before his death how the poem was going to develop.

It is accepted that Hg is the earliest extant manuscript, and the way in which it is put together indicates a first attempt at assembling the material in the poem. Its order has not found favour with modern critics, although it lies behind all subsequent orders. On the other hand, its text has been regarded as of the highest quality, and modern editors tend to rely on Hg as their base manuscript. This has created the curious situation that a manucript with a good text was not copied by later scribes even though those scribes followed its lead in the ordering of the tales. Any explanation of the manuscript tradition must account for this situation. The most satisfactory explanation is that later scribes did not use Hg, but used its exemplar whose parts were arranged in the order found in Hg and gradually modified to suit changing conditions. Hg was not used for the text, because attitudes towards the text changed. Clearly it was felt that 'improvements' should be introduced, and these to judge from El included metre, *rime riche*, parallelism and uniformity. Hence Hg's text may well have seemed somewhat outdated to subsequent scribes. It is possible to see some continuity in the changes in the text just as it is in the ordering of the tales, but in neither case is the continuity straightforward. It is rather as though the changes made by earlier scribes were known to later ones and they could choose which they would follow. So it seems possible that some changes were introduced onto the copytext itself. This would allow later scribes to follow the suggested changes or not, as they wished. Without this kind of explanation one has to assume a large number of vanished exemplars which were juggled with by the subsequent scribes. Quite apart from the inherent improbability of this hypothesis, it does not in fact clear up all the problems in the text. So one is forced to accept a complicated and implausible hypothesis which still leaves certain problems unanswered. The solution put forward here is much simpler and does not demand the existence of a large number of vanished manuscripts. It allows us to explain why a good manuscript was not employed by later scribes and yet why the solutions to tale order which it proposed were developed by those same scribes.

Manly and Rickert divided the manuscripts of *The Canterbury Tales* into four major groups with some left over in an anomalous category. Their attempt to organize the manuscripts into groups is only the last of several by various scholars. However, it is characteristic of all these attempted groupings that they are not watertight. Each group of manuscripts shares certain features with manuscripts in other groups, and one is always left with the uncomfortable feeling that if different criteria had been chosen as the basis for the groupings the manuscripts to be grouped together could well have been different. The Manly–Rickert group which is most coherent is their group *a*, but even in this case certain common features link manuscripts in this group with other manuscripts of the poem. It must be admitted that all the manuscript groupings proposed hitherto share this shortcoming. For example, a manuscript like Lansdowne which may be a copy of Corpus nevertheless contains extra material not in Corpus which is found in other early manuscripts. For a majority of the text it may be appropriate that Corpus and Lansdowne should be associated together in the Manly–Rickert group *c*, but if one were to take the extra passages in Lansdowne as being more significant for its textual affiliations one would have to put it in a different group from Corpus. It is clear that the web of relationships that exists among the manuscripts needs a different approach to the manuscript hierarchy than the one which has been used hitherto. This is why the hypothesis of a copytext, which itself was being modified, as the basis of many early manuscripts appears to be a more satisfactory solution to the textual problems of the poem. It provides a framework for the changes which were developing in the poem, even though those changes are not represented uniformly in all manuscripts. We may assume, therefore, that there was the basic copytext, which formed the Chaucerian draft copy. To that were added additional sheets of paper or vellum containing additional links and even additional tales. Sometimes the additional material contained extra lines or passages, as we may assume happened to the Adam stanza in MkT. On the copytext itself changes would also be indicated. Possible headings or titles, alternative readings, extra lines, and glosses may all have been added in the margins of the original copytext. This would mean that the copytext gradually came to be more difficult to read and also that it presented the scribes with a variety of readings and possibilities. Most would be able to distinguish what was original from what was suggested by later editors, but naturally many would be influenced by the improvements which had been suggested by their predecessors. In this way many of the basic features of the text would remain unchanged, but certain 'improvements' would tend increasingly to occur, though not necessarily in a regular manner.

There are other considerations which help to confirm that the early scribes used the same copytext, which was the author's draft. An important feature of the early manuscripts is the freedom with which the scribes approached the text of the poem. In part this may be because a tradition had grown up that *The Canterbury Tales* was a poem which needed polishing and ordering. Yet such a tradition could develop only in a relatively small circle of scribes in which each knew something of what the others were doing. In part the freedom may have developed because they were all using a copytext which was the author's original, but which was clearly incomplete. The additions to and corrections on it would encourage the scribes to adopt a rather freer hand than might otherwise have been the case. It may be admitted that this manner of handling the text could also occur if the tales had been circulated independently and had been collected by the scribes as they wrote their manuscripts. In this case, however, one would not have expected the tales which form constant sections to have regularly appeared in the same sequence or certain sections to have appeared regularly in the same order. On the other hand, this freedom is not what would have occurred if complete copies of the poem with a fixed text were available in manuscripts in which there was no conjunction of quire and section boundaries. In such cases the scribes might have made small adjustments and alterations, but they are hardly likely to have attempted the relocation of various sections and the adaptation of certain links to impose a different presentation on the poem. It is apparent that the copytext available to the early scribes encouraged a degree of experimentation in the order and contents of the poem; and that copytext is best understood to be the author's original draft.

The relationship among the manuscripts is such that it is not usually possible to say that an individual scribe used a copytext which he supplemented with a single manuscript. In the majority of cases the extra material which is found in a given manuscript cannot be identified with that found in a second one. The extra passages in most manuscripts have affiliations with a range of other manuscripts, as we have noted in the earlier chapters. This feature also points to a more complicated textual development than scholars have been willing to admit previously.

There are many textual features which can also best be explained on the hypothesis that the early scribes used the same copytext. The most intriguing is the misreading of *sterres* (1:2039) in KtT which is found in so many manuscripts. In Hg it appears as *sertres*, and other manuscripts have different readings. It has often been proposed that these misreadings come from a misplacement of an abbreviation for *er* so that scribes were confused as to what the correct reading was. Some tried to represent what was in the copytext and others interpreted it to make sense of the passage. The important point is that many of the early scribes were clearly responding to an identical stimulus, though the way in which they responded was different. The original copytext had a reading that was far from clear and the scribes made what they could of it; some, like that of Ha7334, managed to deduce what the right reading was. Since this ambiguous reading must have occurred in the original copytext, it is most sensible to assume that these scribes had access to that original. There is no need to assume intermediate exemplars in which this ambiguous reading was interpreted in diverse ways.

Similar instances occur in MeT. In Hg at 5:61-2 the scribe included only the first half-line of the couplet and left the rest blank. Hence his text reads here only 'And if thow take a wyf'. At 5:986 Hg has a blank so that only the first line of the couplet is included in his text: 'Folwynge his wyf, the queene Proserpyne'. Since the Hg scribe is conscientious, it is reasonable to assume that his copytext also omitted these lines or else had some writing which was quite illegible. If we assume that the copytext was the author's draft, the latter possibility is more likely, since it would be grotesque to assume that Chaucer composed couplets by thinking of the first half-line and then waiting for further inspiration to complete the couplet. There was evidently an indication in the copytext that the couplets were incomplete for the scribe of Hg left gaps to complete them; an illegible copytext is a likely solution. It is unlikely that he would have omitted lines in the copytext in this way without some stimulus from his copytext; the gaps suggest that he anticipated that something would be provided to fill them in. This indeed did happen, but only at a considerably later stage. The lines introduced to fill these gaps in Hg are in a different hand. Other manuscripts do not, however, have the same readings at these two places in MeT. Different scribes included other possible readings in their manuscripts, and some simply omitted the first couplet altogether. There are as many as eight different solutions to the problem of filling these gaps which are found in Hg and which were presumably in the copytext. This number reveals that many scribes had access to a copytext which had a text identical with that found at first in Hg—and there seems no reason to doubt that it was the same copytext as the one used by the scribe of Hg, for Hg itself was not used as copytext by these other scribes. If the scribes had had access to a copy which had completed or omitted these couplets, they would not have been aware that there was any problem with them and they would simply have copied whatever was in their exemplar. They did not do so and we cannot escape the conclusion that Hg's copytext was also used as a copytext by a variety of other scribes. It is possible that words to fill these gaps were subsequently added to the copytext by some scribes or editors, but this is hardly likely to have occurred immediately. It is also possible, as with *sterres* discussed earlier, that the solutions which we now find in the manuscripts were first incorporated in lost manuscripts; but unless there is some overwhelming need to posit such lost manuscripts, this is a view which has little to commend it as against the hypothesis that it was the scribes themselves of the extant manuscripts who had direct access to the copytext and completed the lines themselves.

Most textual developments are best explained by the theory of a changing copytext, as we have noted during the course of the earlier chapters. As an example consider the addition of the Adam stanza in MkT. Previous scholars have found it difficult to account for this stanza, though it has been suggested it was added in the margin of his draft copy by Chaucer. This view, though possible, does not offer any explanation for its absence in some manuscripts or its potential presence in others. The stanza is not found in Hg and so was not presumably in the copytext when that manuscript was copied. In Corpus, which may be the next oldest manuscript, a space is left for the Adam stanza and its title is given, but the stanza itself is not included. It is possible to imagine that it had been decided to include a stanza on Adam, which was under composition but which was not given to the scribe of Corpus in time. If this is so, it would mean that an indication that there was to be an Adam stanza was included in the copytext and the stanza would have been written on a separate sheet of paper to be included with the copytext itself. It is not surprising that this extra piece of paper did not always get sent with the copytext so that some scribes failed to include the stanza in their manuscripts even though they made allowance for it. Similarly some who knew that there should be an Adam stanza, because there was a note to that effect on the copytext, composed their own stanza to complete the gap which would otherwise be left in their manuscript. This explanation is straightforward and therefore seems much more acceptable than others which have been offered. It does, however, depend upon the existence of a single copytext which was undergoing transformation through editorial intervention.

Another feature of the existing manuscripts is the variety they exhibit in the type of headings they employ and in the variety of glosses. Headings and rubrics differ in wording from one manuscript to the next, and they also differ in language, for they can occur in English, French or Latin. Similarly the place at which headings occur and the provision of sub-headings differ considerably. This diversity indicates that no tradition had developed in the copytexts available as to what headings should be used or where they should be placed. Although a certain amount of variety was inevitable in manuscripts because scribes chose to arrange texts with a different *ordinatio*, the wide limits of this variety in the manuscripts of *The Canterbury Tales* shows that there was no established textual tradition to which the scribes were adhering. It is a situation which is most likely to have developed as a result of their using as copytext a draft copy of the poem rather than a prepared manuscript. The same applies to the glossing which is found in the manuscripts. Like the order of the tales this glossing exhibits both diversity and uniformity, for some glosses frequently recur whereas others are particular to one or two manuscripts.

Another interesting feature of the text concerns the end of CkT. Scribes treated this tale very differently from the way in which they treated the incomplete SqT. Scribes did not generally expect a conclusion to SqT, which they accepted was incomplete. With CkT they behaved differently, and often a gap after the tale was included in manuscripts to allow for a continuation or addition. In some manuscripts Gamelyn was included as part of CkT. The reaction of most modern scholars to this situation has been to indicate that Chaucer did not complete CkT. In the nature of things there is no evidence to support this view, but there are indications that it may not be the correct answer. As SqT and CkT are both considered to be unfinished texts by many scholars, it is natural to assume that the scribes would have treated them in the same way. This did not happen, and it suggests that there was something in the copytext which stimulated them to treat the two texts as different. If SqT finished in the middle of a page it would naturally appear unfinished to the scribes. But if CkT finished at the bottom of a page, it might well have seemed to the scribes that the tale had been finished and its end was now missing. This would account for their leaving a gap at the end of CkT, since they might assume that the end would turn up. There is no need to assume that Chaucer failed to complete CkT. In Hg SqT was initially a tale without links which can readily be understood to be a tale which was in process of composition. CkT, on the other hand, is a tale which is linked with other tales in a constant section. It is bizarre to imagine that Chaucer started on a tale like this without knowing what its conclusion was to be or that he would have included it in a section before it was complete. These factors indicate that CkT was completed and that its conclusion is missing because of the state of the copytext. Clearly this conclusion argues against prior publication. It is unlikely that Chaucer would have allowed an unfinished tale to circulate. If CkT was finished and if pre-publication had taken place, it is improbable that its conclusion would have disappeared so completely. The incomplete CkT argues for the existence of a draft which was in a somewhat untidy state, for some of the final leaves of a constant section were missing and were never discovered. By the same token it is likely that the early scribes had access to this draft for many of them responded to the incompleteness of the tale in a similar way.

Finally it must be remembered that it is generally accepted that Chaucer was still working on his poem when he died and that he therefore left it in an unfinished state. This view has been challenged recently by Benson, who has proposed that Chaucer issued the poem in an incomplete state.[1] He seeks to justify his argument by relying on the evidence of Rt, which he claims would only be added to the poem when it was released for publication. Chaucer, therefore, issued the poem as complete in its incompleteness. The theory that Chaucer actually issued the poem as a complete unit, even though it was apparently unfinished, seems totally unfounded. Why would a poet issue a tale like SqT for publication when it was not even a self-sufficient unit? One might reasonably assume that a poet who had spent many years writing a poem would tidy up these incomplete tales in some way before issuing them to the public. Equally, one might assume that rubrics, headings and glosses would have been put into some order before the text was issued. Furthermore, the evidence of Rt hardly supports the theory advocated by Benson. It is not certain that Rt is by Chaucer; its genuineness is not universally accepted. Because of missing final leaves it is not possible to tell whether it was found in Hg, the earliest extant manuscript. The same problem exists with regard to Corpus, which may be the second oldest extant manuscript. What may be the two earliest manuscripts lack Rt through loss of leaves, and it is possible that they never in fact contained it. Since additions were made to the poem at an early stage in its textual development, it is quite possible to suggest that Rt was one of those additions which were included to give the poem a more finished appearance. Even if we accept that it is genuine, its inclusion need not necessarily signal that the poem was finished in the poet's eyes. The poem was not written in the sequence in which the tales were to appear and so a conclusion might well have been written to the poem long before other parts were begun. Benson himself seems to accept this possibility since he understands there to be two Chaucerian orders, one of which is represented by El though the other is not represented completely by any manuscript.

[1] Benson 1981.

Since the second authorial order contains passages which do not occur in the first, it follows that even in Benson's own theory of the order of the poem the inclusion of Rt did not prevent the author from adding pieces to his poem after the conclusion was written.

The matter is of some interest since it could affect our decision as to whether Chaucer was possessed of a copy of his poem when he died. If he had finished with the poem and was issuing texts of it, it could mean that he himself no longer had a copy in his possession, since the publication of the work would be surely undertaken by others. On the other hand, if he was still in the course of writing the poem, then it is inevitable that he would have a copy in his possession. This latter view was the regular one until Benson proposed his alternative. There does not, however, seem sufficient evidence to support his case and it may be accepted that the poem was in the course of composition when Chaucer died. This would mean that he had the draft in his possession. Naturally, if he did have the draft in his possession, this would not have prevented him from issuing individual tales separately; but we have already indicated that this is unlikely. Indeed, the existence of a draft in Chaucer's possession when he died is a crucial fact since it is bound to influence our attitude towards the textual tradition. It makes the hypothesis of prior publication unnecessary. Why should scribes who knew that a complete set of tales existed among Chaucer's papers go to the trouble of assembling individual tales from a variety of readers? They might have done so if there was some element of competition in the production of the manuscripts, but the evidence from palaeography and the textual tradition suggests that manuscripts were produced co-operatively rather than competitively.

Although some of the points outlined earlier in this chapter may not be very strong in themselves, together they provide good evidence of the following general picture. Chaucer had been composing his poem for some time. He did so by writing individual tales which were gradually amalgamated with other tales through the provision of links. When this happened the two tales may have been physically joined together with some fastening, though that was probably not always very secure. The poem existed only in draft form, which was untidy, and which over the course of time came to lack certain parts which had been written such as the end of CkT. He may have read individual tales in public and he may have discussed the poem with his friends, but the only written copy was in his possession. When he died a friend or some friends decided to publish the poem. To do this they collected the various sections of the draft from Chaucer's house and put them into some order. In the course of this exercise they realized that some necessary linking passages were missing and that their first attempt at organizing the tales had certain flaws. They were therefore obliged to provide links to give the poem a veneer of completeness, and they also found it necessary to experiment with the order of some sections, although the bulk of the poem remained in the order which was first devised for it after Chaucer's death.

If the picture presented in the previous paragraph may be accepted as broadly true, it is necessary to consider the nature of the copytext used by the scribes. Perhaps the most important point is that it was a draft; it was not a finished copy which was clean and which could have been broken down into scribal stints so that the poem could be copied simultaneously by several scribes. There are mistakes in the draft which one could expect Chaucer to have corrected in any revision he made. For example, in MkT there is a line 'Bothe est and west, north and septemtrioun' (10:2371) which is acknowledged by all editors to be wrong for there are two words for north and none for south. The line is always emended to 'Bothe est and west, south and septemtrioun'. This mistake is found in all manuscripts and must have appeared in the copytext. If we assume that editors are right in identifying a mistake here, that mistake is attributable to Chaucer's draft which was used as copytext by the scribes. Other errors would also be present in the copytext, though few are kept by all scribes. As a draft the copytext may sometimes have been hurriedly written so that some things were not clear to the scribes. The best example of this is the word *sterres* in KtT which I have commented on earlier in this chapter. It was written in such a way that scribes did not know what the word was, even though as a word it is one that occurs commonly enough in Chaucer and other Middle English texts. The miswriting, if one may call it that, was such as to prevent most scribes from reaching what seems to us the obvious solution to the problem.

Another feature of the copytext as draft is that bits of the poem had gone missing over the time that the poem was in the course of preparation. This is hardly surprising if one thinks that the poem may have been at least twenty years in production and was composed in a haphazard way in that the poem did not commence at the start and gradually work its way through in the correct order. The tales and links may have been written on disparate pieces of paper or vellum so that the whole consisted of a rather untidy mass. As one tale was joined to another by the provision of a link from the pilgrimage frame, they may have been bundled together in some way. It is hardly surprising that occasionally sheets at the end of these bundles became detached and so were lost. The incompleteness of CkT is best explained as the result of missing pages in this way rather than as a tale which was never completed by the author. But quite apart from such longer pieces as the end of CkT which were missing, several shorter ones were also not available to the scribes. These amount to no more than the odd line or phrase, though in FrT there is a succession of lines which lack their concluding words. It would appear as though the copytext had suffered some damage which made these parts illegible. Either the paper could have been torn so that the words were lost or else ink or some other substance could have been spilt on the pages which made some words illegible. It is clear that the scribes knew something was missing, though in many cases that could easily have been overlooked. For in prose tales like TMel or in poetry when a complete line was missing, it would have been easy for a scribe not to be aware of this fact unless there was something in the copytext to alert him to it. That something is likely to have been a blot or a gap in the copytext. Naturally different causes may be responsible for missing pieces in different places. What seems unquestionable is the rough and unsatisfactory nature of the copytext.

The omissions which I have described so far were accidental, but others may have been deliberate. It is possible that Chaucer composed links which were free-standing and were not related to tales both before and after. Thus PsP was attached to PsT which follows, but it may not have been attached to any preceding tale. If this were so it would mean that its opening line would have contained a blank since it refers to the previous teller. Otherwise one would have to assume that Chaucer inserted the name of a teller even though he had not decided when he wrote PsP whose tale would precede it. Certainly we must allow for the possibility that the method of composition by which tales were composed out of sequence meant that occasionally gaps were left for the names of tellers who would be decided upon as tales were linked together.

Because it is a draft it is quite possible to imagine that the copytext contained authorial corrections and revisions on it, though this theory is extremely difficult to prove. It has been assumed by many scholars that there was no thoroughgoing revision of the text by Chaucer since the poem was incomplete. It is argued that he is unlikely to have commenced any serious revision before he finished the poem as a whole. There is something to be said for this view, but it would not prevent running corrections and other minor improvements being inserted in the draft. Since we cannot know how Chaucer worked, we cannot really decide whether he embarked on revisions of the completed parts of the poem. Its nature as a draft would certainly allow for the possibility of authorial revision and it would also encourage editors and scribes to introduce alterations or alternatives on the copytext. Once that happened, it might have been difficult to decide whether any corrections were authorial or not – and we are in the same position. Consequently, although we can allow the possibility that authorial corrections were made on the draft, the impossibility of deciding which might have been authorial rather than scribal means that we cannot accept changes in later manuscripts to the text as preserved in Hg as authorial. Hg is a reliable text and its scribe was clearly conscientious; it is difficult to see why he would have ignored what were clearly authorial changes, deletions or additions in the copytext.

As a draft the copytext would have no rubrics at the beginning and end of each tale, and there would naturally have been no running heads. The provision of such rubrics and running heads is part of the presentation of a text which in the Middle Ages was the responsibility of the scribe and is today executed by a sub-editor or even the printer. It is possible that in the copytext there was a word like *narrat* in the margin at the beginning of each tale, and the word *explicit* at the end of each tale. The introductory links from the pilgrimage frame had no rubrics. All this seems clear enough from the diversity of languages in which the rubrics appear in different manuscripts and also from the uncertainty as to where the headings should be placed. It is clear that scribes did not know whether to call the linking sequences from the pilgrimage frame prologues or something else, for on some occasions there was more than one such sequence. This uncertainty must reflect the absence of any heading in the copytext. Each scribe as part of the presentation of the text in his manuscript decided what language to use for the rubrics and headings, where to place them, and what to include within them. They therefore imposed on the poem a more fragmented text divided into parts by providing signposts for the readers. It is also fairly certain that the copytext did not break down the individual tales into parts or books, such as we now find commonly in modern editions. This sub-division of the tales is also a part of the scribal presentation of the text. It remains possible that there were paragraph marks or larger capitals which gave the scribes their lead in this sub-division, but the diversity of scribal reactions makes this only a distant possibility. The way in which the scribes responded to the text may be compared with the approach adopted by William Caxton to the presentation of Malory's *Le Morte Darthur*. He divided that text into books and chapters, as he informs us in his introduction, and he consequently imposed a unity of textual presentation on the whole work which may not have been characteristic of it in its original form.

There is finally the question of whether the copytext had any glosses. In general one would assume this to be unlikely as the copytext was a draft, for glossing, like the rubrics, is part of the final presentation of a text. The glosses that are found in the manuscripts occur irregularly and may be divided into three types. The first includes the glosses which refer to the sources or possible sources of the tales. These can either be extensive as is the case of the long Latin quotations found in MLT or limited to a single word or phrase such as the gloss *qi la* to the expression 'Who ther' in ShT. The latter have more the nature of translations, though they appear to be taken from the sources available to Chaucer. These glosses are usually in Latin, but occasionally in French. The second type consists of guides to the reader and have almost the nature of sub-headings. Passages in which the author is deemed to be making a comment may be signified by *Auctor*, and other passages which struck a responsive chord may be signified by *Nota bene* or some-thing similar. The third group consists of short explanatory comments or translations. Examples of *rime riche* may be explicated by the provision of Latin glosses to the two homonyms. Hence 'here' may have a gloss *hic* in one line and *audire* in the next. The first person pronoun may be explicated by the addition of *Chaucer* in the margin; and a reference to 'my lord' in NPT (10:3417) is explained in some manuscripts as a reference to the Archbishop of Canterbury. Of these groups it is not difficult to decide that the last two are additions made by scribes. Yet as they are repeated in various manuscripts which are not otherwise closely affiliated, it is likely that some glosses were added by an editor in the copytext itself. These glosses could then be picked up by the scribes as they wished. The glosses of the first group may be Chaucerian, though the majority of them are likely to be scribal. Sometimes the glosses are not so much sources as quotations from texts which illuminate the tale. Others seem definitely to come from the sources which Chaucer used. Many of the longer quotations were added by some scribes, and these may well have been incor-porated by an editor on the copytext itself. What is significant about them is that the editor who included the glosses had access to the texts which Chaucer used, and this supports the view that the copytext was Chaucer's draft. For the person who was putting Chaucer's papers in order for publication would also have access to the books in Chaucer's library and would be able to draw on them to provide marginal glosses to the tales. These glosses help to give the tales a more learned and rhetorical look as well as providing the text with a finished appearance.

10

The Evidence of Other Chaucerian Texts

In the last chapter I suggested that the textual tradition of *The Canterbury Tales* indicated that many of the early manuscripts were copied from the same copytext, which was Chaucer's own draft that was gradually subjected to editorial changes and improvements. This hypothesis is supported in part by the general scholarly acceptance that this poem was under composition at the time of Chaucer's death, since that fact gives us some understanding as to why the poem was only in draft and why the draft was in a somewhat unsatisfactory state. It may be helpful to consider how far *The Canterbury Tales* differs from the other works of Chaucer in this respect, though naturally it is not possible to consider the textual traditions of the other works in any detail.

Chaucer is often described as a 'court poet'. Precisely what is meant by this is not clear, and it is a description which has been subjected to some criticism lately because it is uncertain what a court culture in England at the end of the fourteenth century was.[1] Chaucer as a young man was attached to the household of the Countess of Ulster; he is later described as a *dilectus valetus* in the accounts of Edward III; he received payments from John Duke of Gaunt and from the Royal Treasury; and he was employed in certain official positions which implies service to the crown.[2] In many of these things he was little different from many other young men of the time, who were attached in some way to the court through some kind of service or occupation. These features would not in themselves indicate that Chaucer was a courtier or even known personally to the King or John of Gaunt. However, it is accepted also that Chaucer wrote his *Book of the Duchess* as a consolation to John of Gaunt for the death of his first wife Blanche, and Chaucer's wife became a lady-in-waiting to Gaunt's second wife. Although it was possible to write a poem for a man one had never met, just as Caxton was to dedicate his printed volumes to members of the nobility he had never met, the evidence

[1]Scattergood and Sherborne 1983.
[2]See Crow and Olsen 1966 *passim*.

available does suggest that Chaucer did have some relationship with Gaunt and his household. It is partly for reasons like this and partly because of the courtly nature of his poetry that many scholars have thought of Chaucer as a court poet.

If he were a court poet one might expect some indication in the extant manuscripts of this position, for one might expect to find manuscripts from Chaucer's lifetime which were presented to members of the court and which were elegant in their production. This is not what one finds. Although there are some de luxe manuscripts, these were almost certainly produced after Chaucer's death and may have been written to present to influential people on a purely speculative or commercial basis in order to make Chaucer's works more familiar among a certain type of person. Although the ownership of several early manuscripts can be associated with members of the aristocracy or gentry in the fifteenth century, there is no evidence to link any manuscript with royal or aristocratic ownership in the fourteenth century. In part this is because almost no extant manuscripts of Chaucer's works were written in the fourteenth century. Those which may perhaps have been written in that century are those of some of his prose works. The Peterhouse manuscript of *The Equatorie of the Planetis* was probably written *c.*1392 and may even be in Chaucer's hand. It was certainly written in Chaucer's lifetime and preserves a spelling system which has been claimed as representing Chaucer's own system more closely than any other extant manuscript.[3] At least one of the manuscripts of Chaucer's *Boece*, Cambridge University Library MS Ii.1.38, dates from before 1400. It is possible to say, therefore, of these two works that they existed in a form that was publishable, if not actually published, before Chaucer's death.

If one excludes the lyrics for the moment, no Chaucerian poem survives in a manuscript which can be dated before Chaucer's death. This is very surprising; it is only the prose texts, which are the least courtly of his output, that can be shown to have appeared in his life-time in a written form. Yet if the *Book of the Duchess* was written as a consolation for John of Gaunt, one would expect some evidence of presentation to John of Gaunt and perhaps to other interested people. There is no evidence that any presentation copies existed, though naturally they could have all been lost, and so one is forced to assume that any presentation of the poem which took place happened orally rather than in any written form. This poem survives in only three manuscripts, Fairfax 16, Bodley 638 and Tanner 346, all in the Bodleian Library. Although these manuscripts cannot be dated with certainty and textual priority established among them, it may not be unreasonable to say that the

[3]Samuels 1983b.

first extant written version of the poem dates from *c*.1440, that is approximately seventy years after the poem was composed. In addition all three manuscripts contain textual imperfections, in particular a passage of some lines is missing after line 30. As it happens the first printed edition of the poem, that by Thynne in 1532, contains a passage which fills this lacuna and amounts in that version to 66 lines. Thynne's edition also contains additional lines to fill the other much smaller lacunae in the manuscripts. It has usually been assumed that Thynne's text includes the genuine Chaucerian parts of the poem which are missing in the manuscripts, though this assumption has been called into question recently.[4] Thynne and other early printers were quite prepared to complete gaps in the poems they printed, and this is what may have happened in the *Book of the Duchess*. What is undeniable and what remains a fact of some importance is that the manuscripts which are extant from the fifteenth century contain a text with important lacunae; and one must therefore assume that these lacunae occurred in the copytext or copytexts available to the scribes. It is consequently possible that these lacunae go back to the Chaucerian archetype which ultimately lies behind these manuscripts. The position with regard to this poem may be equated with that for *The Canterbury Tales*, for as we saw in the last chapter the Chaucerian copy of the latter existed in an unsatisfactory state for parts of it were lost. The reasons for this similarity are not all the same. *The Canterbury Tales* is an unfinished poem which was being written over a lengthy period of time; there is no reason to believe that it ever got beyond the draft stage. *The Book of the Duchess*, on the other hand, is a relatively short poem; it was presumably completed by the author; and it could easily have been published in some form in his lifetime. Nevertheless, if the manuscript copies go back to a version which was in his possession, then that copy suffered the same sort of depredation which the copytext of *The Canterbury Tales* experienced. In other words it is probable that Chaucer did not look after his papers with the care we might have expected, and in the confusion in which they were preserved some bits of them got lost.

Another difference between the short poems and *The Canterbury Tales* is that the latter was issued in many manuscripts shortly after his death, whereas the former appeared rather later in the fifteenth century. This is a question we shall need to look at in a moment. Chaucer's other major poem, *Troilus and Criseyde*, is like *The Canterbury Tales* in that it too was issued in many manuscripts shortly after the poet's death. It resembles the shorter poems in that it had apparently been completed many years before

[4]Blake 1981b.

Chaucer died and could therefore have been published in his lifetime. Indeed, *Troilus* is referred to in the short poem addressed to *Adam scriveyn*. If this poem is Chaucer's, and it has been accepted as his by most scholars, it would imply that *Troilus* had been professionally copied or that it was well enough known to be referred to in another poem; and this would in turn lead one to suppose that the poem had been published in Chaucer's lifetime. That the poem was known of is also indicated by a reference to it in Usk's *Testament of Love*, though that reference (book 3 chapter 4) does not necessarily imply a very close acquaintance with the poem. Nevertheless, since Usk was executed in 1388, knowledge of the poem's existence must have been available to Chaucer's friends and admirers by then. *Troilus* would therefore seem to occupy a position midway between the minor poems and *The Canterbury Tales*. It is like the former in being completed during Chaucer's life-time; and it is like the latter in being issued in many manuscript copies shortly after Chaucer's death.

The position of *Troilus* is that it was apparently finished in Chaucer's lifetime, but that no manuscript of it is extant from before 1400. Although its existence was clearly known to some people such as Usk, there is no evidence that it was formally published in a written form by the author. The manuscripts have important textual differences, and *Troilus* resembles *The Canterbury Tales* in that modern editions of it do not reflect the poem as it exists in any single manuscript, for they conflate several different manuscripts. Earlier in the century an attempt was made to arrange the manuscripts into three groups which contained important textual differences. Some manuscripts contain important omissions and others have rearranged the order of some of the stanzas. Early scholars were uncertain whether to interpret these differences as authorial or scribal.[5] In the former case they were understood to represent different authorial versions, each of which was published as it became available; in the latter the differences were attributed to the scribes who sought to present the poem in a particular way. Some scribal interference seems certain since the three categories are not separate, for many manuscripts represent intermediate positions between the three types. More recently Barry Windeatt has presented a slightly different solution, which he has called the *in-eching* technique. This view sees the differences in the manuscripts as the result of various authorial drafts which were not intended for publication in that form. The drafts represent the way in which Chaucer worked, first using his source, the *Filostrato*, and then adding to it to fill the matter out in

---

[5]See, for example, Root 1916 and Brusendorff 1925.
[6]Windeatt 1979a.

the way in which he wanted to present it. The composition of the poem would thus consist of several different layers, the first of which would be his handling of the *Filostrato* and the later ones his *in-eching* of that basic text to give the resulting poem the tone and emphasis he wished. It would follow from this that, although the layers of the poem's composition can be unravelled through modern scholarship, the early layers were never meant to exist as complete entities for they represent stages towards a final goal that was always envisaged but not immediately executed.

The authenticity of some of these extra parts is argued on literary grounds, for it is suggested that the poem would be incomplete without them and so Chaucer can never have imagined the poem to exist without them. This is naturally a somewhat delicate argument, for it is never really possible to prove authorial intent. What we today consider aesthetically satisfactory and complete may not reflect the views of earlier generations. It is also difficult to understand why the scribes should have been so foolish as to copy out an incomplete poem or to fail to carry out the author's intentions. This shortcoming may be explained through the nature of the exemplar which they copied from. This must have been the author's draft which would have been in a potentially muddled state, if it contained various layers of composition within it. Many of the layers may have occupied separate sheets or marginal instructions which may have been temporarily mislaid or simply ignored. An important element in Dr Windeatt's conclusions is that the author's draft was available to many scribes in the early fifteenth century – a feature which would make it most improbable that the poem had been copied for publication in the previous one.

The existence of a single main source for *Troilus* lends some plausibility to Dr Windeatt's hypothesis, though it fails to explain why no manuscript represents Chaucer's final version which presumably ought to have been recoverable from his draft. *Troilus* differs from *The Canterbury Tales* in that the latter has no single source and so any suggestion of layers of composition would have to work from a different starting point. The theory of *Troilus's* genesis does have many points of similarity with the views put forward about *The Canterbury Tales* in this volume. Neither poem was published in the author's lifetime. Each was published from the author's draft after his death and that draft was clearly in an unsatisfactory state. It was not easy for whoever was responsible for publishing the works to deduce what was the best form for each poem, and several different attempts were made to come to terms with the inconsistencies and irregularities of the draft. It seems likely that the same person or persons were responsible for the publication of both works in the first few years of the fifteenth century. There is, however, one important difference between *Troilus* and *The Canterbury Tales*, for with the former there is no one manuscript which is unequivocally earlier than the others and which might be used as a starting point for the development of the text in this layering process. The position occupied by Hg in *The Canterbury Tales* is filled by no single manuscript of *Troilus*. This may mean that immediately after Chaucer's death the person or persons responsible for the copying of his works started with *The Canterbury Tales*. With that experience he or they were able to experiment with *Troilus* when its turn came for copying.

Naturally much of this is speculation, but it is important to note that there are so many points of similarity in the state of the texts of these two poems. Neither was copied in Chaucer's lifetime and each was copied after his death from his drafts. In each case the state of the drafts was such that the poems came to exist in different forms. In one the draft was incomplete and because it contained fragments from different parts of the poem it asked to be presented in a more complete manner. In the other the draft contained layers of different levels of composition, which opened up the possibility of different editorial response. Each draft encouraged the editor or editors to experiment with the manner of presentation, though naturally the form of each poem was such that the experiments took different forms in each case.

If it was possible to show that *Troilus* had been published in Chaucer's lifetime, one might argue that *The Canterbury Tales* had not been published because it was unfinished. But the example of *Troilus*, to say nothing of the *Book of the Duchess* mentioned earlier, indicates that Chaucer may have published no verse in manuscript form in his own lifetime. He may have recited his poems or even had them recited professionally; but there is no indication that people had access to written copies before 1400. This situation contrasts very sharply with the manuscript traditions of *Confessio Amantis* and *Piers Plowman*. John Gower took an active interest in the publication of his work and he appears to have supervised the copying of some of the early manuscripts. The publication of authorized versions of his poem was part of Gower's overall plan; he did not leave his poem to the whim of later editors or scribes. Langland's attitude to his poem is more difficult to establish, though early manuscripts which probably date from his own lifetime are extant. It is possible to trace at least three different versions of *Piers Plowman*, and it is usually accepted that each version was published when it was completed. The versions arise from three different authorial states of the poem and not from author's drafts that were not meant to be published. In both these cases it is more reasonable to suppose that the poem's popularity arose through the written versions rather than through oral performance. But with Chaucer there is no evidence, as we have seen, that the poems were published in written form in his lifetime. But there was a tremendous surge in publication immediately after his death. This could mean that *Troilus* and *The Canterbury Tales* were known about so that there was a considerable demand for written versions when Chaucer's death made that possible.

With the shorter poems there was a greater delay before they were published. The earliest manuscript of the *Parliament of Fowls* and the *Legend of Good Women* is probably Gg 4.27, and both *House of Fame* and *Book of the Duchess* probably first make their appearance in manuscript form in Fairfax 16. Although Gg 4.27 may be as early as 1420, it is probably a little later than that. It contains a copy of *The Canterbury Tales*, as we have seen, and the scribe clearly had access to the draft available in London for in *The Canterbury Tales* its text is linked with El and Dd 4.24. The scribes of Gg 4.27 were from East Anglia, though the manuscript itself may have been written in London. Whoever was responsible for it had access to many of the poems which must have been available only in Chaucerian draft. The scribes had close links with the people producing Chaucerian texts in London, and the fact that Gg 4.27 contains so many different poems by Chaucer indicates that the London editors, if I may call them that, had access to a variety of Chaucerian works even though they apparently started by producing only *Troilus* and *The Canterbury Tales*. Fairfax 16 dates from about the middle of the fifteenth century and was written in London. It is permissible to assume that it came from the same kind of editorial environment which produced *The Canterbury Tales* and *Troilus* earlier in the century. It is almost as though the two major poems were produced first and only when they were well established were the shorter poems issued.

The interesting thing about these four shorter poems is that they each have textual problems. The *Legend of Good Women* and *House of Fame* are incomplete, and the former exists in two versions for Gg 4.27 contains a prologue which has clearly been revised. The *Book of the Duchess* contains omissions which were referred to earlier, and the *Parliament of Fowls* has a roundel (680-92) at the end which is preserved in its completest form only in Gg 4.27, though there it is written in a different and later fifteenth-century hand. It is generally argued that Chaucer never completed either the *Legend of Good Women* or *House of Fame*, though the only justification for this assumption is that the end of both poems is missing. However, there are suggestions elsewhere that the poems were complete and it could easily be that their endings were lost in the course of textual transmission. Since the earliest extant version in each case dates from at least fifty years after the date of the poem's composition, the loss of the endings would not be surprising. This is all the more so when we consider the state of Chaucer's other poems. Since the drafts of both *The Canterbury Tales* and *Troilus* were in an unclear state, there is no reason to doubt that the same was true of these shorter poems. If the end of CkT was written and subsequently lost, as has been argued earlier in this book, then the same could have happened to these shorter poems. A similar state of affairs probably prevailed with the *Book of the Duchess* and *Parliament of Fowls*. The passages missing in the former cannot be attributed to an incomplete text by Chaucer; they must have arisen through the state of the copytext. Whether the roundel in *Parliament of Fowls* is Chaucer's is uncertain, though one may accept that the text seems to demand something like it at that stage. It reminds one of the omission in some manuscripts of *Troilus* of passages which Windeatt suggests were the result of *in-eching* for they are not found in all manuscripts.

It is usually suggested that the variant prologue to the *Legend of Good Women* in Gg 4.27 is Chaucerian and represents his revised version which appears only in this manuscript. That is possible, though there is no reason for not considering the alternative view that it is a revision made by an editor or the scribe for Gg 4.27. The early date of Gg 4.27 as compared with the other manuscripts in which this poem survives could mean that the references to the court in the prologue were still considered sufficiently relevant to merit adaptation to different political circumstances. Later in the fifteenth century the reign of Richard II would have faded sufficiently for a revision of the prologue at that stage to be unnecessary. If, however, the two prologues are genuine, one might assume that they were both available in draft form and that one scribe copied the revised version while all the others copied the original. It would once more indicate that the state of the draft was such that Chaucer's intentions could not be interpreted unequivocally.

From what has been written in this and the previous chapters certain general conclusions can be suggested. No Chaucerian poem was published in manuscript form in his own lifetime. When the poems were copied, they were at first copied from Chaucer's own drafts. The state of these drafts was such that the copying of the poems caused the scribes problems either because the precise arrangement of an individual poem was uncertain or because sections of it were missing. Because the manuscripts were copied from Chaucer's drafts, there was probably in existence in the early fifteenth century some person or persons who had control of those drafts and who acted in an editorial capacity in issuing the finished poems.

11

Conclusion

One of the important considerations in the textual tradition of *The Canterbury Tales* has been whether Chaucer published any part of the poem during his own lifetime. As we saw in an earlier chapter, the general view used to be that he did not. However, the Manly–Rickert edition claimed that individual tales were circulated by Chaucer and more recently Larry Benson has suggested that not only had Chaucer finished with the poem even though it was apparently incomplete, but also he had arranged and issued it in two versions in his lifetime. Both these views are related to the position of El and to the assumed excellence of its text and order. As most editions have been based on the order and contents of El, there has been an assumption that El represents Chaucer's final position on the poem. To that extent the Manly–Rickert edition and Benson are simply trying to find means to justify what is found in El. The effect has been to prevent the evidence of the manuscripts being organized in a coherent textual tradition, for the manuscripts have not been allowed to speak for themselves. The assumption that what is in El is genuine has dictated the way in which many textual scholars have tried to recreate the textual tradition. Unless we are prepared to approach the evidence of the manuscripts without prior assumptions, we will never be able to make sense of the textual tradition. Despite the editions it has been widely accepted that El is a late and an edited manuscript with a text which has many imperfections. It has recently been shown that it may have been written as much as ten years after Hg. It remains for scholars to accept that El's order and contents may be as edited as its text for progress to be made.

It is naturally possible for a later manuscript to contain the best text, but that is something that can be decided only after the manuscript and textual tradition has been sorted out. The questions of prior publication and the authorial completeness of the text remain important factors to take into account. Benson's view that Chaucer had finished with the poem, though it is apparently incomplete, runs counter to the accepted scholarly position and is supported simply by his interpretation of Rt. In his opinion the inclusion of Rt indicates that Chaucer had finished with the poem. However, the status of Rt is dubious. It is not found in Hg or Corpus, perhaps the two earliest manuscripts, because they lack their final folios. It occurs for the first time probably in Ha7334, but that is an edited manuscript which contains material which is probably not authorial. Its inclusion in Ha7334 cannot therefore guarantee its genuineness. It is dangerous to base textual arguments on a part of the text of such dubious authenticity. Furthermore, one may question whether Rt does indeed imply that Chaucer had finished with the poem. Although the author retracts his secular works, it need not imply he was going to write nothing else. Finally, the poem was not written in the order in which it is now usually read, and if genuine Rt might well have been written before some tales which are included in *The Canterbury Tales*. Benson himself assumes that there are two Chaucerian orders, both of which include Rt. So even Benson does not accept that the inclusion of Rt prevented Chaucer from tinkering further with his poem. We may accept that there is no evidence that Chaucer had finished with the poem. Indeed the incompleteness of SqT and the lack of many links would argue strongly against this presumption.

Whether Chaucer circulated individual tales in manuscript during his lifetime is another matter, though no such manuscripts have survived. Since so many manuscripts are extant from the early years of the fifteenth century, it would be surprising for no pre-1400 manuscripts to have survived if indeed Chaucer did publish any tales in his own lifetime, particularly as one might assume that such copies would be reasonably numerous. In fact the theory of prior publication was proposed to account for features of the textual tradition which the Manly–Rickert edition posited. If those features are eliminated from the textual tradition, the need for prior publication would disappear. Hence the question of prior publication depends upon the textual tradition and not the other way round. In this book a theory of the development of the text has been proposed which does not need the assumption of prior publication.

There are some features of the poem and its manuscript tradition which most, if not all, scholars would accept as facts. The first is that no manuscripts of part or the whole of the poem are extant from Chaucer's own lifetime. This need not mean that no manuscripts were in fact written before 1400 when Chaucer died, but that is also likely to be the case. The second is that Hg is the earliest extant manuscript. Again it does not follow that it was the first manuscript of the poem to be written, for earlier manuscripts could have been lost. It does, however, mean that particular attention should be paid to Hg in the formulation of the poem's textual history. The third is that all the orders of the poem found in the various manuscripts are related. This may not be accepted so readily by all scholars, but is usually implicit in what they write. Even Manly and Rickert accept that all versions of the poem go back to what they called O[1], and so it follows that all versions are variants of that copy. In addition there are sections of the poem which have no internal system of ordering and which nevertheless appear in the same position in all manuscript orders; this is true, for example, of section 9. The uniform position of this section could have arisen only if all orders were interdependent. The fourth is that the poem was not composed in any particular order; tales which are late in a section may have been written earlier than those which come at the beginning of the section. For example, it is generally believed that KtT was written before Pro. It follows from this that Chaucer had no general plan of the poem to which he was working and that he was gradually building up sections from the individual tales he had completed. It is likely that he usually composed a link only when he had two tales to join together, though some tales do have free-standing links which are not joined to any other tale. The framing device of the pilgrimage depends upon the tales.

From these details, related inferences and the surviving manuscripts it is possible to suggest the following picture of the genesis and development of *The Canterbury Tales*. It is not possible to say when Chaucer wrote the first tale which is now included in the poem, though there is no need to assume that it occurred after he had finished all his other poems. It is reasonable to deduce that *The Canterbury Tales* was the major poetic creation of the last years of his life, for he was still engaged on its composition when he died in 1400. He did not write the parts of his poem in the sequence in which it was to be read, for he had no blueprint to which he was working. He composed tales either singly or possibly sometimes in pairs so that at any one time his poem consisted of a series of unrelated parts, each of which might contain one or more tales. As more tales were written he would join some of them together by providing linking sequences from the pilgrimage frame. These sequences were dramatic and may have become increasingly difficult to compose as the various possibilities for character interaction became exhausted. It seems unlikely that incomplete tales would be linked with other tales, unless their incompleteness is noted in the linking sequence as in TTh. So it may be that CkT which is linked to ReT was complete at one stage. Its present lack of an ending may be attributable to the lack of care with which Chaucer kept the parts of his poem. On the other hand, the incompleteness of SqT which was without links in Hg may be the result of Chaucer's death, for it may be the tale on which he was working at the time.

There is no evidence that Chaucer published any part of the poem in manuscript in his lifetime or that he took any interest in the publication of any of his poems. He seems to have kept his drafts in a very untidy state. It is not unnatural to assume that Chaucer made alterations to his draft, parts of which may have been over twenty years old when he died. In such a long poem he could easily have had a change of mind. However, the evidence that he did change his mind and make alterations is not easy to find. For example, the various geographical and temporal references in the links can have been only provisional when he included them, for subsequent groupings could have forced alterations in the progress of the pilgrimage. There is no evidence that these references were ever altered. When he did join tales together by providing a linking sequence, it is likely that he physically united the various sheets in some way. This may have been some form of pinning or sewing. It is not likely to have been very strong, and in some cases it broke.

Although there is no evidence that Chaucer published his poem in manuscript in his lifetime, there is some evidence that it was known of before he died. The best proof of that is the large number of manuscripts produced in the early fifteenth century. They testify to a demand for the poem, which suggests some knowledge on the part of the purchasers though it remains possible the manuscripts were produced speculatively. In addition, there are references to characters in the poem such as the Wife of Bath in other works attributed to Chaucer. These references, if Chaucer's, may be taken to suggest that some people knew about *The Canterbury Tales*. It is, therefore, possible that Chaucer read or had recited some of the tales orally either privately to his friends or even publicly. It is not likely that this was done at court.

The situation when Chaucer died may have been as follows. The poem was extant only in unconnected sections in a draft in his own possession. This draft was in an untidy state and parts of it were already missing. The sections consisted of individual tales, both complete and incomplete, without links, individual tales with links, and sections of at least two tales and their connecting links. We may assume that this draft was in Chaucer's house together with his other works and his library. The existence of the poem was known to his friends, who may have heard bits of it read aloud. When he died one or more of these friends would have taken it upon themselves to publish the poem in a written form. Since there was no Chaucerian plan to guide them, they would have to make editorial decisions on their own initiative simply following the testimony of the actual condition of the individual sections. It is from Hg, the earliest extant manuscript, that we can best understand what happened at this stage. The existence of Pro made it clear that section 1 came at the beginning. Even if Rt is not authorial, there would be little hesitation in accepting that PsT was the last tale, for in PsP the Host says:

> Now lakketh vs no tales mo than oon.
> Fulfild is my sentence and my decree. (12:16-17)

In this prologue there is a reference to the pilgrims entering *a thropes ende* (12:12), though it is doubtful whether the editor (for it is simplest to refer to the arranger as such) had worked out the geography of the journey at this stage or even whether there was an outward journey only. He may not have identified this *throp* with a particular place. After these two points were fixed, the remaining sections were ordered to fill the middle. This was done on a purely arbitrary basis. In section 1, which came first, there is a sequence in the poem of link−tale−link−tale, and the editor would have assumed that this was the pattern of the whole poem. Unfortunately there were insufficient links, because some tales were without them, and some sections of more than one tale did not have links to introduce or conclude them. He therefore arranged the intervening sections into two groups, one with no links and the other with a regular succession of tale−link−tale. This inevitably meant that some of the poem appeared to be incomplete, and it was evidently the intention that the gaps which were created by this ordering should be filled through the composition of appropriate linking passages. To whom this task was entrusted it is impossible to say. There is, however, no doubt that the original intention was to make of the unrelated sections as complete a poem as possible, even though it meant composing new portions for the poem. That need not surprise us, for it was something that scribes and editors were quite accustomed to doing.

It needs to be emphasized that, as far as we can tell, there was never any suggestion that the poem should be issued in parts by the editor after Chaucer's death. This in itself is quite a telling point. If the tales had been circulating independently in Chaucer's lifetime, it would have been more natural for the editor to continue this mode of publication after his death if he also decided to issue a complete edition of the tales. And if the tales had been circulating earlier, the form of such a collected edition of the tales is likely to have been different from the completed poem which finally emerged, for there would have been much less need to string the independent tales together in such a coherent way with new linking passages.

The scribe of Hg was set to copy out the text along the lines indicated above and was ordered to leave gaps for the necessary links and for the end of CkT. The writing of the missing links was also set in train. Unfortunately it was discovered, when Hg was copied, that there were some illogicalities in the order which had been determined on such an arbitrary basis. These had nothing to do with the geographical or temporal progression of the narrative, but simply with the interrelationship of some tales. The Wife of Bath is mentioned in MeT and ClT, and yet her tale in the proposed order came after both these other tales. To maintain any kind of fictional coherence, it was necessary to rearrange the order of these tales. This rearrangement is already prefigured in Hg, for section 2 was moved forward, but its consequences caused most of the later tampering with the order. For if MeT and ClT refer to the Wife of Bath, it suggests not only that WBPT should precede ClT and MeT but also that these two tales should follow immediately after the Wife's. It is for this reason that later manuscripts cannot arrive at the precise order for ClT, MeT, SqT and FkT, for this pressure to rearrange the tales conflicted with the desire to leave things alone. That there was a constant reshuffling of these tales indicates that there was continuity in the matter of order and that in turn suggests many of the early manuscripts were produced for the same editor. In addition, two tales not in Hg were added to the poem at an early stage, namely Gamelyn and CYPT. The latter is woven into the fabric of the poem from its first appearance and consequently has been accepted as a genuine tale. Its importance at this moment is simply that it is keyed in to follow NnT and it refers in its prologue to Boughtoun-vnder-Blee [G556]. This reference was taken to mean the Blean forest which is also mentioned in McP, and so in some manuscripts the inclusion of CYPT also led to the removal of NnT to a later place in the order.

After Hg the manuscripts tend to tinker with the order of ClT, MeT, SqT and FkT, and they also may alter the position of NnT because of CYPT. In addition new links and other new material are added. In the Manly–Rickert edition the subsequent manuscripts were arranged in four main textual groups, *a, b, c* and *d*, with a few anomalous ones which could not be arranged in any group. The implication of these groups was that each came from a separate archetype and it was these archetypes that went back, possibly through several stages, to Chaucer's original. However, the interrelationship of the manuscripts makes these groupings very dubious, as was partly recognised by Manly and Rickert and confirmed by Dempster.[1] Groups *b, c,* and *d* do not exist as separate textual entities. There is so much common to them that it is better to accept that they may be divided up into a larger number of sub-groups, the chief manuscript of each going back to the original Chaucerian draft. It is only in this way that one can

---

[1]Manly and Rickert 1940, and Dempster 1948a and 1949. See also Kane in Ruggiers 1984.

account for the many textual peculiarities and interrelationships. One may also accept that the original draft was gradually being changed under corrections and suggestions made by the editor. Only group *a* has real textual cohesion, and it is possible that this group does share an archetype. Even in this case the group has many links with the other manuscripts, and if there was an archetype it cannot have been used exclusively by the scribes of the group *a* manuscripts. It may be simpler also for these manuscripts to assume that we are dealing with some sub-groups which go back directly to the draft.

Although the editor was responsible for the order and many of the extra passages in the early manuscripts, the scribes themselves were probably responsible for the mise-en-page. This included the presentation of the text through rubrics and glosses, though in both cases some indication may have been provided by the editor or supervisor. Those glosses which occur in many manuscripts may have been introduced by the editor after consulting some of the books available in Chaucer's library.[2] Others were added by the scribes. Equally the editor may have indicated where tales and links began and ended, but it would be up to the scribes to convert those indications into precise rubrics. It was the editor who was responsible for the continuity of the text; and he toyed only once with the idea of arranging the tales in a different system. In Corpus he considered arranging the tales as chapters, which might have obviated the necessity of links for those tales which did not have them. But the presence of so many links elsewhere in the poem may have led him to abandon this attempt which was never tried again.

Since this book has looked at the text through the organization of individual manuscripts, it may be appropriate to consider briefly the additions and alterations to the text, many of which have been noted before as part of an individual manuscript. In what follows I shall follow the text in its Hg order, and I shall consider only the major alterations to the text, paying particular attention to the places where modern editions differ from Hg. The discussion will normally refer only to the eight early manuscripts which have figured centrally in this book.

In Pro Hg includes the couplet 1:253-4 which is not found in any other manuscript. It is probable that the couplet is genuine and was omitted as being too antagonistic to friars, for this attitude can be traced in other changes and additions, particularly in Corpus and Ha7334. Hg omits the couplet 1:639-40, which is almost certainly genuine and which is one of the few examples of eyeskip in the manuscript. In KtT Hg, Dd 4.24, Gg 4.27 and El do not contain the couplet [A2681-2] which appears in Corpus, Ha7334, Lansdowne

---

[2]Caie 1984.

and Petworth. The couplet is proverbial in its drift and was probably added by an editor. Such proverbial statements remind one of the editorial and scribal interest in proverbial and moral statements as indicated through the pointing of such passages by the glosses. The couplets [A2779-82] are found in Corpus, Ha7334, Gg 4.27, El, Lansdowne and Petworth; they do not occur in Hg and Dd 4.24. The lines express some pathos and help to emphasize the moral that virtue should be rewarded; they may be taken as a later addition. In MiP the couplet [A3155-6] is found in Ha7334, El and Gg 4.27, but not in Hg, Dd 4.24, Corpus, Lansdowne and Petworth. It again points the moral in a somewhat proverbial way and is likely to be an addition. In MiT only El contains the couplet [A3721-2], which helps to point the humour of the scene. Its occurrence only in an edited text like El must indicate that it is a later insertion. CkT is incomplete in all manuscripts, though some of the early ones like Hg allowed room for the ending if it should turn up. The behaviour of the early scribes certainly suggests that they believed CkT had been completed by the author at some stage. The incompleteness of CkT led to the inclusion of Gamelyn. This was probably first inserted in Corpus, which arranged the tales as chapters. As the chapter containing CkT was so short, it was felt necessary to enlarge it by including Gamelyn; it is not possible to say where Gamelyn was found, though it is extant now only in manuscripts of *The Canterbury Tales*. When the editor reverted to the tale–link–tale organization of the poem, the presence of Gamelyn was less necessary. So it was dropped in some manuscripts, but it was provided with a link to CkT in others in order to make it fit in with the text more convincingly.

In section 2 the major alterations to the text occur in WBP. Five additional passages are found in Dd 4.24, [D44a-f, 575-84, 609-12, 619-26 and 717-20]. Of these the last four are also in El and the middle three in Gg 4.27. None is found in Hg, Corpus, Ha7334, Lansdowne and Petworth. Though the last passage is slightly more moral in its implication, if slightly tongue-in-cheek, the others make the character of the Wife of Bath even more colourful and suggest an attempt to increase her sexual aggressiveness. The passages fall into line with the glosses which occur in Dd 4.24, and they may be accepted as additions which occurred first in that manuscript. In FrT the ends of the lines 2:1285-94 in Hg have been added later. Since there is no apparent smudge in the manuscript, which caused the lines to be rewritten, it may be that the lines were damaged in the draft and copied incompletely in Hg. If so, the endings must have been added to the draft shortly after Hg was written, for the line endings occur in all subsequent manuscripts and were written in Hg later in a different hand. In SuT there are additions to the friar's sermon in Ha7334. These additions are later and are attributable to that interest in friars by the editor or one of his assistants that we have already noted.

There are no changes of note in MLT which forms section 3. The only point of interest concerns what is now often referred to as ML endlink, though in practice it usually acted as SqP. In Hg MLT was followed by SqT and the scribe left a gap for a link to be provided. No link was added, though the one which is now called ML endlink may well have been written to introduce SqT. The failure to include the link may have been caused by the decision in principle to alter the order of MLT and section 2, though the change could not be carried out in Hg because MLT ended in the middle of a quire. This link would have been left with the original draft, for there was nowhere else for it to be housed. In some manuscripts section 2 was placed directly after MLT. When this happened, there was no need for ML endlink, for WBP acted as the link between MLT and WBT. This is the position in Dd 4.24, El and Gg 4.27. In some manuscripts with this order ML endlink was included, though the reference to the Squire was changed to the Summoner, the next available pilgrim whose name began with S. This happened in Ha7334, though the complete endlink was not included, presumably because of alterations to the plan and uncertainties as to how this link fitted in. In other manuscripts when the order was rearranged, section 2 was placed after both MLT and SqT so that SqT still followed MLT. This order allowed for the inclusion of ML endlink as a SqP, and that is the position in Corpus, Lansdowne and Petworth. It is not possible to say whether the availability of the link determined the order, or whether the chosen order allowed the link to be included.

SqT is incomplete in all manuscripts, and it ends in Hg after the first two lines of part 3. The Hg scribe treated SqT differently from CkT, for he left a small gap after SqT which could accommodate a link, but not the rest of the tale. He did not anticipate that the rest of the tale would become available. We may, therefore, assume Chaucer was working on this tale when he died. Most scribes were content to leave the tale unfinished, though some tidied it up by excluding the last two lines or by including them in part 2. SqT is followed in Hg by MeT and a gap was left for a linking sequence. This gap was later filled in the same hand but in a different ink by the link [F673-708]. This arrangement also occurs in Petworth. In El which has the tales in a different order this link could not be used in this way because FkT follows SqT. The same link is introduced between SqT and FkT but 'Merchant' is changed to 'Franklin' at the appropriate places. It is possible that a similar situation prevailed in Ha7334, Dd 4.24 and Gg 4.27, but missing folios in these manuscripts prevent our knowing precisely what was included. Corpus and Lansdowne have an order of tales that has no use for the link, because SqT is followed by WBP.

In MeT there are two gaps in Hg. At 5:61-2 the scribe included only the first half of the first line; the remaining line and a half were left blank, though they were subsequently filled in a later hand. It is generally believed that this omission was caused by the state of the copytext. Manly and Rickert, for example, write 'The condition of this couplet in the various MSS makes it clear that O[1] contained only the first half of the first line. This is one of the most striking instances of the fact that the CT had not received Chaucer's final touches' (III.474). In fact it is unlikely that Chaucer failed to complete a couplet while he was composing; it is more probable that the couplet had been rendered partly illegible in some way. This passage provides proof that the copytext was Chaucer's draft and that the draft was in an untidy state. Scribes reacted to the gap in one of three ways: they left a gap; they omitted the incomplete couplet so that 5:63 follows immediately after 5:60; or they invented something to complete the couplet. There are at least eight suggested ways of completing the couplet. A similar situation occurs at 5:986, though in this case only the second line of the couplet is missing. Hg left a blank, as did El at first, though the scribe subsequently added a line in a different ink. This line is found in Ha7334, Dd 4.24 and Gg 4.27 as well. The other four early manuscripts have a different line. It is probable that the copytext was illegible at this point, but that instead of eight readings as in 5:61-2 in this case only two emerged. Neither need be considered authentic. Corpus and Lansdowne omit the last hundred lines of MeT. In Corpus this may be caused by the absence of the last few folios of the draft; Lansdowne probably copied Corpus. It is evidence that the means used to pin together the folios of the draft was not very reliable.

In Hg MeT is followed by FkT, and when the scribe copied the manuscript he left a gap to accommodate a link to join the two tales. A link [E2419-40, F1-8] was provided which he copied into the manuscript at a later date using a different ink. In Corpus and Lansdowne the end of MeT is missing, so it is not surprising that this link is also not found. In Ha7334, El, Dd 4.24 and Gg 4.27 the tales are rearranged so that SqT follows MeT, and this link was adapted to join MeT to SqT with the consequent change of 'Franklin' to 'Squire' at [Fl] together with other adjustments. In other manuscripts like Petworth the rearrangement of tales led FkT to follow ClT. In this case the link was adapted for this position by rewriting it in the stanza form found in ClT. This led to a considerable shortening of the link.

In El there are some notable additions in FkT which are found only there, namely [F1455-6, 1493-8]. The first adds extra examples of virtuous women, and the second invites the readers to suspend their judgement of Arveragus until the tale is complete. The first exhibits that interest in learned example which we find in so many glosses, and the second exhibits the same rather fussy moral comment that we have noted as being added elsewhere. They may both be accepted as later additions by the editor. In addition Corpus and Lansdowne omit certain lines which the scribes did not approve of because of their moral implications.

FkT is followed in Hg by NnT, and when the scribe copied the manuscript he left a gap for a possible link. This link was not provided, and as far as can be deduced was never written. Some later scribes made up for this absence of a link by dividing NnT into a prologue and tale, though the resulting prologue has nothing to do with the pilgrimage frame since it concerns the meaning of the name *Cecilia*. In Hg NnT is a free-standing tale without prologue and without any tale joined to it at the end. But in most subsequent manuscripts, CYPT is joined to NnT. The first line of CYP does not refer to the teller of the previous tale, only to its subject matter for it begins:

Whan toold was al the lyf of seinte Cecile [G554]

CYPT also refers to pilgrims who had not started with the others in London, but who joined the pilgrimage at some point on the journey. The question necessarily arises whether CYPT was written by Chaucer or by, for example, the editor who compiled the missing links. The tendency has been to accept it as genuine, though now there are increasingly voices heard which accept that all or some of the tale may not be Chaucerian.[3]

In Hg NnT is followed by ClT, which is preceded by a prologue and concluded by the envoy and the Host-stanza. Because ClT refers to the Wife of Bath and her tale, it was subsequently moved forward in the order in many manuscripts. In Ha7334, Dd 4.24, El and Gg 4.27 this led to ClT being followed by MeT. It was decided that the Host-stanza was not a sufficient link between these two tales, and a new link [E1213-44] in couplets was composed. This link echoes in its first line the last line of the envoy. It may well be that this link was designed to replace the Host-stanza, which it does in Ha7334. But as the Host-stanza is omitted in Corpus and Lansdowne, it may be that the link was written for Ha7334 in ignorance of the Host-stanza. However, once the new link was written it was introduced into those manuscripts which follow ClT with MeT, though in El, Dd 4.24 and probably Gg 4.27, in which some folios are missing, the new link is included together with the Host-stanza. It is somewhat illogical to have both links, which is

3Brown 1983 and Knight 1983.

why modern editors leave out the Host-stanza. But that stanza is original, and the link [E1213-44] is spurious.

ClT is followed in Hg by section 9 which consists of PhT and PdT. In Hg the Host-stanza serves as the link between ClT and PhT, but when ClT was moved forward PhT could occur in a situation where it was not provided with an introductory link. Some manuscripts, though only Lansdowne among the early ones, supplied that loss by a new link. It has always been accepted as spurious by modern editors. PhT and PdT are joined by a link, which was varied in some manuscripts. Corpus was probably the first in which the changes were made. An extra couplet was included at [C297-8] which points the moral that Virginia was killed on account of her beauty. Some of the other changes, which are also found in Ha7334, may have been made to nullify the criticism made of lawyers and other members of the legal profession. In the prologue proper to PdT some lines have been rearranged and others included in some manuscripts, but the changes are spurious and are not usually included in modern editions.

Section 10 follows section 9 regularly in the early manuscripts. Generally the exchange between the Host and the Pardoner at the end of PdT was accepted as a sufficient link between PdT and ShT, which opens section 10. In some manuscripts, however, a separate ShP was included, though it is clearly not Chaucerian. One form of it occurs in Lansdowne; another in Petworth, though that manuscript had disturbed the order by placing ShT earlier in the poem. In TTh only Dd 4.24 has line 10:805, which is usually included in modern editions. It is probable that the line was omitted through oversight in Chaucer's draft and so many scribes did not realize that anything was missing. The line which occurs in Dd 4.24 may be taken as spurious. TMel is a prose tale in which one might reasonably expect omission to occur for various reasons, for Chaucer's tale is a fairly close translation of a French version. Chaucer's version omits 10:1062-3 and 10:1433-4, which appear in no manuscript, presumably because his French version did not contain these lines. They should not be thought of as part of the text. In 10:1000 we may assume that some words were omitted in Chaucer's draft through eyeskip, for they are omitted in many early manuscripts. Other manuscripts may occasionally supply what was missing, though they do so in many different ways. The same probably applies to 10:1335-6, where an omission through eyeskip in the draft was restored in different ways by various scribes. At 10:1777 the scribe of Hg left a gap, which presumably reflects an illegible passage in the draft, for we cannot imagine that Chaucer suddenly left a gap in his translation. This gap was no doubt supplied at some later stage, for many manuscripts contain an appropriate insertion at this point. Others simply omitted some of the surrounding text to make the whole passage more comprehensible.

In MkT and NPT there are some important changes which may well be associated with one another. In Hg there is no Adam stanza in MkT, though in some later manuscripts this was supplied as [B²3197-3204]. In Corpus a gap was left for a stanza and a heading provided, but the stanza was never copied in; it may not have been ready in time. In Hg the four fourteenth-century examples of tragedy known as the Modern Instances come at the end of MkT; in several other manuscripts they are placed in the middle of MkT between Zenobia and Nero. This seems to occur for the first time in Corpus, though there are marginal letters there indicating that the Modern Instances should come at the end of the tale. Finally in NPP Hg has what is sometimes referred to as the short form of the prologue; several manuscripts have a longer version which includes lines [B²3961-80]. These extra lines increase the role of the Host and contain echoes to the final lines in the tragedy of Croesus, the final story in MkT when the Modern Instances are in the middle of the tale. It seems probable that the inclusion of these extra lines is related to the moving forward of the Modern Instances, though some later manuscripts include the extra lines without changing the position of the Modern Instances. The moving of the Modern Instances makes the tale seem less complete because the logical order of the tragedies is interrupted. The extra lines in NPP accentuate the sense of incompleteness, because the Host's words to the Monk are far from polite and imply that he has been cut off in the middle of his tale − an implication that is found in the Knight's words in this prologue too, but much less strongly. The Adam stanza was no doubt added to MkT because it was usual to start such lists of unfortunate people with Adam, as indeed occurs in Boccaccio's *De casibus virorum illustrium*, the principal source for MkT. It is clear that Hg contains the original form of both these tales, for it is easy to understand why these additions and changes to its text were made, whereas it would be difficult to account for the deletion of these passages if they were part of the original text. It may consequently be assumed that the extra passages are spurious additions made fairly early in the poem's textual history.[4] Corpus allowed for the addition of the Adam stanza, but did not have it. It changed the position of the Modern Instances, but it did not include the extra lines of NPP. In Ha7334 the Adam stanza and the extra lines of NPP are included and the Modern Instances are in the middle of MkT. The lack of correlation between the forward position of the Modern Instances and the inclusion of the extra lines in NPP may be attributed to the fact that the former meant

[4]See further Blake 1984b.

rearranging the text through following marginal annotations whereas the latter simply meant including more text, presumably written on separate, inserted sheets. The former would take far more scribal organization and attentiveness than the latter.

In Hg NPT which concludes section 10 is followed by McPT which forms section 11. McP acts as a link between the two tales. But in some manuscripts the inclusion of CYPT which contains a reference to *Boghtoun-vnder-Blee* meant that it and NnT were moved to a position between NPT and McT. This meant that NnT followed NPT, but as NnT had no introductory link there was nothing from the pilgrimage frame to join NPT and NnT. This is a problem that arises in Dd 4.24, El and Gg 4.27, for the move of NnT and CYPT occurs essentially in group *a* manuscripts. As Dd 4.24 may be the earliest extant of these manuscripts, it is not surprising that we find in it a new link [B^{2}4637-52], now usually known as NP endlink. This link does not serve as a prologue, for it does not refer directly to another teller; its concluding couplet reads:

> And after that he with ful merie cheere
> Seide vnto another as ye shuln heere.

It was added later in Dd 4.24 in a gap which was left for it, though it would appear as if it was designed to have a further passage to act as prologue to the next tale. As this extra section was not written, the endlink itself served no useful purpose and was not included in El or Gg 4.27. Instead the first lines of NnT were designated as a prologue and served as the link between the two tales.

There is nothing of much textual interest in McT or PsT, and much of the latter is lost in Hg because of missing folios. In modern editions PsT is followed by Rt. It is not possible to say whether it was found in Hg or in Corpus, because both are incomplete at the end. Dd 4.24 and Gg 4.27 have also lost their final folios. It occurs in the other four early manuscripts. It may be Chaucer's, but it is the sort of passage that one can also readily imagine was added by an editor to finish the book off. Since the text was in a fragmentary state and since the editor was trying to make it seem as complete as possible, the provision of an ending would be a logical step for him to take. It cannot be stated with certainty that it is spurious, but its authenticity is dubious.

From this picture it is possible to deduce that the editor was trying to present a finished text to the readers which at the same time did not offend fictional propriety by referring to something before it had actually been narrated. As part of this attempt to present a finished text, the various pieces of the poem were arranged in a standard way. Usually this consisted of prologue and tale, sometimes of just link and tale, and once of chapters. As part of this presentation headings were provided for the various pieces, and concluding rubrics were also gradually introduced. Many of the tales were divided into books, and many of the proverbial or poetic utterances in the text were signalled by glosses. Even some of the sources were consulted to introduce passages and short quotations from them to prevent the reader misunderstanding the moral implications of the tales. Many of the changes to the text were embarked upon in the same spirit. Attacks on the clergy and the professions which were felt to be too harsh were toned down; proverbial and other moral comments were added; learned touches increasing the number of examples of a particular theme were included; and occasionally even the point of a story or passage was emphasized by an inclusion. As has been said of the glosses, many of the additions were made perhaps 'by a learned contemporary who probably had access to Chaucer's own source manuscripts, and who may have had less confidence than Chaucer in the moral acumen of his readers'.[5] There was no root and branch modification to any tale; the tales were simply subjected to a tidying up in their moral and fictional presentation. In the link passages one may note the frequency with which the editor uses echo as a technique, for many passages take their point of departure from the last lines of the tale to which the link is appended. In addition, the role of the Host is greatly enlarged in these new links and his character is, if anything, made more grotesque and outrageous. Whereas in the original links other pilgrims like the Knight may play a prominent role, this is not true of the additional links.

Perhaps the most difficult aspect of the development of the poem outlined above for modern scholars to accept is that there existed a person or persons who acted as editor of the text and was prepared to arrange its pieces in accordance with his own whim and to write or have written additional pieces to supplement the text. While it is possible to accept that Gamelyn was not written specifically for *The Canterbury Tales* and need not therefore be attributed as a composition to the editor, this cannot be true of CYPT, if it is accepted that it is not Chaucerian. So in addition to CYPT, there are several links and a number of smaller passages which are attributable to this reviser, whether he was the editor himself or someone known to him. In itself the composition of this number of lines is not a problem; it is merely that as so many of them at one time or another have been ascribed to Chaucer, modern scholars may well find it too difficult to assume that such passages could have been written by a Chaucerian imitator. This arises simply because we put Chaucer on a pedestal and assume that

[5]Caie 1981 p. 84.

no one else could write like him. This assumption may be true for complete poems, but it is clearly unrealistic for shorter passages. Even as regards whole poems, there are works such as *The Boke of Cupide* and *The Flower and the Leaf* written by his contemporaries or immediate successors which are of considerable literary merit and were for many years attributed to Chaucer. The history of scholarship suggests that we are unable today to tell with confidence what was written by Chaucer and what was not, for the canon has been gradually whittled away over the last century. For the most part attribution of a text to Chaucer is made on other than purely literary grounds.

This point brings us back to the whole question of genuineness which has so bedevilled discussions of *The Canterbury Tales*, because scholars start with certain assumptions about what is Chaucer's and try to make their textual work fit in with these prior assumptions. In this book I have tried to suggest a textual history of the poem through the development of the various manuscripts. The implication of that enquiry is that whatever is not in Hengwrt is most convincingly interpreted as a later edition to the poem and hence not by Chaucer. It is, however, much more important to focus on the textual tradition than on the question of genuineness. Until the textual tradition is established with a reasonable degree of unanimity, there is little point in considering which portions of the text are Chaucer's. This book has been written in order to expedite the achievement of such unanimity.

Bibliography

Allen, Judson B. and Theresa A. Moritz. *A distinction of stories.* Columbus: Ohio State University Press, 1981.

Anderson, J.K. 'An Analysis of the framework structure of Chaucer's *Canterbury tales.*' *Orbis literarum* 27 (1972): 179-201.

Anderson, Robert. *A complete edition of the poets of Great Britain.* Vol. 1. London: Arch, Edinburgh: Bell and Bradfute, 1793.

Baker, D.C. 'The Bradshaw order of the *Canterbury tales:* a dissent.' *NM* 63 (1962): 245-61.

—— *The Manciple's tale.* A variorum edition of the works of Geoffrey Chaucer, vol. II part 10. Norman: University of Oklahoma Press, 1984

Baugh, A.C. 'The original teller of the Merchant's tale.' *MP* 35 (1937-8):16-26.

—— *Chaucer's major poetry.* New York: Appleton-Century-Crofts, 1963.

Bell, Robert. *Poetical works of Geoffrey Chaucer.* London: Griffin, 1854.

Benson, L.D. 'The order of *The Canterbury Tales.*' *SAC* 3 (1981):77-120.

Blake, N.F. 'Caxton and Chaucer.' *Leeds studies in English* n.s. 1 (1967):19-36.

—— *Caxton's own prose.* London: Deutsch, 1973.

—— 'The relationship between the Hengwrt and Ellesmere manuscripts of the *Canterbury tales.*' *Essays and studies* n.s. 32 (1979):1-18.

—— *The Canterbury tales edited from the Hengwrt manuscript.* London: Arnold, 1980.

—— 'Chaucer manuscripts and texts.' *Review* 3 (1981): 219-32

——'Chaucer's text and the web of words.' *New perspectives in Chaucer criticism.* Edited by Donald M Rose. Norman: Pilgrim Books, 1981, pp. 223–40.

—— 'Critics, criticism and the order of *The Canterbury tales.*' *Archiv* 218 (1981):47-58.

—— 'On editing the *Canterbury tales.' Medieval studies for J.A.W. Bennett aetatis suae LXX.* Edited by Peter L. Heyworth. Oxford: Clarendon, 1981, pp. 101–19.

—— 'The textual tradition of *The book of the duchess.' ES* 62 (1981):237-48.

—— 'The text of the Canterbury tales.' *Poetica (Tokyo)* 13 (1982 for 1980):27-49.

—— 'The Wife of Bath and her tale.' *Leeds studies in English* n.s.13 (1982):42-55.

—— 'The editorial assumptions in the Manly–Rickert edition of the *Canterbury tales.' ES* 64 (1983):385-400.

—— 'Geoffrey Chaucer: the critics and the canon.' *Archiv* 221 (1984):65-79.

—— 'Editorial assumptions and problems in The Canterbury Tales.' *Poetica* 20 (1984):1-19.

—— 'The debate on the order of *The Canterbury Tales.' Revista Canaria de Estudios Ingleses* 10 (1985): to appear.

Blodgett, J.E. 'Some printer's copy for William Thynne's edition of Chaucer.' *Library* 6th ser 1 (1979):97-113.

Bradshaw, H. 'The skeleton of Chaucer's *Canterbury tales.' Collected papers of Henry Bradshaw.* Cambridge: University Press, 1889, pp. 102–48.

Brewer, D. 'Observations on the text of *Troilus.' Medieval studies for J.A.W. Bennett aetatis suae LXX.* Edited by Peter L. Heyworth. Oxford: Clarendon, 1981, pp. 122–38.

Brown, C. 'The evolution of the Canterbury "marriage group".' *PMLA* 48 (1933):1041-59.

—— Review of Manly and Rickert 1940. *MLN* 55 (1940):606-21.

—— 'Three notes on the text of the *Canterbury tales.' MLN* 56 (1941): 163-75.

—— 'Author's revision in the *Canterbury tales.' PMLA* 57 (1942):29-50.

Brown, P. 'Is the 'Canon's Yeoman's tale' apocryphal?' *ES* 64 (1983):481-90.

Brusendorff, Aage. *The Chaucer tradition.* Oxford: Clarendon, 1925.

Burnley, J.D. 'Inflexion in Chaucer's Adjectives.' *NM* 83 (1982):169-73.

Caie, G.D. 'The significance of the glosses in the earliest manuscripts of *The Canterbury tales.' Papers from the first Nordic conference for English studies, in Oslo 17-19 September 1980.* Edited by Stig Johansson and Bjorn Tysdahl. Oslo: Institute for English Studies 1981, pp. 25–34.

—— 'The significance of the marginal glosses in the earliest manuscripts of the Canterbury tales.' *Chaucer and the scriptural tradition.* Edited by David L. Jeffrey. Ottawa:

University of Ottawa, 1984, pp. 337–50.

Caldwell, R.A. 'The scribe of the Chaucer ms, Cambridge University Library, Gg.4.27.' *Modern Language quarterly* 5 (1943):33-44.

Caxton, William. [*The Canterbury tales*. Westminster, 1476.] (STC 5082).

—— [*The Canterbury tales*. Westminster, 1482] (STC 5083).

Chapman, R.L. 'The Shipman's tale was meant for the Shipman.' *MLN* 71 (1956):4-5.

Child, F.J. 'Observations on the language of Chaucer.' *Memorials of the American Academy of Arts and Sciences* n.s. 8 (1862):445-502.

Clawson, W.H. 'The framework of *The Canterbury tales*.' *University of Toronto quarterly* 20 (1951):137-54.

Cohen, E.S. 'The sequence of the *Canterbury tales*.' *ChR* 9 (1974-5): 190-5.

Cook, D. 'The revision of Chaucer's *Troilus*: the beta text.' *ChR* 9 (1974-5): 51-62.

Cooper, Helen. *The structure of the Canterbury tales*. London: Duckworth, 1983.

Cox, L.S. 'A question of order in the *Canterbury tales*.' *ChR* 1 (1966-7):228-52.

Crow, M.M. 'John of Angouleme and his Chaucer manuscript.' *Speculum* 17 (1942):86-99.

Crow, M.M. and C.C. Olson. *Chaucer life records*. Oxford: Clarendon, 1966.

Dempster, G. 'Manly's conception of the early history of the *Canterbury tales*.' *PMLA* 61 (1946):379-415.

—— 'A chapter in the history of the *Canterbury tales*: the ancestor of group *d*, the origin of its texts, tale-order, and spurious links.' *PMLA* 63 (1948):456-84.

—— 'On the significance of Hengwrt's change of ink in the Merchant's tale.' *MLN* 63 (1948):325-30.

—— 'The fifteenth-century editors of the *Canterbury tales* and the problem of tale order.' *PMLA* 64 (1949):1123-42.

de Worde, Wynkyn. *The boke of Chaucer named Caunterbury tales*. Westminster 1498, (STC 5085)

Donaldson, E. Talbot. *Chaucer's poetry: an anthology for the modern reader*. New York: Ronald press, 1958.

—— '*Canterbury tales* D 117: a critical edition.' *Speaking of Chaucer*. London: Athlone, 1970, pp. 119–30.

—— 'The ordering of the Canterbury tales.' *Medieval literature and folklore studies: essays in honor of F.L. Utley*. Edited by Jerome Mandel and Bruce Rosenburg. New Brunswick, N.J. University of Rutgers Press, 1970, pp. 103–204.

—— 'The manuscripts of Chaucer's works and their use.' *Geoffrey*

Chaucer. Edited by Derek Brewer. London: Bell, 1974, pp. 85–108.

Doyle, A.I. and M.B. Parkes. 'The production of copies of the *Canterbury tales* and *Confessio amantis* in the early fifteen century. *Medieval scribes, manuscripts and libraries, essays presented to N.R. Ker*. Edited by Malcolm B. Parkes and Andrew G. Watson. London: Scolar, 1978, pp. 163–210.

Dunn, Thomas F. *The manuscript source of Caxton's second edition of the Canterbury tales*. Chicago: University library, 1940.

The Ellesmere Chaucer reproduced in facsimile. 2 vols. Manchester: University Press, 1911.

Elliott, C. ' "The Reeve's prologue and tale" in the Ellesmere and Hengwrt manuscripts.' *Notes and Queries* 209 (1964):167-70.

Fisher, J.H. 'Chaucer's last revision of the *Canterbury tales*.' *MLR* 67 (1972):241-51.

—— *The complete poetry and prose of Geoffrey Chaucer*. New York and London: Holt, Rinehart & Winston, 1977.

Fletcher, B.Y. 'Printer's copy for Stow's Chaucer.' *SB* 31 (1978):184-201.

Furnivall, Frederick J. *A temporary preface to the Chaucer Society's six-text edition of Chaucer's Canterbury tales*. Chaucer Society 2nd ser 3. London: Trübner, 1868.

—— *The six-text edition of Chaucer's Canterbury tales*. Chaucer Society 1st ser 2 etc. London: Trübner, 1868-84.

—— *The Harleian MS.7334 of Chaucer's Canterbury tales*. Chaucer Society 1st ser 73. London: Trübner, 1885.

—— *The Cambridge MS Dd. 4.24 of Chaucer's Canterbury tales*. Chaucer Society 1st ser 95-6. London: Kegan Paul, Trench, Trübner, 1901-2.

Garbaty, T.J. 'Wynkyn de Worde's "Sir Thopas" and other tales.' *SB* 31 (1978):57-67.

Gardner, J. 'The case against the "Bradshaw shift": or the mystery of the manuscript in the trunk.' *Papers on English language and literature* 3 (1967):80-106.

Greg, W.W. 'The early printed editions of the Canterbury Tales.' *PMLA* 39 (1924):737-61.

—— 'The ms sources of Caxton's second edition of the *Canterbury tales*.' *PMLA* 44 (1929):1251-3.

Hammond, E.P. 'On the order of the *Canterbury tales:* Caxton's two editions.' *MP* 3 (1905-6):159-78.

——*Chaucer: a bibliographical manual*. New York: Macmillan, 1908.

Hartung, A.E. and G. Dempster. 'The Clerk's endlink in the *d* manuscripts.' *PMLA* 67 (1952):1173-81.

Hellinga, Lotte. *Caxton in focus*. London: British Library, 1982.

Hench, A.L. 'Printer's copy for Tyrwhitt's Chaucer.' *SB* 3 (1950): 72-5.

Jones, R.F. 'A conjecture on the Wife of Bath's prologue.' *JEGP* 24 (1925):512-47.

Kane, G. 'The text of *The legend of good women* in CUL MS Gg.4.27.' *Middle English studies presented to Norman Davis in honour of his seventieth birthday*. Edited by Douglas Gray and Eric G. Stanley. Oxford: Clarendon, 1983, pp. 39–58.

Kase, C.R. 'Observations on the shifting position of groups G and DE in the manuscripts of the Canterbury tales.' *Three Chaucer studies*. Edited by C. Robert Kase, Russell Krauss and Haldeen Braddy. Oxford: University Press, 1932, pt. 1.

Keiser, G.R. 'In defense of the Bradshaw shift.' *ChR* 12 (1977-8): 191-201.

Kilgour, M. 'The manuscript sources of Caxton's second edition of *The Canterbury tales*.' *PMLA* 44 (1929):186-201.

Knight, S. 'Textual variants: textual variance.' *Southern review* 16 (1983):44-54.

Koch, John. *The Pardoner's prologue and tale*. Chaucer Society 2nd ser. 35. London: Oxford University Press, 1902.

—— *A detailed comparison of the eight manuscripts of the Canterbury tales as printed by the Chaucer Society*. Chaucer Society 2nd ser 47. London: Kegan Paul, Trench, Trübner, 1913.

Lossing, M.L.S. 'The order of the Canterbury tales: a fresh relation between A and B types of mss.' *JEGP* 37 (1938):153-63.

McCormick, Sir William and Janet E. Heseltine. *The manuscripts of Chaucer's Canterbury tales: a critical description of their contents*. Oxford: Clarendon, 1933.

Manly, J.M. 'Tales of the homeward journey.' *SP* 28 (1931):613-17.

—— and Edith Rickert. 'The "Hengwrt" manuscript of Chaucer's Canterbury tales.' *National Library of Wales journal* 1 (1939): 59-75.

—— *The text of the Canterbury tales*. 8 vols. Chicago: University Press, 1940.

Moore, S. 'The position of group C in the *Canterbury tales*.' *PMLA* 30 (1915):116-23.

[Morell, Thomas.] *The Canterbury tales of Chaucer, in the original, from the most authentic manuscripts*. London: privately ptd, 1737.

Muscatine, Charles. *The book of Chaucer: an account of the publication of Geoffrey Chaucer's works from the fifteenth century to modern times*. San Francisco: Book Club of California, 1963.

Olson, G. 'The terrain of Chaucer's Sittingbourne.' *SAC* 6 (1984): 103-19.

Owen, C.A. Jr 'The *Canterbury tales:* early manuscripts and relative popularity.' *JEGP* 54 (1955):104-10.

—— 'The development of the *Canterbury tales.*' *JEGP* 57 (1958):449-76.

—— 'The earliest plan of the "Canterbury tales".' *Medieval studies* 21 (1959):202-10.

—— 'The design of *The Canterbury tales.*' *Companion to Chaucer studies.* Edited by Beryl Rowland. New York: Oxford University Press, 1968, pp. 192–207.

—— 'The alternative reading of *The Canterbury tales:* Chaucer's text and the early manuscripts.' *PMLA* 97 (1982):237-50.

Pace, G.B. 'Speght's Chaucer and ms Gg.4.27.' *SB* 21 (1968):225-35.

Parkes, M.B. 'The influence of the concepts of *ordinatio* and *compilatio* on the development of the book.' *Medieval learning and literature: essays presented to R.W. Hunt.* Edited by Margaret Gibson and Jonathan J.G. Alexander. Oxford: Clarendon, 1976, pp. 116–41.

—— and Richard Beadle, *Geoffrey Chaucer: poetical works; a facsimile of Cambridge University Library Gg.4.27.* 3 vols. Cambridge: Brewer, 1979-80.

Pearsall, Derek. *The Nun's Priest's tale.* A variorum edition of the works of Geoffrey Chaucer, vol. II part 9. Norman: University of Oklahoma, 1983.

The poetical works of Geoffrey Chaucer. Revised edn by Richard Morris. London: Bell & Daldy, 1866. (Aldine edition)

Pollard, Arthur W., H.F. Heath, M.H. Liddell and W.S. McCormick. *The works of Chaucer.* London: Macmillan, 1898. (Globe edition).

Pratt, R.A. 'The order of the Canterbury tales.' *PMLA* 66 (1951):1141-67.

—— 'The development of the Wife of Bath.' *Studies in medieval literature in honor of A.C. Baugh.* Edited by MacEdward Leach. Philadelphia: University of Pennsylvania Press, 1961, pp. 45–79.

—— *The tales of Canterbury complete; Geoffrey Chaucer.* Boston, Mass.: Houghton Mifflin, 1974.

Pynson, Richard. [*The Canterbury Tales.* London, 1492.] (STC 5084)

—— *Here begynneth the boke of Caunterbury tales, dilygently corrected and newly printed.* London, 1526. (STC 5086; cf. STC 5088, 5096).

Ramsey, R.V. 'The Hengwrt and Ellesmere manuscripts of the Canterbury tales: different scribes.' *SB* 35 (1982):133-55.

Robinson, Fred N. *The works of Geoffrey Chaucer.* 2nd edn. Boston, Mass.: Houghton Mifflin, London: Oxford University Press, 1957.

Rogers, F.R. 'The *Tale of Gamelyn* and the editing of the *Canterbury tales.*' *JEGP* 58 (1959):49-59.

Rogers, H.L. 'The tales of the Merchant and the Franklin: text and interpretation.' *Studies in Chaucer.* Edited by G.A. Wilkes and A.P. Riemer. Sydney studies in English. Sydney: University Press, 1981, pp. 3—27.

Root, Robert K. *The Textual tradition of Chaucer's Troilus.* Chaucer Society 1st ser 99. London: Kegan Paul, Trench, Trübner, 1916.

——*The book of Troilus and Criseyde by Geoffrey Chaucer.* Princeton: University Press, 1926.

—— 'The text of the Canterbury tales.' *SP* 38 (1941):1-13.

Ross, Thomas W. *The Miller's tale.* A variorum edition of the works of Geoffrey Chaucer, vol. II part 3. Norman: University of Oklahoma Press, 1983.

Rowland, Beryl. *Companion to Chaucer studies.* 2nd edn. New York: Oxford University Press, 1979.

Ruggiers, Paul G. *The Canterbury tales. Geoffrey Chaucer. A facsimile and transcription of the Hengwrt manuscript.* Norman: University of Oklahoma Press, 1979.

——*Editing Chaucer: the great tradition.* Norman,Oklahoma: Pilgrim Books, 1984

Rydland, K. 'The meaning of "variant reading" in the Manly—Rickert *Canterbury tales*: a note on the limitation of the corpus of variants.' *NM* 73 (1972):805-14.

Samuels, M.L. 'Chaucer's spelling.' *Middle English studies presented to Norman Davis in honour of his seventieth birthday.* Edited by Douglas Gray and E.G. Stanley. Oxford: Clarendon, 1983, pp. 17—37.

—— 'The scribe of the Hengwrt and Ellesmere manuscripts of the *Canterbury tales.*' *SAC* 5 (1983):49-65.

Sayce, O. 'Chaucer's "Retraction": the conclusion of the Canterbury tales and its place in literary tradition.' *Medium AEvum* 40 (1971):230-48.

Scattergood, V.J. and J.W. Sherborne. *English court culture in the later Middle Ages.* London: Duckworth, 1983.

Severs, J.B. 'Author's revision in block C of the *Canterbury tales.*' *Speculum* 29 (1954):512-30.

—— 'Did Chaucer rearrange the Clerk's envoy?' *MLN* 69 (1954):472-8.

Silvia, D.S. 'Some fifteenth-century manuscripts of the *Canterbury tales.*' *Chaucer and Middle English studies in honour of Rossell Hope Robbins.* Edited by Beryl Rowland.

London: Allen & Unwin, 1974, pp. 153–63.

Skeat, Walter W. *The complete works of Geoffrey Chaucer.* 6 vols. Oxford: Clarendon, 1894.

—— *The evolution of the Canterbury tales.* Chaucer Society 2nd ser 38. London: Kegan Paul, Trench, Trübner, 1907.

—— *The eight-text edition of the Canterbury tales with remarks upon the classification of the manuscripts and upon the Harleian manuscript 7334.* Chaucer Society 3rd ser 43. London: Kegan Paul, Trench, Trübner, 1909.

Speght, Thomas. *The workes of our antient and lerned English poet, Chaucer newly printed.* London: Islip for Bishop, 1598. (STC 5077)

—— *The workes of our antient and learned English poet, Geffrey Chaucer, newly printed.* London: Islip, 1602. (STC 5080)

—— *The workes of our antient, learned & excellent poet, Jeffrey Chaucer.* London, 1687.

Stevens, M. 'The royal stanza in early English literature.' *PMLA* 94 (1979):62-76.

Stow, John. *The workes of Geoffrey Chaucer, newlie printed, with divers addicions whiche were never in print before.* London: Kyngston for Wight, 1561. (STC 5075)

Stroud, T.A. 'A Chaucer scribe's concern with page format.' *Speculum* 23 (1948):683-7.

—— 'Scribal errors in Manly and Rickert's text.' *MLN* 68 (1953): 234-7.

Sudo, J. 'The order of the *Canterbury tales* reconsidered.' *Hiroshima studies in English language and literature* 10 (1963):77-89.

Tatlock, John S.P. *The development and chronology of Chaucer's works.* Chaucer Society 2nd ser 37. London: Kegan Paul, Trench, Trubner, 1907.

—— *The Harleian manuscript and revision of the Canterbury tales.* Chaucer Society 2nd ser 41. London: Kegan Paul, Trench, Trubner, 1909.

—— 'The Canterbury tales in 1400.' *PMLA* 50 (1935):100-39.

Thynne, William. *The workes of Geffray Chaucer newly printed with dyuers workes neuer in print before.* London: Godfray, 1532. (STC 5068)

—— *The workes of Geffray Chaucer newly printed, with dyvers workes whych were never in print before.* London: Bonham, 1542. (STC 5069)

—— *The workes of Geffray Chaucer newly printed, with dyvers workes whiche were never in print before.* London: Bonham [1545]. (STC 5071)

Tyrwhitt, Thomas. *The Canterbury tales of Chaucer.* 5 vols. London: Payne, 1775-8.

Urry, John. *The works of Geoffrey Chaucer, compared with the former editions and many valuable mss.* London: Lintot, 1721.

Wilson, J.H. 'The Pardoner and the Second Nun: a defense of the Bradshaw order.' *NM* 74 (1973):292-6.

Windeatt, B.A. 'The scribes as Chaucer's early critics.' *SAC* 1 (1979): 119-41.

—— 'The text of the *Troilus*.' *Essays on Troilus and Criseyde.* Edited by Mary Salu. Cambridge: Brewer, 1979, pp. 1–22.

—— *Geoffrey Chaucer: Troilus & Criseyde. A new edition of 'The Book of Troilus'.* London: Longman, 1984.

Work, J.A. 'The position of the tales of the Manciple and the Parson on Chaucer's Canterbury pilgrimage'. *JEGP* 31 (1932):62-5.

Wright, Thomas. *The Canterbury tales of Geoffrey Chaucer. A new text with illustrative notes.* 3 vols. Percy Society. London: Richards, 1847-51.

Young, K. 'The plan of the Canterbury tales.' *Anniversary papers for George Lyman Kittredge.* Boston, Mass: Ginn, 1913, pp. 405–17.

INDICES

INDICES

(a) Index of lines from **The Canterbury Tales** quoted or referred to:

1:8	18	1:2839	94
1:49	67	1:2917	133
1:253−4	9, 17, 19−22,	1:2954	115
	94, 104, 106,	1:2983	94
	114, 116, 129,	1:3013	147
	136, 141, 148,	1:3017	147
	193	1:3023−4	94
1:292	136	1:3041	73, 94, 119
1:311	65	1:3059	136
1:338	109	1:3085−6	67
1:638	94	1:3157	134
1:639−40	65, 94, 129,	1:3227	134
	141, 148, 193	1:3297	134
1:640	94	1:3686	134
1:861−94	143	1:3726	94
1:895	92, 143	1:3316	64
1:1166	93, 133	1:3411	134
1:1357	143	1:3605	134
1:1468	133	1:4347−50	115
1:1776	94	1:4367−8	115
1:1883	143	1:4405−6	110
1:1833−4	67	1:4407−14	115
1:2013−20	115	2:77	137
1:2019	115	2:115	94
1:2039	30, 55, 169	2:180−1	134
1:2042	115	2:193	146
1:2062	136	2:228	134
1:2277−8	67	2:333	118
1:2299	146	2:336	118
1:2350	146	2:453	146
1:2375	146	2:503	146
1:2485	143	2:509	134
1:2689	146	2:519	134
1:2753−8	129	2:575−8	69
1:2760	133	2:598	134
1:2771	133	2:633	134

2:635	134	5:539	94
2:754	134	5:571−4	106
2:802	101	5:625	94, 118
2:803	114, 144	5:813	94, 118
2:831	101, 144	5:985−6	65, 116
2:954	134	5:986	20, 22, 106,
2:1083	94, 134		109, 116, 130,
2:1151	134		137, 141, 160,
2:1269−70	115		170, 196
2:1282	115	5:1022	135
2:1285−94	64, 194	5:1026	135
2:1465−6	137	5:1074	37, 61, 72, 99
2:1499b−1501a	137	5:1075	37
2:1705−6	105	5:1109−10	2
2:1762	65	5:1112−13	116
2:1845−8	105	6:1	99, 101, 158
2:1846−8	105	6:1−20	2, 20, 121, 144
2:1881−6	137	6:21	99, 102, 121,
2:2022	65		140, 158
2:2132	153	6:21−2	106
2:2198	141	6:209−10	131
2:2217	144	6:401−4	137
2:2268	68	6:402	147
3:33−4	85	6:421−4	138
3:99−133	144	6:439−40	106, 131
3:134	144	6:483−8	106, 131
3:197	115	6:557−8	131
3:322	140	6:715−16	106
3:386	144	6:725−7	106, 131
3:876	144	6:763−4	138
3:952	140	6:813−14	106
4:61−4	131	6:840−2	106
4:583−4	116	6:851−2	106
5:43	135	6:867	99
5:49	98	7:1−119	2, 121, 145
5:61−2	x, 10, 13, 20,	7:37	99
	65, 105, 116,	7:73−4	107
	130, 137, 141,	7:120	121
	160, 170, 196	7:120−553	2, 145
5:63−4	116	7:155	117
5:73	135	7:156−9	107, 138
5:98	135	7:207	102
5:113−16	141	7:210−16	117
5:217	94	7:213−14	107
5:240	137	7:326−37	107
5:309	118	7:389−90	107
5:357	135	7:432	107
5:403−4	105	7:879−86	106
5:511	135	8:6	143
5:533−4	105	8:622	134

8:887	147	10:1395	156
8:937	135	10:1433−4	198
8:995	135	10:1463−4	108
8:1170−6	153	10:1506−7	108
8:1176	144	10:1556−7	142
8:1177−1212	x	10:1777	65, 119, 132, 138, 142, 198
8:1183	135		
8:1189	98	10:1957−8	142
8:1195−1200	153	10:2015−22	118
8:1212	10, 153	10:2109	93
8:1213−19	x, 2, 5, 20, 73	10:2166	118
9:103−4	142	10:2238	118
9:287−326	2	10:2371	175
9:291−2	107, 117	10:2557	118
9:296	107	10:2656	133
9:299	107	10:2665−70	21
9:303−4	117	10:2670	11, 21
9:327	128	10:2671−94	2
9:330	131	10:2671−758	2
9:344	131	10:2759	100
9:461	128, 139	10:2893−6	108
9:476−7	117	10:2918−19	118
9:485−6	107, 117	10:2974	147
9:486	132	10:3015−20	108
9:601−2	107	10:3135−8	133
9:715−16	117	10:3162	118, 133
9:741−2	138	10:3261−2	118
10:114−19	138	10:3417	178
10:165	117	11:215−16	138
10:176	94	11:256	94
10:186−9	117	12:4	118
10:214	93, 107, 132, 147	12:9	118
		12:12	191
10:453−87	145	12:16−17	191
10:487	129	12:28	61
10:488	102, 132	12:168	142
10:488−690	145	12:273	142
10:694	93	12:511	94, 142
10:805	75, 132, 138, 142, 198	[A2681−2]	17, 20, 22, 104, 115, 129, 136, 141, 193
10:852−4	108	[A2779−82]	20, 22, 104, 115, 129, 136, 141, 194
10:915−18	108		
10:918	197		
10:1000	142, 198	[A3155−6]	9, 17, 20, 22, 115, 129, 137, 141, 159, 194
10:1062−3	198		
10:1138−72	108		
10:1254−5	117	[A3721−2]	9, 17, 20, 22, 129, 137, 141, 148, 157, 159, 194
10:1320	108		
10:1329	108		
10:1335−6	108, 198		

[B¹1163−74] 111
[B¹1163−90] 1, 3, 8, 11−12, 17, 136
[B¹1776−83] 111
[B¹1179] 1, 3, 6, 11, 16, 20, 71, 97, 111, 121, 152, 157
[B²3197−3204] xi, 21, 99
[B²3961−80] xi, 21, 73, 113, 136, 154, 199
[B²3972] 11, 72
[B²4637−52] xi, 17, 21, 75, 127, 136, 200
[C103−4] 17
[C297−8] 17, 21−2, 117, 160, 198
[D44a−f] x, 1, 3, 10, 13, 16−17, 20, 22, 75, 130, 135, 137, 141, 194
[D575−84, 609−12, 619−26, 717−20] x, 1, 10, 16−17, 130, 194
[E1213] 10
[E1213−44] x, 1−3, 5−6, 10, 13, 17, 20, 65, 73, 112, 136, 141, 156, 197−8
[E1233−4] 10
[E2419] 17
[E2419−40] x, 10, 13, 17, 20, 45, 60, 68, 88, 125, 136, 141, 196
[F1] 196
[F1−3] · 125−6
[F1−8] x, 2, 9−10, 13, 17, 20, 45, 60, 68, 88, 125, 136, 141, 157−8, 196
[F673−708] x, 2−4, 6, 10, 12−13, 17, 20, 60, 136, 141, 156, 195
[F675] 6, 10, 20
[F682] 10
[F1455−6] x, 10, 13, 21−2, 131, 138, 142, 148, 160, 196
[F1493−8] x, 10, 13, 21−2, 138, 142, 148, 160, 196
[G554] 197
[G554−719] 121
[G555] 165
[G556] 192
[G562−3] 133
[G564−5] 133
[G711] 133
[G720] 114, 121
[G972] 145
[G1046−7] 138
[G1121] 138
[G1282−3] 117

(b) General Index

Note: Titles of individual tales and passages in Hg are not generally listed as individual passages may be more conveniently located by using the line reference in (a).

Absolon 94, 134
Adam xi, 100, 171, 199
Adam scriveyn 48, 54, 182
Adam stanza xi, 2, 4, 6, 11, 13, 21, 54, 65, 73, 100, 109, 121, 132, 138, 142, 160, 168, 171, 199
Adventure of Pardoner and Tapster 14
Alison 94, 134, 141
All England 34, 150
Alma redemptoris mater 91, 102
Anderson, R. 14
Arcite 51, 94, 104, 133, 146
Arveragus 106−7, 136, 138, 142, 197
Astrolabe 76
Aurelius 106−7, 142

Beadle, R. 76, 78
Bell, J. 14
Bell, R. 14
Benson, L. 40−1, 51, 173−4, 187−8
Bentley 18
Black Prince 13
Blanche, Duchess of Gaunt 179
Blean Forest 26−7, 89, 192
Bobbe-vp-and-down 27
Boccaccio 199
Boece, Boethius 48, 180
Boke of Cupide 202
Book of the Duchess 179−81, 184−6
Boughton under Blee 10, 22, 26, 28−9, 32, 44, 124, 192, 200
Bradshaw, H. 26, 28−9, 32, 44
Brusendorff, A. 33−5
Burnley, D. 43
Bukton 52

Cambiuskan 131
Cambridge 9

Canon's Yeoman 6, 10−11, 13, 17, 21−2, 164
Canon's Yeoman's Prologue and Tale xi, 2, 4, 22, 26−30, 34−5, 40, 46, 65−6, 69, 71−2, 84, 86−7, 89−90, 99−100, 102−3, 111, 113−14, 117, 121, 123−4, 126−7, 129, 133, 136, 138−41, 145, 150, 154−6, 162, 164, 192, 197, 200−1
Canterbury 27, 39, 47−8, 62, 83
Canterbury, Archbishop of 178
Canterbury Tales, The ix, 1, 5, 7−8, 12, 14−15, 17, 19, 24, 28−9, 31, 35, 40, 42−3, 46−7, 50−2, 54, 57−8, 66−8, 76−7, 84, 89, 97, 103, 109, 148, 150, 165−6, 168−9, 172, 179, 181−90, 194, 196, 198, 201−2
Cato 109
Cawley, A.C. ix
Caxton, W. 1, 3−5, 8, 177, 179; 1476 edition 1-6, 155: 1482 edition 3−6
Cecilia 33, 71, 73, 87, 100, 102, 120, 124, 127, 145, 197
Chaucer: A Bibliographical Manual 32
Chaucer, G. *passim*
Chaucer society 15−20, 22, 24, 27−8, 31, 50
Chaucer's wife 179
Chantecleer 133, 145
Christ 107
Clerk 5−6, 8, 10, 16, 20, 22, 26, 29, 32, 38, 45, 96, 113, 120
Companion to Chaucer Studies 39
Confessio Amantis 41, 59, 68, 90, 109, 184
Constance 85
Cook 8, 97, 104, 110, 145

Croesus xi, 4, 11, 21, 113, 132, 199

Damian 2, 94
Dartford 25
De casibus virorum illustrium
  102, 120, 129, 139, 145, 199
Dempster, G. 33, 35–8, 40, 48,
  154, 162, 192
de Worde, W. 5–6
Diana 146
Donaldson, E.T. 47–8
Dorigen 107, 142
Doyle, A.I. 41–2, 61, 63, 90, 96,
  109

East Anglia 76, 185
Egeus 94
Emily 133, 146
Edward III 179
England 1, 136, 179
Envoy to Bukton 52, 61
Epicurus 109
Equatorie of the Planetis 180
Eve 130

Filostrato 182–3
Flower and the Leaf 202
Franklin 4, 6, 8, 10, 17, 22, 26,
  32, 38, 45, 84, 86, 88, 96,
  113, 125, 144, 195–6
Friar 100–1, 144, 153
Furnivall, F.J. ix, 15, 24–30,
  34–5, 44–5

Galathea 147
Gamelyn 7–9, 13–14, 19–20, 28,
  30–1, 34, 46, 62–3, 65–6,
  68–9, 71–2, 74, 90, 97, 101,
  103–4, 110–13, 120, 123–5,
  136, 140, 151–2, 155–6,
  160–3, 172, 192, 194, 201
Globe Chaucer 18–19
Godfray, T. 5
Gower, J. 59, 90, 184

Hammond, E.P. 17, 32
Henry VIII 5
Hoccleve, T. 42, 59
Host xi, 2, 6–7, 11, 17, 19, 21,
  61, 81, 83, 85–6, 88, 90, 92,
  101, 125, 140, 146, 154, 190,
  198–9, 201
House of Fame 185

January 93–4, 105–6, 135, 144
Job 137
John Duke of Gaunt 179–80

Keiser, G. 41
Knight 6, 100, 146, 199, 201
Koch, J. 31–3, 51, 53

Langland, W. 184
Legend of Good Women 51–2,
  76, 78, 185–6
Le Morte Darthur 177
Lenvoy de Chaucer x, 2, 4, 10,
  18, 20, 26, 73, 92, 98–9, 112,
  114, 121, 125, 128, 139, 141,
  144, 155, 157–8, 197
London 5, 9, 41, 53–4, 59, 68,
  76, 97, 109–10, 136, 139,
  185, 197

Malory, T. 177
Manly, J. 33, 36, 96
Manly, J. and E. Rickert 1, 19–24,
  35–8, 40, 42–3, 50–1,
  53–4, 58–61, 63, 65–7,
  69–70, 73–4, 96, 119, 123,
  151, 155–6, 161–2, 164–5,
  168, 187–9, 192, 196
Man of Law 3, 6, 8, 32, 85, 92
Manciple 61, 85
Manuscripts:
  Additional 5140 9
  Additional 35286 21
  Bodley 638 180
  Bodleian Musaeo 116 76
  Cambridge Ii.1.38 180
  Cambridge Mm.2.5 70
  Corpus 15, 31, 37, 50, 54,
    68–74, 79–80, 96–127, 129,
    131–2, 134, 136, 141, 143,
    148, 150–2, 154–6, 158–9,
    161, 163, 168, 170, 188,
    193–200
  Dd.4.24 xi, 9, 15–16, 20, 31–2,
    50, 58, 74–9, 123–37,
    139–42, 144, 147–8, 160–1,
    185, 193–8, 200

Egerton 2726 9
Egerton 2864 9
Ellesmere ix–xi, 5, 9, 15–23, 26–7, 30–44, 50, 54, 57–9, 65–70, 74–80, 85–6, 88, 123, 129–30, 137–48, 167, 173, 185, 187, 193–7, 200
Fairfax 16 180, 185
Gg.4.27 7, 15–16, 31, 50, 58, 76–8, 123, 129–30, 136–43, 148–50, 185–6, 193–7, 200
Harley 7334 5, 9, 12–15, 18, 20, 27, 29–31, 33, 35, 37, 39, 50, 54, 57, 67–72, 79–80, 96, 103, 109–27, 129–32, 136–7, 141, 143, 148, 151, 155, 157, 161, 170, 188, 193–6, 198–9
Harley 7335 9
Helmingham 37, 155–61
Hengwrt ix–xi, 2, 5, 9, 15, 17, 20–1, 23, 29–45, 50, 54, 57–70, 72, 76, 79–100, 103, 105–8, 111–12, 115–20, 124, 129, 131–5, 137, 139, 141–4, 146–8, 150, 152–4, 156–9, 161, 163, 165–7, 170–2, 187–200
Holkham 164
Lansdowne 15, 30–1, 50, 58, 68, 72–4, 79–80, 96, 99, 106, 118–24, 131–2, 141, 151–2, 154, 160, 168, 193–8
Lincoln 156–60
Merthyr Fragment 58, 148
Peterhouse 180
Petworth 15, 30–1, 37, 50, 58, 73–4, 79–80, 131, 150–6, 158–60, 165, 194–6, 198
Royal 18.C.II 162
Selden 11, 16
Sloane 1686 99
Tanner 346 180
Trinity College R.3.2 59
Trinity College R.3.15 3
Mars 146
May 2, 106, 135
Melibeus 60, 145–6
Merchant 2, 5, 6, 8, 10, 16, 22, 26–7, 29, 38, 45, 84, 86, 96, 113, 195

Merchant's Second Tale 14
Mery Adventure 8, 13
Midas 134
Modern Instances xi, 2, 4, 9, 13, 16, 21–2, 72, 75, 100, 109, 113–14, 132–3, 138, 142, 154, 160, 199
Monk xi, 6, 146, 199
Morell, T. 9, 17
Morris, R. 14, 28

Nero xi, 100, 199
New Aldine Edition 14
Nicholas 134
Nun (Second Nun) 2, 4–6, 10–11, 17, 21–2, 25, 33, 73, 86, 113, 127, 145, 154
Nun's Priest 2, 10–11
Nun's Priest's Epilogue xi, 6, 21–2, 72, 77, 127–8, 136, 200

Orleans 106
Ospringe 26–7
Owen, C. 39–41
Oxford 9, 34, 150
Oxford English Dictionary 14

Palamon 51, 133, 146
Pamphilus 147
Pamphilus de amore 136
Pardoner 2, 11, 81, 100, 127, 131, 198
Parkes, M. 41–2, 63, 76, 78, 90, 96, 109
Parliament of Fowls 185–6
Parson 7, 61
Pedro the Cruel of Aragon 13
Percy Society 12
Pertelote 145
Physician 2, 11, 154
Physician's Prologue 6, 10, 12, 17, 121, 136, 154
Piers Plowman 184
Ploughman 7
Ploughman's Prologue 7–8
Ploughman's Tale 7–8, 11, 14
Pluto 135
Pollard, A. 19
Prioress 145

Proserpina 106, 131, 135, 160, 170
Prudence 146
Pynson, R. 5–6, 8

Ramsey, R.V. 42
Retraction xi, 2, 5–8, 11, 17, 21, 46, 58, 63, 93, 100, 114, 121, 127, 154, 156, 160, 163–4, 173–4, 187–8
Richard II 186
Rickert, E. 19, 76, 96; *see also under* Manly, J. and E. Rickert
Robinson, F.N. ix
Rochester 10, 26
Ruggiers, P. 39

Sampson 118
Samuels, M. 42, 59
Second Nun *see under* Nun
Seneca 108–9
Shipman 2, 11, 16, 20, 49
Shipman's Prologue 6, 12–13, 16, 22, 121
Skeat, W.W. ix, 1, 14–22, 29–33, 69
Southwark 27
Speght, T. 7, 9
Squire x, 4, 6, 8, 10–12, 17, 22, 26–7, 29, 32, 38, 45, 66, 71, 84, 86, 96–7, 104, 111, 121, 125–6, 141, 144, 152, 157, 195–6
Squire's Yeoman 8
Statius 101, 113, 143
Stilbon 107
Stow, J. 7

Summoner x, 20, 62, 111, 115, 144, 157, 163, 195

Tabard Inn 164
Tale of Beryn 8, 13
Tatlock, J.S.P. 31, 33, 35, 69
Temporary Preface to the Six Text Edition 24
Testament of Love 182
Text of the Canterbury Tales 19
Thomas, T. 8
Thopas 90
Thynne, W. 5–9, 29, 181; 1532 edition 5–7, 181; 1542 edition 7; 1550 edition 7
Thynne, Mrs 8
Troilus and Criseyde 48, 76, 181–6
Truth 66
Tyrwhitt, T. 1, 5, 9–15, 17–28

Ulster, Countess of 179
Urry, J. 6–8, 14
Usk, T. 182

Variorum Edition 23–4, 39
Venus 105, 132, 146
Virginia 107, 198

West Midlands 68
Westminster 1, 8, 41, 54, 59, 69, 96
Wife of Bath 10, 22, 26, 49, 52, 83, 98, 101, 111–12, 130, 134, 144, 153, 190, 192, 194
Windeatt, B. 182–3
Workes of Geffray Chaucer 5
Wright, T. 12–14, 28
Wytton 75, 128

Zenobia xi, 13, 199